DATE DUE

DEC 0 96			

ARE YOU A CANDIDATE FOR THE FAST TRACK BLUES?

1. Are you extraordinarily competent? Do you feel exhilarated by the control you exercise over your work, other people, important events?

2. Have you successfully competed for rewards, resources, and recognition?

3. Have your bosses or knowledgeable peers told you that you are a "comer," a "whiz kid," or somebody with "the right stuff"?

4. Do you feel driven to attain ever higher goals? Does their attainment often lead to short-lived satisfaction, followed by an uneasy discontent?

5. Are you frequently bedeviled by self-doubt over what you have not yet accomplished? If you have such feelings, do you conceal them from your family and colleagues?

If you have answered "Yes," "Maybe," or "Sometimes" to any of the above, read on. This book could save your career—and your life!

COPING WITH THE FAST TRACK BLUES

ALSO BY ROBERT M. BRAMSON, PH.D.

Coping with Difficult People

QUANTITY SALES

INDIVIDUAL SALES

Robert M. Bramson, Ph. D.

COPING WITH THE FAST TRACK BLUES

A Survival Guide for Your Climb to the Top

A DELL BOOK

Published by
Dell Publishing
a division of
Bantam Doubleday Dell Publishing Group, Inc.
666 Fifth Avenue
New York, New York 10103

ISBN: 0-440-21175-1

Reprinted by arrangement with Doubleday

Printed in the United States of America

Published simultaneously in Canada

March 1992

10 9 8 7 6 5 4 3 2 1

OPM

Contents

Preface

I wrote this book because I could not find another like it. As a consultant to men and women who were alternately sprinting and stumbling their way through fast track careers, I found little to choose from among the current books that were written for and about them. There were gloomy tracts that equated worldly success with an obsessive and unfulfilled life. Or there were equally extravagant motivational epics that promised an easy hop and skip for anyone who acquired the proper kind of "winning attitude" or learned the latest secret of good management. While there was some truth in many of these offerings, none seemed in touch with the realities that I was seeing in the work lives of my clients.

A hunger to be "somebody," and at least a modicum of professional skill and self-confidence, *are* sine qua non for leaping on the track in the first place, but talent and enthusiasm alone are not enough to keep you out of trouble. Fast Trackers *do*, at times, find themselves derailed and depressed; their paths are indeed filled with blocks and hazards. But it is equally true that with knowledge and reasonable care most of the hazards can be avoided or, if unavoidable, overcome. What *is* needed by these adventurers is a map of the territory with the hazards clearly marked, and specific ideas about how to stay clear of them. Ergo, this attempt at a practical, yet not superficial, guide (some have suggested that "guerrilla manual" might be a more apt term) to a successful, but still properly balanced, life. I intend it as a resource for those who are already embarked on a demanding, busy life as well as for students en route to careers in business and the professions.

A word about the cases and examples you'll find throughout the book. The conversations in them are as close to those that actually occurred as almost verbatim note taking, or hurried scribbling shortly after they had taken place could make them. While I selectively chose the cases to illuminate points made in the book, I have done my best *not* to change either substance or form just to make them fit the text perfectly or testify to the efficacy of a suggested approach. I have, however, to protect both their privacy and my future ability to serve as a consultant, taken pains to disguise the identities of both individual clients and the organizations of which they were a part. These efforts have included changing names, first and last; sex—when it would not alter the meaning of the example; professional identity; and the location, setting, or kind of organization.

Through the years I have drawn on the ideas and research of many others to make sense of the always complex and sometimes paradoxical predicaments people get themselves into, and to point the way to more effective consulting techniques. Among the most helpful of these rich sources of information have been the recent applications of brief therapy and cognitive approaches to the resolution of family problems. There are many similarities between the dynamics of families and those of work groups, and the methods developed in one setting are often applicable, with modification of course, to the other (elsewhere, in fact, I've made the case that families are a special kind of mini-organization and are, therefore, subject to the same institutional forces that affect their larger cousins*).

Among the individuals whose thoughts have found their way directly into these pages are: my wife Susan Bramson, a talented consultant in her own right and a brutally frank editor; my partner Lucy Gill, and our current associates, Joanne Smyth-Vartanian, Richard Terrell, and Wendy Waits. Nicholas Parlette and Allen Harrison, former partners in consulting, added to my store of useful perspectives. From Wilson Yandell, counselor, mentor, and colleague, I learned both consulting technique and the most useful skill of all—how to recover from self-induced disasters. Marni and Eric Welch, Don Waits, and my sons Robert, Sean, Patrick, and Jeremy have shared their own experiences with organizational life, and have been a continuing source of useful ideas.

Margaret Smith turned my erratic dictations, scrawled notes, and sketchy instructions into a beautifully typed manuscript. Then Kevin Groom, and especially John Bergez, provided frank but supportive editorial assistance and kept my bifurcated mind within reasonable boundaries.

My Doubleday editor Loretta Barrett, Marilyn Abra-

*Bramson, R., and S. Bramson. *The Stressless Home*. Garden City, N.Y.: Doubleday, 1985.

ham, and my friend and agent Carol Mann helped with the basic design of the book and with their usual encouraging enthusiasm.

Finally, my earnest appreciation to my clients, past and present. Without their willingness to share thoughts, fears, and wishes with me, there would be no book.

1

Coping with the Fast Track Blues
Introduction

For twenty years I have been consultant, father confessor, and management guru to men and women caught up in the stress and excitement of the fast track— executives and senior managers in Fortune 500 companies, high-flying salesmen and -women, professionals in medicine, education, and law, entrepreneurs who had successfully birthed both high- and low-tech enterprises, science mavens, and jet-setting academicians—and, not infrequently, their spouses and families. This panoply of fast-tracking clients included some who were in it for the sheer fun of it. Some had never chosen to pursue success but had been catapulted by their talents into a life of ambitious achievement. A few had been pulled, at times reluctantly, from peaceful backwater niches by the luck of having been in the right place at the right time.

All were successful in a worldly way, and rightfully proud of their achievements. But many also felt depressed, emotionally troubled, driven, angry, resentful, and ambivalent about their futures. Here are Virginia and Mark, two examples of "proven successes" who found themselves personally derailed.

VIRGINIA

"The corporate treasurer's job—that's what I want, as soon as Ted [Virginia's boss and the current treasurer] moves up," Virginia declared at our first meeting, with a confident nod and the kind of clear, piercing eye contact that they teach in executive presentation classes. She had been referred to me by her boss, who was trying to decide whether to fire her or promote her.

"I was near the top of my class at B-school," she went on, "and I'm the youngest portfolio manager in the company. I've seen the view from Mount Olympus, and I like it. Hey, if you don't aim high, what's the point of taking a shot? I don't know why Ted thinks I need help from a consultant. I'm the best brain on his staff, and he knows it."

"Virginia's the most technically competent person I've seen in a long time," Ted had told me. "But I'm fed up with her moody ups and downs. She's good, and she knows she's good. She's had three promotions in the last two years. But I keep getting complaints about her arrogance from my boss, from her peers, and recently even from her subordinates. I don't really know what's happened to her. As a first-line supervisor, she was great. As a functional manager, she stinks. She wants me to promise that I'll promote her to assistant treasurer, but that's an officer-level job, and I'll need the CEO's OK. What she doesn't know is that she's getting a reputation on high as a defensive, calculating opportunist who is only interested in her own success. Of that kind of press, corporate treasurers are seldom made."

MARK

I recall the tense brightness of Mark's eyes as he abruptly shifted from topic to topic at our first meeting. Ernie, his boss, had described him a bit wryly as "a terribly bright guy, who meets every deadline with first-rate work and has enough charisma to lead an army, but who's stuck with a growing reputation as an empire builder." As Ernie had guessed he would, Mark at first turned his charm on me. Whether or not he knew he needed help he wasn't about to let me know it. What he wanted from me, he said, was "just a few ideas on how I can handle some priority problems. Ernie mentioned that you'd really helped him out with some new management ideas—so I thought I might as well take advantage of what you have to offer."

When I did not rise to Mark's flattering bait, but instead asked him to tell me something about himself and his job, he walked to the door of his office to check that it was shut, asked his secretary to hold all calls, and commenced an hour-long litany.

"I'm doing twice as much as anyone else around here, except maybe Ernie. Our reports are used everywhere. I ought to be a department head, but all I get from the vice president is 'be patient.' I think Ernie is on my side, but I don't know. I'm getting tired of not having this place recognize what I'm giving it."

Mark paused a bit, looked down at his hands, and then continued.

"I'm in the office till 8:00 P.M. most days, and I'm worried about the effects of all this on my family. Jeanna knows how much my career means to me, but I think that her patience has about run out. It's hard to have a deepening relationship—that's what she keeps talking about—when all we have are shreds and patches of time together."

THE FAST TRACK BLUES

Certainly tensions, conflicts, and moody ups and downs are frequent concomitants of achievement, but the degree of personal distress experienced by competent and respected people like Virginia and Mark far exceed what might be expected, even from the scramble of a full and busy life. That such people usually avoid—often quite creatively—facing the degree to which they are affected is troubling in itself. Of even greater concern is the self-defeating nature of their attempts to make things right. Some, like Virginia, driven by suspicion that their progress has been stymied, lash out and jeopardize their future prospects. Others, like Mark, feel out of balance, or, worse, out of control. Often they also feel trapped by the "necessity" of choosing between an exciting job and the development of deeper relationships and a richer family or personal life. Usually their impulsive efforts at instant recalibration, driven by guilt, anger, and frustration, only make things worse.

While the life of each of these interesting people was unique, over the years I began to see a common theme to this set of debilitating symptoms that I have come to call the Fast Track Blues. They were the predictable, almost unavoidable, consequences of encounters between the energy, optimism, and oversized need to excel or to win that most high achievers bring with them, and some ubiquitous characteristics of the crowded world in which they must do business.

Understanding these Fast Track Blues and visualizing how and why they might happen to you is the first step toward coping with them. The second step is using that understanding to minimize—or, even better, prevent—the serious effects they can have on your career and well-being.

That is what this book is about: how to cope with the predictable hazards that capable, ambitious people encounter on the high-gear road to occupational success.

The book is not a brief for, nor a judgment against, life in the fast track. It simply recognizes that the phenomenon I call the Fast Track Blues exists and is spreading. The accelerating tempo of life, fueled primarily by the ease and speed of communication, has drawn most of us into running through our workdays, and even seems to be eroding most of those quiet oases of reasonably paced and modulated activity that are left. Nor is this book a treatise on the psychology of success, or a collection of exercises for stress relief, or a manual on how to organize your time and your life, although, of necessity, it will touch on some aspects of each of those areas. Rather, it is a warning look at the often subtle pitfalls into which many people have slipped and a compendium of ideas and methods that will help you to cope with their predictable consequence, the Fast Track Blues.

ARE YOU A CANDIDATE FOR THE FAST TRACK BLUES?

A most important question for anyone in a rapidly upward-bound career is "How much at risk am I of stumbling—or leaping—into one or more of these pitfalls?" The Fast Track Blues do not announce their presence. They sneak up without fanfare until one night you find yourself lying awake after another rewarding day at your fascinating job, feeling bored, disappointed, and uneasy. Or even worse, you wake up the next morning to an empty bed, an empty bottle, or a drawer full of unpaid bills, and a headache from trying to figure out how anyone who's making such good money and who is so accomplished at work could have such a messed-up life.

While it's never too late to realign aspects of your life that aren't working well, it's far easier the earlier you start. To assess the degree to which you might be at risk, read through and mentally answer the fourteen questions that follow. Try to test yourself against each question as deeply and honestly as you can.

1. Are you extraordinarily competent? Do you feel exhilarated by the control you exercise over your work, other people, important events?

2. Have you successfully competed for rewards, resources, and recognition?

3. Have your bosses or knowledgeable peers told you that you are a "comer," a "whiz kid," or somebody with "the right stuff"?

4. Do you feel driven to attain ever higher goals? Does their attainment often lead to short-lived satisfaction, followed by an uneasy discontent?

5. Is your work demanding: multiple tasks; unremitting long hours; rapid decisions made in complex environments; high visibility, even celebrity? Do you feel stimulated, even intoxicated, but also overloaded and anxious about doing all of it well?

6. Are you frequently bedeviled by self-doubt, over what you have not yet accomplished? If you have such feelings, do you conceal them from your family and colleagues?

7. Do you work in an atmosphere that at times feels highly political or grounded in favoritism and personal bias?

8. Do you have access to, or control of, great sums of money?

9. Have you recently bent rules, fudged facts, or lied a little to get the funds you "needed" to attain your goals or to "make your numbers"?

10. Do you sometimes notice symptoms of "jet lag" even when you haven't been traveling: forgetting or double-scheduling appointments; sudden attacks of sleepiness at odd hours; difficulty in concentrating on what others are saying; difficulty in falling asleep at night?

11. Have you noticed, or have you been told, that you're more angry, indecisive, overly social, withdrawing, or intimidating lately?

12. More than occasionally, do you feel that your life has lost its savor, that it is out of balance, that family, friends, or your "true" interests have been neglected?

13. Have you increased your use of alcohol and other drugs to get temporary relief from overload or to have a little fun out of life? For example, have you

started to pour 2½-ounce drinks because a standard shot no longer gives you enough lift? Do you use alcohol or any other drug every day?

14. Do you discover yourself rationalizing expenditures that overreach your personal income as deserved compensation for too-long hours, too-short vacations, and too-heavy responsibilities?

If you have answered "yes" or "maybe" or "sometimes" to more than half of these questions, read on. You fit the fast track template well enough to benefit from learning more about it. Remember, the earlier you are alerted to the dual nature of occupational success—stimulating but also disabling—the easier it will be to minimize the deleterious effects and maximize the fun.

True, some Fast Trackers seem immune to the tensions and stresses that trouble their fellows. If you are such a one, you may find yourself puzzled and perhaps a little saddened that, for others, success has brought so little satisfaction. Perhaps your career path has been smooth because you were simply lucky enough to avoid the deepest pitfalls. Or perhaps you're one of those fortunate few whose early life has toughened them against the emotional strains of a rapid climb up the occupational ladder. Either way, you may still find this book useful. It will forewarn you of unpleasantnesses that you may yet encounter farther along your way. It will also provide a framework that will help you ease the way of subordinates, friends, or family members who have not been as lucky as you.

If, on the other hand, you already find yourself a bit frantic, resentful, or disappointed, or simply puzzled about why you're feeling so poorly when you're doing so well, reading this book can bring you several related benefits. First, you'll better understand how and why strong, bright people can be derailed, or can derail themselves. Second, you'll learn ideas and practical methods for pursuing your own goals in a more effective, human, and satisfying way. The methods are neither untested "bright ideas" nor guaranteed cure-alls that will forever resolve complex human problems. Rather, they are the distillations of close and careful observations, by both myself and my associates, of what actually helped the immensely capable but perplexed people who have been our clients, buttressed by recent findings about how we can hurt, and help, ourselves along the way. Finally, and perhaps most satisfying of all, you may find in these pages a validation of your unease that is not solely due to the vagaries of your own psyche, and a confirmation that some of the steps you have been taking on your own are on target.

A PERSONAL WORD

Moving up in the world of affairs is a bit like high-mountain climbing. At first you move through familiar territory, choosing a trail that best fits your climbing style, energetically taking advantage of every opportunity to move up the slope as quickly as you can. At a certain point, however, the terrain starts to become hostile: the trail narrows, dangerous crevasses must be leaped or gone around, the only routes available demand skills you've not yet developed. As if a perverse mountain weren't bad enough, as you climb higher, increasingly your body and mind react to these new hazards in ways that foil you even more. The air thins, your breathing labors. Unused to these strange and unforgiving tasks, your fatigued muscles cramp. Anger—at yourself, the mountain, and whoever talked you into the climb—clouds your judgment, disrupts your climbing technique, and gives you a stomachache to boot.

Was your choice to climb the mountain to blame for your miseries, was it the hazards the mountain threw in your way, or was it simply that you were not well enough prepared for the task? Of course, to an observer safe on the ground, it's obvious that it was the interaction of all three that left you tired, anxious, and discouraged on that craggy mountain. Unfortunately, when it is you who are climbing either a Swiss Alp or the pyramid of occupational success, it's all too easy to lose sight of that fact. Then, as you ascend the heights, the perils you encounter—some new to you, some familiar but now more subtle and slippery—may challenge your strengths and magnify your liabilities in ways you didn't anticipate. After all, if you had known in advance about vertical walls and icy rocks, you might have gotten some tips from expert climbers and learned some new techniques to make yourself less vulnerable to the anger and self-doubt that kept you from functioning at your best. It is my hope that this book can serve that purpose for you.

In the chapters that follow, we'll examine the coping methods that can help you to deal with the personal and organizational barriers that have most frequently derailed the Fast Trackers with whom I've worked: killing work schedules, a nonsupportive atmosphere, the squeeze at the top, power pathologies, and unhealthy organizational practices, as well as the personal costs that can accrue from the largely unavoidable encounters with them. In the final chapter, we'll turn to broader strategies for regaining a better balance in your life and that will help you determine when the fast track, as exciting as it can be, may not be for you.

2

Slowing Down the Squirrel Cage:
Getting Control of Overload

It was five o'clock when Jon's secretary finally nodded me into his office. He sat with his back toward the door, gazing out at an orange sun, just setting on a clear December day. When he realized that I was in the room, he waved me into a chair.

"When you get back to your office, Dr. B.," he began, "they'll tell you that I tried to cancel out for this afternoon. Well, maybe it's just as well they couldn't reach you, 'cause I've about had it. Yesterday, I got back from a ten-day tour of the district offices. I wasted today in stupid meetings. I still need at least two hours to finish the capital expenditures budget for an 8:00 A.M. meeting tomorrow. My dear wife is expecting to be taken out to dinner tonight—it's her birthday—and I still haven't gotten up enough nerve to call her. And this job is just shit."

Although they may not have put it quite so succinctly as Jon, most of my fast-tracking clients have realized that they were working harder and longer than they wanted to. They have known that the twelve-hour days and many weekends were taking their toll, but they have all insisted, sometimes angrily, that they had no choice. Their jobs, their boss, or their own pride required them to work at superhuman levels.

By and large, these clients were right. As one who has chosen or been dumped in the fast track, you will avoid an unpleasant surprise if you expect more work than you can handle. Problems will generate work. Opportunities will generate even more work, as anyone tied to the tail of a small business that has suddenly taken off can attest. The higher you rise, the more you find that *everything* that arrives on your plate is important (a fact that sometimes seems to elude those management authorities who urge "delegation" as the solution to all overload problems).

Bradley, the handsome but harried head of a prestigious Beverly Hills law firm, put it this way:

"The way things are going, I'm on the way to complete exhaustion. When I started in as an associate, I understood that I was cheap labor, and I expected to run my ass off. When I became a junior partner, I knew I would have to supervise most of the preparation work, as well as scramble for new clients, so I expected to work even harder. What I didn't expect was that as the managing partner I'd be working harder than ever, and everything I do has got to be done by me. I dump everything I can on the others, who are all good lawyers, and I've got an administrator who handles the office stuff. But for some deals—the big ones—I'm expected to be there. I'm the only one who seems interested in planning for future growth, and you wouldn't believe the time it takes to jolly a bunch of fifty-year-old senior attorneys out of bickering with each other. I'm on the far side of middle age, I work until nine o'clock most nights, long weekends are the only vacations I've had in years. I just can't seem to find my way out of a squirrel cage that keeps traveling faster and faster."

Of course hard work, in itself, is not necessarily a fast track pitfall. Most people have a physical capacity for exhausting labor. While they may become exceedingly tired in both body and mind—recent studies of how the brain works have provided some hints as to the physical basis for "mental fatigue"—hard work in itself does not seem to have long-term deleterious effects. Indeed, when the work is interesting and the company is congenial, hard work is a genuine tonic and has often been prescribed as such. But prolonged overwork, and, in particular, the sense of being frantically and unremittingly overloaded is a pitfall, and its victims are plentiful.

The distinction between working long and hard and feeling chronically overloaded is an important one. The exhaustion of hard work is temporary and easily cured by rest. The kind of overload experienced by Jon and Bradley is more complicated. True, at times I have been tempted to dismiss complaints such as theirs as the quibbles of those whose magical seven-league boots are beginning to pinch a little. But the facts are plain. The physical effects of relentless work combine with a sense of internal rebellion to overwhelm the natural processes of recovery. As a result, overload feels terrible. Those who experience it show most of the effects of emotional stress even as they continue to put in long hours on the job. They feel sullen, lethargic, uncaring, irritable, and even incompetent. Worse, because they are coping less well, they are likely to exacerbate their own overload and thus feel even more overwhelmed.

In every organization I have studied or consulted with, an unremitting load of work does, in fact, afflict those who attain the heights. Even in the worst situations, however, there has always been some room to maneuver. How to find that room and which maneuvers seem to help the most is the subject of this chapter.

We'll begin our exploration with a checklist of the signs that you might be verging on or already experiencing overload. Next we will briefly review some nonobvious pressures in the fast track environment that make long hours an unavoidable concomitant of any starring, leadership, or entrepreneurial role. Understanding that it's not *just* the work that leaves you feeling overloaded can, in itself, be stress-relieving. Doing something about it is even better. While a complete escape from work pressures will probably remain a Monday morning fantasy, we'll review techniques that provide at least a modicum of control. They are especially valuable, because even a 10 percent reduction in the flood of projects can lift you out of overload and into a state of stimulating challenge. Our third undertaking will be to examine a variety of *internal* pressures that both contribute to your capacity for work and make you a prime candidate for those "I'm tired to the bone and my spouse is going to kill me" blues. Finally, we'll take a brief look at prevention and the notion of front-end time as a constructive alternative to that exhausting game of "Frantic," better known in some circles as "crisis management."

ARE YOU SUFFERING FROM OVERLOAD?

The transition from hard work to overwork can be a gradual one, so it pays to know what the warning signs are. As you review the following checkpoints, I urge you to be as honest as you can in asking whether they apply to you.

Checklist of Overload Symptoms

- Frequent bouts of what feels like jet lag, even when you haven't been traveling; difficulty in concentrating; listening, but not grasping the content of what you have heard; flashes of extreme tiredness, even early in the day; feeling discouraged or emotionally down without an obvious reason.

- An increase in the usual panoply of stress-related physical symptoms, such as an over- or underactive digestive tract; difficulty in sleeping; an increase in smoking (or any other behavior you indulge in when you feel nervous or stressed); unusual forgetfulness; increases in heart rate or blood pressure.

- Recurring thoughts, accompanied by feelings of guilt or sadness, about neglecting your family or your hobbies and other interests. Anger at your job because it never seems to let go of you.

- Complaints from those at home about being ignored or being left with the entire burden of raising the family; or that you're forgetful; or that "you love your job more than you love me."

- Anger and disappointment because your family or significant others don't appreciate all you're doing for them.

- Ambivalence about your successes, that is, feeling proud when you have brought in a successful project and at the same time feeling oddly disappointed.

- A nagging sense that the quality of your work is suffering. Specifically:

  — You're spending less time on preparation and follow-through. Thus, perhaps you find yourself putting off coaching subordinates or not making the effort to listen to your staff or customers. In other words, you're letting the urgent—financial reports, say—drive out the important.

  — You're unusually impatient about the time it takes to solve problems, because you want to move on to the next one. You've begun to fall back on tried-and-true solutions just to dispose of issues rather than searching for new and better approaches.

  — Squeaky wheels and a constant sense of urgency are ruling your days. You're tending to give equal attention to every aspect of your job without discriminating between the key tasks and those that are less important.

  — You find yourself doing more of exactly those things that you know, or have been told, are the least effective behaviors in your repertoire. For example, you're starting to: analyze things to death; sell your bosses, subordinates, or customers too hard; back away from dealing directly with poor performers; or otherwise indulging what you know to be the flaws in your own style of working.

— Even though you're aware that these behaviors constitute poor management (of your life as well as your work), you feel trapped. You continue to slog along, feeling tired and anxious, but convinced that there is nothing that you can do about the pressures bearing down on you. You tell yourself or others that "it comes with the territory" or "I'm only doing what I'm getting paid for," while ignoring hints from others that your effectiveness is falling off.

If most or all of these warning signs are showing up in your life, it's time to learn how to cope with overload. The first step is to understand why it's happening.

ENVIRONMENTAL SOURCES OF OVERLOAD

The obvious reason for the whirlwind life of Fast Trackers is the amount of work to be done. But there are a number of less obvious reasons, some quite real and some the products of commonplace—but wrong— beliefs about how people and organizations ought to behave. These environmental sources of overload add increments to the workweek that do not stem from either the number or complexity of the tasks themselves. They include the budgeting process itself; unexamined organizational traditions; work-team pressures; myths about the nature of work and accomplishment; and the inefficient use of resources.

The Budgeting Process

There are some singular characteristics of the typical budgeting process that, especially in fast-growing organizations, can propel everyone involved into a long-distance sprint, even when no one consciously sets out to cause mischief.

Budget Catch-Up. When an organization is growing rapidly, budgets often lag behind the need for new resources because funds are appropriated only after it has been amply demonstrated that not enough hands are available for the work assigned. (There is much good sense in this, as will be ruefully acknowledged by anyone who has begged, borrowed, or approved funds to staff up for rapid growth that never materialized.) The result of this catch-up approach, however, is predictable: the incumbent staff will constantly be scrambling to keep up.

Resources Inadequate for the Job. Most of us have been stuck at some point in our careers with the task of staying within a budget that was plainly inadequate for the quantity or quality of work that those who set the budget insisted was required. The most common example is the undercapitalized small business, whose owners try, often desperately, to make a go of it by supplementing their inadequate cash with "sweat equity," enduring eighteen-hour workdays until either a stroke of good luck brings in the money needed for adequate staffing, or bankruptcy ends their suffering. (Ironically, as anyone knows who has started a small business, when the stroke of good luck does hit, the fast growth of the business still keeps noses to grindstones.)

The problem of inadequate resources is exacerbated when tightfisted, incompetent, or timid supervisors underestimate the size of the budget that is needed. Because of their understandable, though not constructive, reluctance to acknowledge the mistake or their fear (sometimes justified) of being scolded if they ask for more money, they will usually refuse to return to the well. Such supervisors create a suffocatingly pressured atmosphere for high achievers who are faced with either doing an inadequate job or trying to do the work of two. The other side of this coin, of course, is an overly ambitious set of objectives that far exceeds the reach of a budget whose amount is either fixed or was easily predictable (the sad state of most household budgets).

When Feast and Famine Becomes Feast and Feast. Some workloads are "seasonal"; that is, at certain times of the day, or on certain days of the week, or in certain months of the year, workloads are very heavy or very light. The staffing rationale in these situations assumes that the alternating periods of light work rejuvenate employees so that they will be able to handle—and won't mind—the ultrafast pace required during the periods of heavy workload. Service in a restaurant provides a clear example. The "feast times" of serving patrons during the rush hours is preceded and followed by "famine" periods in which staff will work at a more orderly and moderate pace to ready the dining room for patrons, perform clean-up functions, and make preparations for the next mealtime. The budgeting problem in this situation is clear. If the restaurant staffs up for the rush, some workers will be left puttering around during the more leisurely preparation and clean-up periods. On the other hand, if staffing is based on the "famine" period, service to the patrons during busy hours will be rushed at best and possibly abusive—a phenomenon with which most of us are all too familiar.

Most organizations whose workload has a feast-or-famine quality try to find just the right compromise between too much and too little staff. My perception is that the compromise works well when the organization is doing well financially. However, during lean times, units with variable workloads frequently are seen as ripe sources for salary savings, especially after one of the financial moguls peeks in during a "famine" time and wonders why no one is even breathing hard. At a stroke times of famine disappear—with a reduced staff the "cycle" has become feast and more feast.

Unexamined Organizational Traditions

Traditions are powerful mainstays of any culture, whether ethnic or organizational. They transmit fundamental values across generations of citizens, workers, and leaders. Much of their power to mandate how people should think and behave comes from their acceptance as "givens," precepts that are not to be questioned, in part because they represent the specialness of the nation or organization. At times, however, these traditional and unquestioned tenets can be seriously out of step with social or technological changes, until a gap opens up between traditional expectations and the realities of the situation. The recent reevaluation of sex roles in our society is a major example of this phenomenon, but there are some less weighty role expectations that often contribute to work overload.

For example, many organizations have a tradition that

anyone in our culture would agree is so absolutely clean-cut and American that its goodness can never be doubted. It is that key employees must be (or at least must seem to be) "dedicated" to their jobs. Whether the favored adjective is "dedicated," "committed," or "hardworking," an obvious way of showing that you meet the traditional expectation is by being the first to arrive at the plant, office, or studio, and the last to leave. Similarly, most organizational cultures have delineated a role model for "good manager" or "real contributor" that somewhere along the way metamorphoses into "always works late." These unstated "rules" of organizational life are frequently complained about but seldom disputed. For one thing, there always is—or seems to be—more work to be done. For another thing, the role is continually reinforced, since those at higher levels believe it's poor form to leave before their subordinates do, and those below are afraid they won't fit the model if they seem less "dedicated" than their bosses. Never mind that the long hours might actually be counterproductive in terms of the organization's real objectives—or the well-being of its prized "contributors." At that point, the trap closes on everybody.

Work-Team Pressures

Work groups that are filled with first-rate people often develop an amazing spirit that can boost the group to superlative performance. To be a member of such a group is both exciting and demanding. The group members begin to see themselves as special, and—particularly when they have been successful in a keen competition with other groups—they may develop a group fantasy of omnipotence, feeling themselves immune to fatigue, illness, and other "human weakness." This sort of group loyalty, in concert with the always hefty workload, can make team members feel painfully guilty or ashamed about the slightest relaxation of effort. As a result, they push themselves past their own individual limits. The same group loyalty makes it difficult to turn down work or to get support within the group for protests about the workload, even when many in the group privately report feeling overloaded.

Faulty Notions About the Nature of Work

There are two commonly held notions about the nature of work that confuse the question of how much work is too much: the belief that if you work long and hard enough you can finish every job set before you, and the idea that twelve hours of work are twice as productive as six hours.

Work Is Infinitely Expandable. The amount of time and labor it makes sense to devote to any task is determined, not by the limits of the task itself—since those limits do not exist—but by how much time and effort the project is worth. But what should be a matter of costs and benefits too often turns into the endless pursuit of chimerical task boundaries—a vicious circle of grubbing away at a pile of work that never seems to diminish.

Take writing a report, for example. The report can always be made more thorough, more detailed, more descriptive, and so on without end. One can pursue the history of the matter, document the results of others' efforts, or develop countless action plans in exquisite detail. Technological advances in information storing and processing that make topic expansion so easy have helped to blur the line between what is possible and what is necessary. It is now feasible to make any report about anything into a four-hundred-page book, and some organizations are doing just that. In the practical world, however, the size and complexity of the report ought to be governed by the time available to write it, the kinds of information needed to make decisions, given the backgrounds of the readers, and the prevailing customs of the profession or the organization. But that reality can be pushed aside by a conviction that there is only one right way to do anything—fully and completely.

Some years ago, I consulted with an organization staffed primarily by engineers, members of a profession noted for thoroughness and detailed accuracy. The senior managers in this agency, who were not engineers, finally gave up any attempt to obtain brief, succinct reports from the technical divisions they supervised. They resigned themselves to receiving book-length documents—and books they were, ranging from one hundred to four hundred pages—even when the purpose of the reports was solely to aid internal decision making. When asked about their reasons for the development of such lengthy reports, the staff members at every level cited the complexity of the problems, the need to include all relevant data, the legal liabilities involved, and the varying degrees of technical knowledge on the part of the readers, which required that everything be explained at least twice. When it was pointed out to them that those most immediately concerned with using the information, the agency director and his deputies, depended almost entirely upon summaries and a brief skimming of the report itself, they accepted that reality as a basic weakness of the system but insisted that it was not reason enough for them to be satisfied with less than "a really good job." While the staff of this agency, which had been experiencing a period of rapid growth, continually complained of manpower shortages, they saw the efforts of senior management to "lean down" their reports as "an attack on their professional integrity" by an outsider.

What those brave, if somewhat mulish, engineers did not appreciate was that a report, like any other job, ought never be done as well as it might be done, because if that were the goal, there would never be an end to it.

Twelve Hours of Work Are Twice as Productive as Six. When things get exciting at the workplace, and new tasks seem to multiply themselves, conscientious and highly motivated people simply tighten their belts and work as long as necessary to get the projects completed. At least that's the way most "hero" scripts are written. Although no one outside of those engaged in organizational research thinks about it very much, an underlying assumption of this buckle-down resignation is that the ratio of time spent at work to actual accomplishment always stays the same no matter how long one has been in the traces—a nice thought, but not true.

Because my own experience has told me that twice the time spent working did not produce twice the results, I have frequently pursued this point with clients. I've concluded that most of us, even with all our wonderful human adaptability, have limits, and our bodies and unconscious minds know them even if we don't. We may accomplish more in twelve hours than we do in six, but the increment of additional accomplishment is likely to be much smaller than the simple arithmetic would lead us to expect. Two human characteristics vitiate the assumption that twelve hours are twice as good as six: the tendency of workers to unconsciously pace themselves and the demonstrated effects of overload on effectiveness.

Let's consider pacing first. Short-distance runners expend many more ergs of energy per second than their marathon-running colleagues, who know that their strength will have to sustain them over a much longer course. Although we may not be fully aware of it, most of us establish a work pace that we can maintain throughout the anticipated working period. Thus, when compelling situations require us to speed up, and we know that the race will be a long one we use our internal brakes to slow down the pace. These "rest stops" may masquerade as headaches, digestive troubles, or sleepiness, misplaced papers, time spent in arguments that otherwise might not have occurred, sidetracked forays into relatively unimportant issues, or in other guises devised by our ever-resourceful unconsciouses. In short, because we naturally pace ourselves, working twice as long won't produce twice the results.

Even if we didn't pace ourselves, we would still confront a point of diminishing physiological and psychological returns brought on by overload. Whether the last two hours worked are as productive as the first two depends upon many factors, one of which is the degree to which our work schedules are meshing with our individual biological clocks. Recent research has shown that working periods that are too far out of synch with the body's natural rhythms of alternating periods of activity and rest—the so-called circadian rhythms—can leave many individuals feeling disoriented and mildly depressed. This interesting new research made sense for me of some puzzling personal experiences—sudden bouts of foggy-mindedness and discouragement that followed sustained periods of burning the midnight oil. I had been mystified because these feelings of disequilibrium often occurred when I'd been able to scratch out a normal amount of sleep. It was while listening to a client who had been forced to spend long evenings nursing a troublesome manufacturing process describing his state of mind as resembling jet lag that I realized that my reactions were not the result of some unique aberration in my own internal balancing mechanisms. Rather, I'd created my own "jet lag" by letting my sleep and waking cycle drift from my body's natural schedule.

Now we know that such experiences are common, although the number of overlong workdays required to produce disorientation seems to vary greatly from individual to individual. (As with conventional jet lag, incidentally, when the fogginess hits, avoid making important decisions, attempting complex problem solving, or engaging in other activities that require sharp judgment and keen sensitivity. Executives whose subordinates need to be alert should encourage or even order them to take planned respite breaks.)

Like unconscious pacing, the jet lag induced by overwork is an inherent limitation on how much we can do for how long. Clearly, a befogged mind can't accomplish what a fresh one can—another reason why, in the arithmetic of overload, twelve is not two times six.

Inefficient Use of Resources

It is stating the obvious to say that people frequently don't use time or money efficiently. But because advice on both of these topics is easily available, and our focus is on the *special* hazards of the fast track (while sloppy work habits are seen everywhere) we will not delve much into the mechanics of efficiency. However, the reference list for this chapter includes several books that clients have said were helpful in making them more efficient.

Unfortunately, although common sense and most seminar brochures say they should, time-saving techniques will seldom reduce your workload pressures to any significant degree. Recall that any piece of work can and, if you're not careful, will expand indefinitely to fill all of the space you may conscientiously squeeze out of your crowded day. My point here is that increased efficiency will reduce overload only if it goes hand in hand with the other techniques we'll be covering in this chapter.

HERE'S HOW TO COPE

I have yet to encounter a client who did not scoff at the suggestion that it might be possible to gain some measure of control over the size of his or her workload. "I'm already not doing half the things I ought to be doing," is a common response. "Sure, I'd like to delegate more," the overloaded Fast Tracker will admit. "But . . ." There's always that "but," followed by ". . . since I'm responsible for this division, there are some decisions that I must personally make" or ". . . the bureaucracy around here forces me to decide on everything." Whatever the reasons, they are invariably delivered persuasively and backed by numerous examples.

Interestingly, however, within six months, those clients who have been willing to work with me admitted, if grudgingly, that their workload seems somewhat lighter and that their feelings of overload have diminished even more. As you will see from the collection of techniques on the following pages, the effort to cut workload often seems like scraping away at a mountain range with a teaspoon. Yet there are several reasons why the attempt usually pays off.

The first reason is that great friend of humankind, Pareto's Law. In general terms, Pareto's Law poses a

20/80 relationship between effort and results, such that 20 percent of any investment will generate 80 percent of the potential return. Equally provocative is its reciprocal: it will take an 80 percent effort to muster up that last 20 percent of whatever might be accomplished. Whether or not those exact percentages always hold, the basic notion that each added increment of time or effort tends to produce less and less actual impact has been demonstrated in a dozen fields. For example, walking a brisk mile three or four times a week is certainly not as health-enhancing as walking five miles five times a week. But repeated studies have shown that the former gives almost as much aerobic benefit as the latter, even though to the five-mile walker (let alone his jog-ten-miles-a-day cousin), the one-mile walk seems a paltry effort. In short, if you succeed in reducing your workload a bit, you'll gain more in renewed energy and well-being than you'll lose in accomplishment.

The second reason why even a small reduction in workload pays off is that it may not take much of a lessened workload to transform a state of demoralization into an exciting sense of leading an energetic life. A heavy workload is just that—a lot of work to do, up to a point. Beyond that point, which varies with each individual, the debilitating effects of overload will set in. If your personal overload point is fifty hours per week—not an uncommon dividing point—a regular dose of fifty-five hours per week will likely drag down your effectiveness disproportionately. And the effects are cumulative. Think of it in terms of Dickens's Mr. Micawber's essay on money and contentment: if your income is $100.00 and your outgo is $99.00, the result is happiness; if your income is $100.00 and your outgo is $101.00, the result is disaster. Though you will surely doubt it at first, the fact is that a small decrease in your workload *can* make the difference between one that stimulates you and one that lays you flat.

Here, then, are some techniques that many Fast Trackers have found helpful in gaining control over both the size and the pace of their workloads. Many of them, as you'll see, are simply ways of sorting out the good sense from the nonsense about what it takes to be successful in a demanding job.

Check Out the Reality of What's Expected

In many, perhaps most, organizations, workers—particularly supervisors and managers—are indeed judged by how hard they seem to be working. Yet there are often cooler heads who know that the customary long hours don't equate with quality work. If you're lucky, your bosses might be among that perceptive group.

Questions such as the following may help you sort out myth from reality in the expectations that are operative in your organization.

1. In truth, do *all* of your most successful and highly regarded peers stay at their desks until eight o'clock every night except New Year's Eve?

2. Have you come to consider long hours a sign of commitment, responsibility, and devotion to duty? Is that consonant with the fact that your superiors talk mostly about bottom-line objectives?

3. Has a legitimate expectation that you put in any *necessary* hours transmuted into an assumption that you'll work late every night?

If you answered "no" or "I don't think so" to the first question and "yes" or "I guess so" to the latter two, a quiet conversation with your supervisor might be indicated. The subject will be the degree to which the number of hours spent on the job is the critical indicator of your worth to the organization. A mistaken assumption that long hours are a necessary prerequisite to advancement is more a rule than a rarity. For example:

In the central research division of a major corporation, almost every project manager believed that both the department director and the vice president for R & D expected them to work sixty to seventy hours a week on a continuing basis. When a succession of resignations and a suit for stress-induced illness provoked an all-day "retreat" for the purpose of finding ways to reduce staff overload, these assumptions were brought out into the open. They turned out to be untrue.

Both the director and the vice president had been aware of the excessive workload, and for months they had struggled frantically but unsuccessfully to find ways to alleviate it without damaging the division's mission. Consequently, they had kept to themselves their concern about the overload and the resulting rushed and sometimes less-than-quality work. Ironically, even after implementation of several workable ideas that were developed at the retreat, the project managers continued to believe that their bosses assumed that sixty hours was a normal workweek.

Try Something Different
To differentiate what is necessary from what is not in your work routine, experiment with different approaches to structuring your workday. Change your work patterns in any ways you can think of. If you normally start your

day by plunging into paperwork, try walking around and talking to people instead. If that's what you usually do, start off by attacking the pile of phone messages that were yesterday's effluvia. Vary your lunch hour, if you've been taking one (if you're like many of the Fast Trackers I know, most of your lunches are eaten on the freeway, off of a tray in your office, or in your imagination). If you're a "night person," purposely work until 11:00 P.M. for several nights and then leave at 3:00 P.M. the next day. Spend the rest of the day with your family or in another activity that is personally satisfying to you. Be sure to talk with your boss about what you've done; maybe he or she will learn something new.

Your purpose will be to break up a mental set that can make whatever you've been doing, including coming early and staying late, seem absolutely necessary. Chances are, it isn't—but you won't know that until you dare to break out of your routine.

Is Everybody Doing It?

Are there role models in your organization or among your business or professional associates who have learned to control their workloads rather than merely responding to them? If so, try to find out what they do and modify it to fit your own situation. Don't let yourself be put off by the fact that the work they do is different from yours or that their places in the company allow them to take liberties. Look for specific ideas or techniques that you might use.

Ask for Help

There is an all-too-common belief that sharp managers and rising superstars should never have to ask for help. Such a belief assumes that promotion from the ranks is an anointing that bestows or certifies perfection on the chosen one (even though, interestingly enough, subordinates seldom believe that of their own bosses).

Reporting on a study of the qualities found in superior managers, Michael Lombardo of the Center of Creative Leadership pointed out that compared with less promotable managers, the superior ones asked for advice and help much more frequently (from peers, subordinates, and mentors), built mutual-help networks in the organization, and used consultants and technical assistants to (1) avoid reinventing the wheel, (2) think through and manage complex undertakings, and (3) get perspectives on how well they were doing their own jobs.

By asking for help, you can actually strengthen your image if you do it right. Here are some rules of thumb that can get you help and at the same time build your relationships with potentially important people.

1. Ask for help as early as you can; don't wait until you've run into an insurmountable obstacle. It is almost always easier to prevent problems than it is to solve them, and invariably less costly in time and resources. Although this flies in the face of the prevailing wisdom that you should draft your plan in such a way that others will "have something to shoot at," I believe that most of the available evidence is on the side of getting certain kinds of help before proceeding with the development of a plan. (Professional writers learn painfully that a piece that is not structured properly often cannot be saved, even with great editorial effort. But a bit of editorial feedback during the outlining phase can save them from having to dump hundreds of thousands of words in the round file.)

2. When asking for more money or staff, show how those resources will benefit clients, customers, or the organization itself in addition to helping you or your people. While this seems to me to be an obvious step, I've frequently found it, understandably but unwisely, omitted. It's natural, when you need help, to emphasize the trouble that the help is designed to get you out of. But too often, regardless of the polish with which the message is delivered, your plea—and it will be heard as that—may engender just the reaction you don't want: "here's another hungry mouth to feed. Why can't you take care of yourself?"

   Keep in mind that the resources you want must invariably be taken from someone else, and those with the power to give them to you need all the positives they can get to justify their decision or to counter those who will say that they can make better use of the resources than you can. Stress the positive, because, as psychologists Kahneman and Tversky have shown, most people will invest more on the chance to get something good than they will to prevent something bad from happening.

3. In the same vein, carefully monitor yourself for a complaining, whining, or an accusing tone of voice. Complaints and accusations almost always get reactions rather than actions. If you have doubts about that, keep an eye on your own response the next time one of your subordinates or family members complains. If you react typically, you'll initially try to placate the complainer with a little sympathy or an understanding jibe. If that doesn't work, you're apt to hear yourself defensively justifying your part

in the problem, ending up with your own accusation "If you did a better job of organizing, you wouldn't need any more help." Your potential benefactors are likely to react the same way.

4. Ask helpers for ideas and alternatives rather than answers. If you force others to tell you what to do—of course some people will feel compelled to do so even if you don't ask—they often feel annoyed if you fail to carry out their instructions, thereby leaving you with a dilemma. Do you follow their ill-advised orders and end up with a bigger mess than you had before, or risk being seen as an arrogant upstart who doesn't take good advice when it's given. Requests such as "I'd like any thoughts you have about what might work" or "What alternatives have you seen work in this kind of situation?" make it easier to avoid being pinned down about the course of action you plan to take.

5. Unless there are specific reasons for not doing so, always follow up significant requests for help with a note or a verbal acknowledgment. You might indicate how you finally resolved the problem, mention the need for additional future help, or simply express your appreciation. I suggest that you complete the communication process in this way whether or not your request for help was truly productive. Most senior managers secretly want to be seen as "elder statesmen" and often privately bemoan the fact that younger managers do not seem to realize what a store of experience and wisdom they have acquired. Studies have shown that they are pleased

to be asked for help (if, of course, it is a request and not a complaint).

Remember, asking for help is also a form of relationship building. Consequently, any requests for help should show respect for the helpers' positions and attainments, acknowledge their competence—even if they don't always act competently—and leave them feeling good about themselves. The five points given above should help you accomplish these objectives.

Set Priorities

Developing priority lists—that is, arranging tasks or objectives in some order of importance—must be the most lauded, misused, and unused planning device known to man. The reason priority lists are so often ineffective, I believe, is that managers are urged to focus on the useless end of the list, the top, rather than the helpful end, which is the bottom. If you've done a good job of establishing your priority list, it is the bottom of the list that will tell you what you are to do poorly or not at all, so that you will have the resources to do whatever is at the top of the list exceptionally well.

Studies of successful managers have repeatedly demonstrated that they purposely allocate varying levels of time and attention to the tasks that face them, focusing on minutiae in some and dealing cavalierly with others. They work some projects all the way through to completion while letting others bounce along as best they can. What these peak-performing managers have learned is that you can't do the former unless you also do the latter.

At the very least, a good priority list can keep you from succumbing to that most importuning of all phrases, "It's important."

Of course it is: most people with demanding jobs are only asked to do "important" things. But it is inexorably true that when there is insufficient time to do all of the "important" things, some of them either won't be done or will be done poorly. The question is, which ones? Usually those that get short shrift are the ones around which there is the least amount of squeaking, even though they may be of the greatest long-term significance. Similarly, a well-considered priority list will give you permission to take a step that is often agonizing for most conscientious Fast Trackers: giving a lick and a promise to the important items at the bottom so that you can do those at the top well. By matching every new task that is thrown at you against your priority list— particularly the bottom—you will have a better sense of the trade-offs involved when something new is added to a load that is already full. For the list to work, you'll need to have confidence in the way you've set the priorities. For that reason, several references to particularly useful priority-setting methods can be found in the chapter 2 reference list in the back of the book.

The next step is to use the cold logic of your priorities as a communication device to educate others to the fact that paying most attention to what's *most* important and giving minimal attention to what's least important is your way of not frittering away time and money. A good priority-setting method not only helps you list items in an appropriate descending order of importance but helps you explicate to others the reasons for the placement of each item on the list.

Learn to Say No

For most people the stickiest stratagem for gaining breathing room is saying no to what are sometimes called messages from God—those special "requests" from highly placed superiors and other powerful people. Whether it's a casual (but disruptive) "can you come to my office right now?" or a memo asking you to "please find out about _____ as soon as possible," the custom in most organizations seems to make "right away" the only possible reply. Awe of high rank, leftover whispery childhood fears of punishment, and a simple wish to please the ultimate givers (and takers away) of rewards, make this automatic response understandable but unfortunate, because it shuts off one avenue of workload control. In reality, if you do it skillfully, you can sometimes get away with saying "no" (or, at least, "not right now") when the message from on high clashes with your own priority commitments.

If you're like most well-brought-up people, your first hurdle will be your own belief that when the boss "requests" anything a decent respect for eminence requires that you say yes. Here are some ideas about saying no that reduce the possibility that you will be seen as rude, insubordinate, or (worse) as lacking an awareness of the requester's importance.

1. *Check out the urgency of the request.* The higher one goes, the greater the tendency to assume that one's time is always more valuable than that of those lower in the hierarchy. In a literal sense the notion of decreasing value is accurate—CEOs *are* paid more than lesser functionaries. But this does not mean that hour for hour what the CEO is doing is always more important to the needs of the enterprise. While some executives—the wise ones, of course—have learned that there are times when they should sit on their heels while an employee of lesser rank who is doing

real work carries on (ignore the sarcasm—top executives do, at times, perform useful functions), most
have not. Consequently, a request that you "come
to my office as soon as you can" usually is made
without much thought of the costs of your dropping
whatever you are doing. I have not infrequently sat
in company with as many as ten disconcerted managers, in limbo, while awaiting the return of a key
executive who had been plucked from the meeting
by a "could I see you for a minute, Charlie?" call
from the CEO. Since such calls often elicit a rapid
reflex action, the CEO never even has the opportunity to judge whether "right now" is really worth
the cost of idling a roomful of managers and an expensive consultant.

To give your own top people a chance to make an
informed choice, politely check out the urgency of
requests for your time. Something like this should
do it: "Could you make it at three o'clock instead,
Tom? I'm meeting with my sales managers, and they
all have planes to catch." While some chief executives may secretly enjoy an instantaneous response
to their royal commands, when faced with a choice
between wasting money or waiting a bit, their good
sense usually prevails.

2. *Check out exactly what's wanted.* Who has not been
   the perplexed recipient of a demand for information
   from an important person who did not specify the
   kind, quality, and scope of the desired information?

   Take a telephoned question such as "Mary, can
   you get me a comparison of our last three years'
   travel expenses with those of the previous three
   years?" Is a time-consuming, detailed report, com-

plete with backup data wanted, or is the caller
merely asking for a glance at year-end summaries
and a handwritten note to the effect that "we've
spent about 30 percent more for travel over the last
few years."

Sure, there is a certain tingle when one is asked
to do staff work by a very important person. But I
have seen too many earnestly researched reports laid
on the desks of senior managers who had forgotten
why they had asked for them. An automatic check
on the use to which the information will be put can
save you time and disappointment.

3. *Pause before saying yes.* Try to substitute a phrase
that forces you to pause and consider for an immediate "yes sir." "Let me check on a few things with
some of my staff. I'll call you back in ten minutes."
During those ten minutes you can (1) review these
points about how to say no, (2) think hard about
what effect taking on another task will have on you,
and (3) not ask anyone else about what you should
do, because they will usually be very brave with your
blood.

4. *Say no decisively and as soon as you can.* If you
decide to say no, say it without equivocation and as
soon as you can. The longer you wait, the harder it
will be to stay convinced that you're doing the right
thing. Further, most people will assume that if you
haven't said no, you're probably going to say yes. If
they make their plans on that assumption, you may
find yourself stuck with filling in the gap left by
someone who "was sure you would be able to do it."

5. *Give as few reasons as possible.* Volunteering reasons why you can't fulfill a request simply stimulates problem-solving "help" to overcome whatever is keeping you from saying yes. Embellishing your "no" with explanations, a temptation that most of us find hard to resist, can make you sound ambivalent or defensive. An arbitrary "do it!" to counter what is perceived as your indecisiveness may be the result.

6. *Say "it can't be done."* You may be specifically asked to give reasons why you cannot respond as requested. Instead, reply first with a statement reinforcing your good intentions and your recognition of the requestor's importance: "I hate to say no to this, Norm, and I know you're the boss, but . . ." Follow that with a matter-of-fact reiteration that you cannot comply. The words of choice are "Sorry, Norm, but it's just not possible right now."

7. *Offer an alternative.* When you must say no, you can often prevent an angry or irritated response by offering a reasonable alternative, such as "I can't have it for you in two weeks, Edith, but I can have it for you in three" or "I can't meet with you tonight—how about first thing in the morning?"

Don't important people sometimes ask for a response that really *is* critical? Of course they do, and even if you put these steps into practice, you may end up saying yes frequently. But if you can cut even one out of five "yeses," you'll have gained a significant step on your sense of an overload. You may also find that you have gained respect in those important people's eyes. That was certainly true with Nick Brodski.

The CEO of Ridex Corporation was known to expect spirited and enthusiastic responsiveness from his executive staff and their immediate subordinates. He asked for reports or project proposals on very short deadlines and was annoyed by any attempt to change them. So it was with some surprise that more than once I observed Nick Brodski, general manager of one of the larger divisions, dealing with the CEO as if he had never heard of the rules that he was supposed to follow. For example, in a company in which almost all executives stayed late, he was in his car and on the way home by six o'clock, unless he was personally needed to meet a customer's request. If his boss or the CEO "suggested" a late session, he would smile and say, without explanation, "Sorry, it's impossible tonight; how about seven-thirty tomorrow morning?" On two of the three occasions I was privy to, the CEO paused, looked around—for what, I'm not sure—and then proposed a new time. On the third occasion, Nick canceled his evening plans after hearing a brief explanation of the purpose of the meeting and stayed with the rest of us until close to midnight to head off a potential loss of business.

It's true that Nick was an exceedingly competent executive with a well-earned reputation for turning losing propositions into winners. However, I was also told that since his first management job he had somehow contrived to maintain a forty-eight-hour workweek.

INTERNAL SOURCES OF OVERLOAD

However much it may seem so, sometimes the world doesn't deserve all of the blame for our work-related stresses. For most of us—although our wish may be to deny it—some of the sources of overload are within ourselves. At best, they conspire with environmental pressures to intensify the effects of those pressures on us. At worst, they move us to sabotage our own rational efforts at solution.

Findings such as the following, and my individual work with a variety of Fast Trackers have moved me to a conclusion I would have vehemently denied during my days as a rising manager: *many, perhaps most of the people who find themselves consistently overloaded have driven themselves to that state, and it usually isn't necessary if the sole criterion is competence in the job.*

Out of thirty-five middle and upper managers in one group I studied, twenty-five indicated that they would continue to work long hours regularly even if their supervisors did not require them to. Of that same group, three said that the question was irrelevant because they did not *regularly* work more than forty hours per week. Of these three, two were considered equally as competent as their fellow managers, and one was exceptionally productive and innovative. Keep in mind that the key word here is "regularly." Most interesting and worthwhile undertakings require periods of intense concentration and effort, and the issue we're getting at is not hard work, it is that state of mind we've been calling *overload*.

If you recognized yourself in more than a few items in the Checklist of Overload Symptoms, I suggest that you spend some quiet time ruminating over the sections that follow. I do *not* mean simply admitting that you are a "workaholic" and then turning back to that magnetic pile of work in your in basket. While such labeling may give the illusion of having explained something, it actually prevents you from achieving the kind of understanding that is helpful. Rather, try to identify which of the ensuing "inner drivers" to overwork might be keeping you hopping when you should be sitting still and thinking.

Lessons Learned Too Well

Childhood is a time for having our heads filled with assorted proverbs, sayings, and social injunctions that on the surface make sense. But when these operating orders are internalized in childish minds, they are often interpreted uncritically. The result is a set of unexamined standards that it is seldom productive to achieve.

One such maxim that has often rung true with my Fast Trackers is "Anything worth doing is worth doing well." In an ideal world, it would be difficult to argue with that notion, but it flies in the face of the reality of limited resources. Have you found yourself repeating or simply thinking this or similar slogans? (The platitudes you bore your children with are clues to those you were indoctrinated with yourself.) If you do, list them as you learned them and then reword them, from your adult perspective, keeping the sensible part and letting go of the nonsense. For example, a more realistic version of "Anything worth doing . . ." would be "Only the most important tasks are worth doing well," together with its corollary: "And the way you get time to do the most important things well is by doing the less important ones just well enough to get by." That, of course, is what priority setting is all about. (If the notion of *purposely* doing some tasks poorly has distressed you, you're on the right track. Each of these parentally transmitted "instructions for being a good person" has attached to it a further injunction: "never question the truth of this rule.")

Impossible Parental Expectations

As psychologist Alice Miller has poignantly shown in her seminal book *The Drama of the Gifted Child*, bright children often receive an unwanted gift from their parents, an especially painful disease called "Never Good Enough." Miller has pointed out that this disease sometimes leaves immensely talented people dragging their feet against their own inner drive toward competence at the cost of personal regrets over wasted years and much disappointment to those who expected better things of them. Paradoxically, this same disease often produces superachievers, who, despite kudos from everyone around them, feel neither gifted nor successful.

The telling symptom of the Never Good Enough disease is a nagging sense at the edge of your awareness that whatever you accomplish isn't enough.

An interesting secondary symptom of this fascinating condition can be evoked by an inordinately high level of compensation or celebrity (what defines "inordinately," naturally, will differ for people of varying backgrounds). It shows up as an inner doubt that you (or anyone, for that matter) could ever be worth the money or adulation coming your way. This doubt can lead to the unconscious assumption that if you're not perpetually exhausted, you must not be working hard enough to justify all the "rewards" you're receiving.

To be infected with this disease, you have to have been a bright child of parents who themselves were bright children, for the Never Good Enough affliction seems to be one that is passed on from generation to generation. It incubates in the nursery, when each childish accomplishment is met by that qualified sort of approval that says "That's nice, but you could do better." The teenage equivalent is "Sure, five A's is good, but how about that

B?" Sadly, even though your parents eagerly anticipated their child's triumphs, they could no more savor them than they can their own, for always there remains that nagging thought, "I/you could have done better."

Those who suffer from this chronically frustrating condition attempt to find relief in one of two equally unsatisfying remedies. Some simply fight their impulses toward true achievement, knowing in advance that "success" must always elude them. Most do the opposite and become productive but perpetually dissatisfied overachievers, driven without their knowledge or informed consent toward a goal they can never reach—an unambiguous and unqualified parental approval. (Remember that the "parents" here are not the actual, flesh-and-blood people who were trying to cope with life as well as they could, but your memories of those powerful, all-knowing figures as seen through three-year-old eyes.)

This is not to say that parental teaching and example alone account for the stubbornness of the Never Good Enough disease, for it is nurtured by both our social and work environments. As dysfunctional as this cultural inheritance is for individuals, there is little doubt that society gains from the productivity of its victims—at least in the short run—for the social rewards for those who stay in the fracas are large. Certainly a society whose best and brightest cannot allow themselves to be content will achieve much, consume much, and glorify both the achievement and the consumption. It will also build into its traditions efficient and powerful mechanisms for ensuring that the key message—whatever you are, it isn't enough—will continue to do its job of whipping overachievers to accomplish more and more, even as they enjoy it less and less.

If you have been conditioned to have this insatiable

appetite to do better and still better, what can you do? Your first and most important task is deepening your awareness of this tension with which you've lived for so long that it seems a part of you. Expect to shed a few tears over years of discontent, or inner resistance to "living up to your potential." And then what? One possibility is to accept your perpetual discontent as a given and relish the edge it has given you in a competitive society. A second alternative is to test out the realism of that old parental injunction from your present adult perspective. Then decide whether you now want to make your career goals both ambitious *and* consonant with your other needs—for the warmth and intimacy of family life, for the expansion of self that comes from community service, and for those other arenas of enjoyment that can be closed to you when you are overly focused on work achievements. I'll say more about how to do this later in this chapter.

Co-dependency

Recent attention, much of it stimulated by the need to better understand alcoholism and other forms of substance abuse, has been paid to the reciprocal relationships that often develop between those who are excessively dependent and those who have been called "co-dependents." Most of us are aware of the characteristics of dependency: an unwillingness to accept responsibility; the assumption that one ought to be cared for by others, and a willingness to engage in almost any sort of finagling to ensure that care will be given. Co-dependents are dependent persons' partners in crime: well-intentioned people who have grown up believing that they are responsible for seeing that everything comes out right for others. They are internally driven by many "shoulds" that tell them it's their job to save other people from the consequences of their own behavior.

What makes co-dependency so seductive in the executive suite is that it is reinforced by most definitions of what a good manager does. If you have a proclivity for co-dependency, you will feel motivated to make sure everyone's work gets done, whether by giving advice, lecturing, throwing occasional tantrums, or doing it yourself. As you might guess, while co-dependents are usually highly competent and hardworking people, they often feel deeply resentful of the very people they spend their valuable time bailing out. Partly true and partly nonsensical beliefs, such as "A good person always helps those who are anxious, upset, or in need" can lead you to respond to your boss's or your subordinates' longing for someone to lighten their load, so that you may lose sight of the dividing line between what is indeed part of your commitment and what isn't. Sure, "We all have to work hard until the package is out the door" is the stated goal of the group, and seeing that the package gets out the door is your contracted responsibility. But if you make a habit of picking up the slack, others will let you especially if they tend to be dependent people—and you'll find it "necessary" more and more often. The result is that everyone loses: you lose because you're suffering the diminished competence and other symptoms of overload. They lose because they never profit from having to face the consequences of their behavior or learn how to carry their share of the load.

The Excitement Disease

Some people get a kick out of living on the edge of catastrophe. As managers, they crave excitement and arrange things so that something is always happening, for example, by putting off important tasks until the last moment, overscheduling themselves so that they breathlessly arrive at meetings ten minutes late, and similar assorted moves that keep the day lively. If you happen to be what some psychologists have called a "sensation seeker," you will realize in your quiet moments that as tired and frantic as you sometimes feel, underneath it all, at the moment of bursting into the meeting room and riffling through the appropriate papers to get caught up with the rest of the group, you are having as much fun as if you were skiing down a steep slope, almost out of control. Obviously, there's nothing wrong with a little excitement—as long as you stay on the right side of the overload line and the costs to rest, relationships, and the patience of others aren't too great.

Work Is Fun

Most Fast Trackers enjoy their work, or, more properly, they enjoy parts of it. Some get such a charge out of those challenging aspects of their work that they are reluctant to let go of them in order to tend to the dull, routine chores that accompany almost any job. Unfortunately, this behavior can add to overload, because the boring work will not have gone away. If you are one of these "really love my work" people, you may frequently find yourself slaving away at 8:00 P.M., checking travel claims or dictating correspondence because the time that should have been devoted to these uninteresting but necessary tasks was spent having a wonderful time fooling around with fascinating problems, reveling in brilliant but nonessential conversations, chatting with customers who were already sold, or doing whatever else is fun.

CONFRONTING INTERNAL SOURCES OF OVERLOAD

As you can see, some of these inner forces that lead to overload are more powerful and deeply ingrained than others, and choosing to learn more about them is not a casual decision. A few of my clients have questioned whether they wanted to risk quenching some of their inner fire by probing too deeply into its sources. I've always assured them that they were quite right to hold back until their doubts were resolved. Not all change is, on balance, for the best, and only they could say whether and when profound changes were called for.

Others, however, motivated by curiosity about what made them what they were, or by an overload they found too heavy to endure, decided to look further. That sort of delving can usually be done best with the help of a consultant, counselor, or therapist, preferably one who is knowledgeable about both intrapersonal psychology and work-related problems.

To decide for yourself whether you want to pursue this line of inquiry with or without help, I suggest you take the following steps:

1. Identify your own beliefs about how you "ought" to behave as a worker, a leader, or a "success." Briefly list the thoughts that seem most true and important to you. Try to capture the injunctive quality usually found in words like "always" and "never." For example, "I must *always* be completely competent, adequate, and achieving in everything I do."

2. Next, challenge the elements in these thoughts that seem nonsensical, exaggerated, or unrealistic. Ask yourself: is this really true? What evidence is there to support it? When and how did I learn the truth of this statement?

3. Now restate the elements of these thoughts in a form that has less of a "driving" quality. Instead of words like "should," "must," "always," and "never," use words like "prefer," "want," and "sometimes."

Here is an example:

UNREALISTIC OR IRRATIONAL DRIVER	MORE REALISTIC OR RATIONAL RESTATEMENT
I must *always* be completely competent, adequate, and achieving at everything I do. When I am not I am a terrible person.	I prefer to do things competently, because then I feel good. When I make a mistake and it's costly, I wish I hadn't; however, I expect that I will make mistakes sometimes because I am a human being.

Try for a list of at least ten of these inner nettles that were put in place long ago. Keep reminding yourself that you didn't really choose them, even though it seems they've always been a part of you. Expect to feel uneasy at some point—bored, irritated, angry at yourself for wasting your time and at me for suggesting such non-sense to a proven success such as yourself. Such feelings are largely inescapable. They are your punishment for daring to violate a tricky little commandment—never, under any circumstances, question these parental and societal mandates.

On the more positive side, you may feel some immediate relief as you begin to glimpse the unrealistic and almost obsessive quality of these marching orders that for years have been enforced with guilt, anxiety, or fleeting depression. As one of my clients put it, "All I could see was that I had been carrying around a twenty-ton weight on my shoulders that I might possibly be able to drop. It got even better when I began to go back and pick up just the pieces that made sense to me and reason out for myself when and where those long hours were *really* needed to do the job. Actually, I'm working just as hard as I ever did, because the situation's just as crappy as it was before—but still I'm closing up the shop earlier, I'm working fewer weekends, and, strangely enough, actually getting more accomplished."

A WORD ABOUT PREVENTION: THE VALUE OF FRONT-END TIME

Front-end time is what you do at the start of a project to avoid spending twice as much rear-end time fixing things that have gone wrong because you didn't plan, prepare, train, clarify, communicate well enough before you got under way. It's difficult to tease that kind of time out of busy schedules already crowded with projects that seem more urgent. Besides, like most movers and shakers you will be eager to get started moving and shaking, instead of thoughtfully considering contingencies and fallback options. Indeed, in many organizations the term "planning session" is a misnomer, since from the very beginning most of the discussion is about who's going to do what rather than how we know what we should do, how we can test it out before we really get moving, or what might go wrong if we do what sounds good right now. Some of this kind of leaping to the top of the mountain—and falling off of its precipices—is set in motion by the otherwise practical-seeming device of asking someone to "put your thoughts on paper to give us something to chew on."

While that technique does indeed save much milling around, it also tends to focus the discussion on the pros and cons of one initial idea. Even worse, it guarantees the unwitting acceptance of the assumptions underlying that idea as well as precluding a full exploration of the problem and of options for dealing with it. This is, by no means, a brief for milling around. Rather, it is a reminder that time invested before you or your group go into action can reduce one source of overload by saving time later that would otherwise be wasted on emergency repairs.

Here are some examples of savings gained from skillfully using a little front-end time.

Getting Input from Customers

The manager of a service unit in a large brokerage house met with each of her internal customers to get their views on contemplated procedural changes. In addition, she asked for any thoughts they might have on how the service from her unit could be improved. As a result, the procedures were implemented with little of the resistance she had experienced before.

Preventing Fast-Growth Problems

When I told Vice President of Customer Service Norma Forges that her boss and some of her peers were concerned about what they saw as her moody and emotionally charged behavior, she not only didn't deny it, but expressed her own worry that her job was getting out of hand. Among the unremitting pressures she catalogued were a rapidly growing workload, accompanied by a reduced budget, the deteriorating morale of her first-rate staff, and unheeded requests to central-office people about reducing the paperwork. She was thwarted in her efforts to delegate some of her own work—already delayed by her guilt about adding to her subordinates' already burdensome load—by a corporate policy that expenditures had to be personally approved by a vice president. Without doubt, Norma felt overwhelmed, out of ideas, and willing to grasp at straws. Otherwise, she never would have agreed to an all-day meeting of her entire headquarters group centered on the question of how to deal with the division workload.

The format was simple. They identified the most frustrating issues, further explicated them in small groups, and came up with alternative solutions. The meeting produced these results:

• The managers involved learned from one another specific techniques for cutting the fat out of an individual unit's workload. None of them had been using all of the techniques, some had been using none. They had simply slogged away at the ever-increasing work.

In addition, they assembled specific data about the hidden costs of three procedures mandated by corporate finance. The data were so convincing that within a week following the meeting Norma was able to get temporary relief from those time-consuming tasks (two years later, the "temporary" relief was still in place). Throughout the day, Norma's staff pointed out ways in which she was contributing to her own stress, as well as theirs (they knew she was overloaded before anyone else did, and not only did they hate to see a first-rate manager lose her effectiveness, they also didn't like being yelled at). Interestingly, they suggested that the one new position that had survived the cost-cutting process should be utilized for direct assistance to Norma.

Implementation Intelligence

Although most college-bound school kids have heard Bobby Burns's lament about "the best laid plans of mice and men . . ." they don't seem to remember it when they become leaders, or they might appreciate that one of the most useful versions of front-end time is what is sometimes called "implementation intelligence."

The essence of this obvious, when you think about it, method is looking to see what unplanned-for effects have fallen out of your highly planned-for projects. It is not quite the same as checking to see if your project was properly implemented—naturally it was; you saw to that personally—although that is better than no checking at all. Either, however, is a better alternative than a usual practice of simply waiting six months to see if the project has paid off. By the time the six months is up, it will be too late or too expensive to fix. Here is an example of someone who avoided a minor humiliation by taking an early look at the effects his program was creating.

The department of highways in a major Midwestern state had a history of failed attempts to engage its managers in leadership training. The most successful effort, a well-planned program implemented by the agency's Training Bureau, had remained in place for a year and a half, until mumbled complaints about "more important things to do" and noticeable nonattendance brought it to a quiet close.

Toby Ronald, the new agency director, was convinced of two things: first, that management quality needed to be upgraded and, second, that previous programs had failed because top management had not continued its support throughout the program. (He was right on both counts.) Consequently, Toby had his human resources staff prepare a plan for a broad-gauge developmental program beginning with a fanfare of speeches and even a ten-minute videotape in which he expressed his personal interest and enjoined all managers to participate. Luckily, two months after the program commenced, he was also persuaded by his consultant to gather some informal data on how it was being received. The consultant was not too surprised—although Toby was—to discover that its major positive effect had been to provide a new topic for coffee-hour humor.

Realizing that something different was needed, Toby dismissed, with thanks, his human resources planning group and proceeded to design a new leadership program himself, using his own training experiences as a guide. Yellow pad in hand, he met with several layers of subordinate managers, especially those he had been told were the most skeptical. Although he recognized that he lacked the expert knowledge of his quite capable human resources people, he also knew that he had to get the attention of those who had good reason to believe that his support of the program was only verbal.

When he announced that he and his executive group were going to be the first ones to go through the training, he broke what seemed to be the last barrier of resistance. The management development process, considerably modified to be sure, was still in place when he left office four years later.

While taking front-end time is decidedly useful, it does seem quite contrary to the ebullient fast track nature, perhaps because of the optimistic perspective of most Fast Trackers. When poised to get started on a carefully planned project, only a pessimist would take the time to anticipate disasters that might never occur. Of course, as you might have guessed, I've only mentioned this as a way of urging you to try it anyway.

3

The Squeeze at the Top

"The higher you go, the less 'up' there is."
"There are fewer chiefs than there are Indians."
"There is far less room at the top of any pyramid."

No matter how you say it, the discouraging fact is that the farther you've climbed, the fewer the places there are left for you to go. Here is how it looked to Alex, an assistant vice president in a moderate-sized Midwestern bank.

"I ran my ass off to get to this job. I've been here four years now, lots of interesting assignments and plenty of positive feedback, but no clear notion about when and how I'm going to make the big jump to vice president. You know, there are four of us assistant VPs in this division, and at least two of them are pretty smart guys, but it's not the competition that's getting me so down. It's the fact that the guy who promoted me to this job was hired away by one of those hotshot West

Coast banks, and the new VP—who, by the way, is a woman—seems a little cool toward me. Now she's moved one of my old buddies out and brought in a gal from her old company. Frankly, it's not nearly as clear to me as it was ten years ago that merit and hard work are the most important keys to the executive suite, even if they ought to be."

Whether they are almost at the hierarchical peak, or, like Alex, trying to break out of the middle, accepting the squeeze at the top is especially irksome for the very people who most need to accept it—those with the potential to move even farther.

SLOWDOWN ON THE TRACK

Disbelief, perhaps, better describes their almost bewildered complaints about the long interval between their last promotion and the one they have led themselves to expect. They tick off the succession of two-year, one-year, or even six-month incumbencies in previous jobs, and speculate anxiously about "what's going on"—and for a very understandable reason. Most successful people bring energy and ability into the fray. Their early successes reinforce the notion that good sense and hard work pay off. And to some extent, their perceptions are quite right.

Alex, whose plaint started this chapter, had indeed risen rapidly. A computer whiz kid in high school, he had majored in math at a prestigious university and had brought to the data processing division of his bank an unusual knack for getting faltering programs to work. At thirty-two years of age, he supervised twenty-seven technical people, consulted regularly with senior management throughout the bank, and had initiated and brought to completion several innovative new systems projects. He was, he was certain, distinctly ready for promotion to the executive ranks. Why, then, had he spent three and a half years as an assistant vice president, with no end in sight?

To an outside observer, the reason seems obvious—there are many climbers and not many places at the top. But it's the very qualities of those who take the fast track—ambition, a desire for power and recognition—that make it so difficult for them to accept a fact that may consign them to a lesser status. They're puzzled when they see less-competitive coworkers seemingly content with their current jobs, unconcerned about advancement to power and glory. The obvious danger (once again, to others, not themselves) is rampant impatience. Their frustration at "the system," or at "the politics of it all," or their anger at that person who did not choose them for promotion may induce them to react in self-defeating ways. This chapter is about how not to do that.

We'll start with a glance at the world as it might look when and if you begin to experience the squeeze at the top. Then we'll consider those actions that will help you with the twofold challenge you need to meet in order to keep your chosen career from going into a permanent stall: accepting the reality of the squeeze while at the same time positioning yourself to take advantage of an opening when one does occur. As you explore each of the coping steps, remember that you need to pay attention both to the realities you face and to your reactions to what you think is happening.

After discussing the when and how to consider seeking a greener pasture, we'll end with a look at the special trauma of mergers and acquisitions.

HERE'S WHAT TO EXPECT

Just as predictable as the slowdown itself are your potential reactions to it, and the reactions of others about you.

Disbelief and False Confidence. If you're like most Fast Trackers, you have an abiding confidence in your talents and abilities, which you trust will at length be recognized and rewarded. Like Alex, you will point with justifiable pride to projects successfully completed, dollars saved for your company, and increases in revenue that were due to your sagacity. Certainly a belief in the ascendency of your own star is valuable, perhaps essential, for anyone who is bound for the heights. Such an optimistic perspective, even if it is rosier than a colder explanation of the facts might justify, can insulate you from being overwhelmed by possible disasters. Such a beneficial effect has often been observed in people who for a time refuse to accept the diagnosis of a life-threatening illness: a few weeks of comforting denial provides them with time they need to come to terms with the worst. The obvious negative side is that, if taken cold turkey, the unpleasant facts might have shocked you into taking preventive action of the sort we'll look at in the next section.

Patronizing Platitudes. Unfortunately, superiors and mentors often collude with you in ignoring what's really going on. They typically respond to your initial queries about when and how you will start moving again with placid evasions of the "there, there" variety. They may point out that "it just takes time" to become thoroughly seasoned into a job, and add heartfelt assurances that your worth will be recognized in due course.

"You're Not Ready." At length, you can expect subtle and indirect—or, if you're lucky, unvarnished and blunt—comments that "you're not ready yet." As we'll see later, these comments can provide leads to your real prospects. However, you'll need to gird yourself against these well-meant but undermining reactions.

"Maybe They're Right." When that longed-for promotion remains elusive, you may begin blaming yourself. Fleeting doubts that you really can "play with the big kids" may pop into your mind, perhaps at odd moments of being alone with your thoughts—in the car, on the commuter train, or when you're trying to sleep.

"Those SOBs!" Whether or not you've gone through a period of losing faith in yourself, you are likely to feel anger and suspicion that others are to blame—your boss, who hasn't supported you, certain peers or subordinates who have undermined you (one of my clients was certain that *all* of her subordinates were in league against her), assorted golf or tennis partners of the CEO or agency director who have toadied their way into "your" job, even your spouse, who didn't have faith in you.

If you find that you've begun to blame yourself or others, take heart. Remember that both of these reactions are natural sequels to being jarred out of your comfortable conception of your rightful place in the world. On the other hand, don't underestimate the ease with which the combination of wavering confidence and a slightly paranoid view can propel you into shooting yourself in the foot. For example, I've sadly witnessed angry, whining attacks on supervisors mistakenly thought to be responsible for a denial of promotion, gossiping about the ineptness of a superior with peers and subordinates, and emotion-driven (and consequently inept) attempts at politicking and maneuvering. Not only were these actions crude and unplanned, but they were so transparently self-seeking that they turned off the very people whose approval was crucial for the frustrated Fast Tracker to get unstuck.

Getting Out or Dropping Out. If this dispiriting cycle continues, the highly likely result is a more direct attempt to get free from such an emotionally untenable situation: a frantic search for "a way out" through transfer to another part of the organization, or even a resignation. While either of these actions might be quite constructive if part of a well-thought-out developmental plan, impulsively done, they often lead to more trouble of the same kind. Later in this chapter we'll consider useful guidelines for judging when you would indeed be better off leaving the situation and how to do so in a way that minimizes risks.

A second and sadder result is bitter "acceptance" by the Fast Tracker of the untrustworthiness of people, and of life in general, quite frequently followed by the transfer of these still talented, but now burdened and grumbling individuals to dead-end jobs.

Adopting a New Perspective

Thus far, we've considered a set of unfortunate and not very healthy responses to the predictable slowdown in your move upward. Much of the rest of this chapter develops the coping steps that will enable you to escape the vicious circle I've described and respond in a more positive—and career-enhancing—way. But to take advantage of these steps, you first need to develop an alternative perspective to the blame others/blame your-self syndrome that derails so many Fast Trackers.

No Better, but No Worse than They Are. It takes appre-ciable courage to see things, including ourselves, as they are, neither better, nor worse. Recent psychological re-search has shown that most people—and I believe that this is particularly true of Fast Trackers— have a view of life that is more optimistic than realistic. Ironically, the studies also show that pessimists tend to be far more accurate in their assessments of what's actually going on!

While the rosy view most of us adopt certainly makes it easier to explore unknown frontiers, or embark on am-bitious projects, it also sets us up for a certain amount of running into brick walls. Perhaps that's not too great a price to pay for the willingness to rise to a challenge. But troubles can arise when the victories you most hoped for don't materialize. For our pessimistic friends, disas-ters at least provide the satisfaction of confirming a dark view of the world. For us optimists, every discovery that the world is not always cooperative brings stinging dis-appointment. If caught in the squeeze at the top, you may save yourself from artistically blaming yourself or others, if you recall these "pessimistic" realities:

.   You are not the only one in the world who is able, highly motivated, skillful, and energetic.

2.   *Situational factors, mostly out of your control, may favor a competitor* for the very plums you've had your eye on and for which you may very well be best suited. For example, when sales in your com-pany are up but profit is down, your competitor from finance will get the nod for the next vice pres-

idency even though you, the marketing whiz, are generally more qualified.

3. *The closer to the top you are, the more you and your competitors will be of about equal competence.* Sure, there will be differences, but remember that the nearer people are in ability, the less likely that relatively small differences will be noticed. Therefore, such things as image, friendship, and general comfort will play a more important part in who gets the prize than they did when you were competing at lower levels. In the 1988 summer Olympics, the three 400-meter medalists were only one second apart. While those seconds loomed large for the competitors in that event, if you were simply looking for a carrier of messages, you would see all three as being plenty fast enough. Your real interest would be in other characteristics that might be nice to have in a message carrier, such as the ability to tell entertaining stories around the nighttime campfire.

In short, though we might all agree that virtue should always be rewarded, the plums of life do not always go to the most deserving.

HERE'S WHAT YOU CAN DO

Now that you've inoculated yourself with a little medicinal pessimism, let's look at constructive ways of dealing with the squeeze at the top.

Realistically Size Up Your Situation
To operate effectively and even ethically in the world, you need to see things as they are, not as you think the

ought to be. Consequently, your first task in coping with the squeeze at the top is a reality check of your chances for advancement. Amos Hardy is one who did not take this step.

Amos Hardy had been executive vice president for the Praxis Corporation for six years. During that time, he had managed the three largest divisions in the corporation, bringing to the job vigor and enthusiasm, and, even more importantly, a tremendous belief in the possibilities for rapid growth of the company. A highly positive person, several times he had pushed ahead on projects that did not produce the results he had expected, but in each case he had bounced back with an even more optimistic view of what the future might bring. Amos's enthusiasm and dedication earned him the loyalty of his direct subordinates, and when he was promoted to executive vice president, he felt sure that he was a shoo-in for the presidency. True, he had often been in conflict with the chairman, who was also the CEO, over a variety of issues, but he dismissed these head-on collisions as "part of the game" and ignored charges by some of his peers that he was a "black-and-white thinker who didn't understand how to compromise in a world that was mostly made up of shades of gray."

When the CEO hired a president and chief operating officer from the outside, Amos was both incredulous and furious. At first, he seemed to accept the patient explanation of his boss that Praxis needed an operating officer with broad corporate-level experience, and that Amos, who had, as the CEO put it, "never been able to get your nose out of operations," needed to develop a corporate-wide view. Two years later, the new president suddenly resigned. Amos, who in the interim had taken on a number of corporate-level staff responsibilities, once again expected the nod. When yet another outsider was brought in, Amos abruptly resigned.

My conversations with Amos's boss, peers, and subordinates led consistently to the same conclusion—without a dramatic change in his outlook and behavior, Amos would never have been asked to take the presidency. The CEO, who had a genuine liking for Amos, saw him as an impulsive risk taker who would not listen to advice that contravened his own sense of what should be done. Indeed, it was the CEO's fondness for Amos that had led him to bring up the possibility of his promotion to the presidency with several influential board members. All but one, he told me, were adamantly against the move. The puzzle was, as one of Amos's peers put it, "How could such a smart guy be so blind about the way things were stacked?"

Amos Hardy was not, as his friends knew, a stupid man. Nor was it solely his burning wish for promotion that kept him from seeing unpleasant realities. His own need to see possibilities where they did not exist was helped along by the unwillingness of his boss and his friends to confront him with the hard truth and, especially, to risk losing a person of his undisputed capabilities. His boss believed—with some justification, it turned out—that if he had been completely candid, Amos would have resigned in a huff. However, it was also true, as I pointed out to this perhaps too-kindly man, that if he had been completely straight two years earlier, Amos might have changed enough to become a serious candidate for the presidency. The CEO quickly assured me that anyone who had to be told about such obvious behavioral flaws was not presidential material. With that opening, I proceeded to ruin the rest of his day, as a good consultant should.

As in Amos's case, setting unrealistic targets for yourself can make you appear out of touch and even fanciful to your superiors and others whose support you need. Remind yourself that questions like "What jobs can I do?"; "What am I ready for?"; and especially, "What do I deserve?" although often touted in "Aim for the Top" seminars, can lead to rational self-deception. They set you up for misreading of others' reactions, ignoring relevant facts, unnecessary disappointment, and a not very constructive escalation of anger at your bosses, your organization, and yourself.

Being realistic means apprising the situation objectively, but to do that, you need to counter some natural human tendencies that can interfere with your effort to perceive clearly and accurately. Here are the worst offenders.

It's Easy to Be Overmotivated. Cautionary words to the wise for ambitious people are not hard to find. Almost every Sunday newspaper carries heartwarming articles by well-known figures in the sports, entertainment, or literary worlds reminding us that success, once attained, turns out to be hollow and that the real satisfaction of life is in running the course. Most people who have profited by their own experience enough to become wise endorse the truth of that statement, and even those who are not yet wise (or successful) have been known to sagely nod their heads. The rub is, most people, particularly ambitious people, don't feel that way. As the popularity of athletic contests attests, most people prefer winning to losing, even when the battles are fought by surrogate warriors, as they are in sporting events. While playing the game for its own sake has its rewards, the inhabitants of any sort of fast track really do wish very much to be the ones to capture the prize, and the closer they get to the winner's circle, the greater is its appeal.

The fly in the ointment for those who would stay calm and objective is that as their emotionality increases, their ability to see things clearly and thus find the best path through thorny problem thickets diminishes. So if your prime task is to see yourself, others, and the general lay of the land as clearly as possible, and to find creative ways of dealing with obstacles, your best bet is not to want what you're going after too much. The confounding paradox is that the more you want some potential outcome, the more the power of your mind will be severely constrained.

We have learned a good deal about the nature of that constraint recently. Convincing research has pointed up these effects of excessive emotionality:

1. When emotions are strong, tunnel vision sets in. That is, as soon as the emotional overload strikes, your circle of awareness constricts and is aimed solely at the task immediately at hand. It is easy to understand the evolutionary value of such concentration. When the saber-toothed cat started to leap at our cave-people ancestors, the ability to concentrate on getting the spear in the right place was obviously the ticket to a longer life. But that same useful response becomes dysfunctional when a broader view of shifting sands of modern organizational life is called for.

2. Under conditions of emotional arousal, people act to get rid of whatever they think is causing that surfeit of feelings, often leading them to take action too quickly. If Alex, for example, upon first being passed

over for promotion, had rushed in to confront the bank president, he would have been behaving in a perfectly understandable and human way. He also would have made his situation worse.

3. When feelings are running high, people tend to fall back on whatever tried-and-true, well-practiced, habitual behavior is in their repertoires. This approach works well when a rapid response is essential—that saber-toothed cat is about to pounce—and when the problems aren't too complicated. But most of the situations that stall your drive to the top are complex rather than simple, subtle rather than obvious. Thoughtful, well-considered solutions are what you need, not a "hit it if it moves" approach. The following steps will help you to avoid the worst of these very human reactions.

Check Out Your Suspicions. Even if you're "certain" that there is plotting and manipulation going on, check out your suspicions with a cooler head—a mentor, your boss, or a friend. A caution: keep in mind friends' general tendencies to tell you what they believe you want to hear as a sign of their support.

Reframe Your Irrational Dilemmas. One of the most difficult realizations to accept is that we all have had our heads filled with beliefs about life that are unrealistic or irrational. After all, to each of us, life appears to be as it appears to be—a universe of happenings that we see, hear, touch, and feel, that have some physical reality. If we didn't feel sure that what we believe to be true is true, how would we ever have the confidence to take any action at all? Fortunately, at least in the practical world, there is enough correspondence between our own inner vision of the world and what's out there so that most of the time we don't fall down the stairs. However, a great deal of convincing evidence shows that many of our beliefs about what people are like have been tainted by misperceptions that were deeply imprinted in childhood and carried, virtually unchanged, into adult years. What makes these beliefs even more pernicious is that we are largely unaware that we have them, so we misjudge what's happening around us.

For example, it was not until my forty-second year that I discovered a deeply held belief that if I was not the very best at anything I attempted, then I must be, by definition, a failure. I had posed for myself an irresolvable conflict of a sort I've come to call irrational dilemmas, a problem posed in a way that precludes any solution. If I didn't try I was a failure. But, however hard I tried, whatever I achieved, it wasn't going to be good enough. I've found that people who strive for high position are often plagued by similar irrational beliefs—such as, "If I don't win the prize (or promotion), then I'm a loser"; or its cousin, "If one of my competitors wins the prize, then someone must be to blame"; or the best one of all, "If you win, I lose."

It is hard to discard such notions, because they seem to be consonant with so much that occurs in organizational life. Consider the following case.

Tess was a first-rate industrial-hygiene chemist who had moved as quickly through government ranks as civil service regulations would allow. At age thirty-two, she saw herself as a prime candidate for promotion to laboratory chief, a politically visible job with responsibility for enforcing unpopular and often newsworthy regulations. After Tess had been considered, but not selected, for two laboratory chief positions that had opened up, she began seriously to think about moving out of public employment to someplace "where people were promoted for merit rather than for how old they were or how well they got on with the director."

When we met, Tess said to me, "If I don't get a directorship the next time around, others in this agency, including my own staff, will begin to wonder what's wrong with me. And if Arnie [another well-respected lab supervisor] gets the nod, everyone will see him as the winner and me as the loser. I don't think I can live with that."

Whether you win or lose is defined by the rules of the game that you're playing. Many authorities have pointed out that American workplaces often confront employees with contradictory expectations. On the one hand, much is said about the value of cooperation, coordination, and teamwork; on the other hand, the informal but far more important rules make promotion a game—a win-lose, zero-sum undertaking. Nonproductive competition is fostered that both impedes effective performance by individual managers and other aspirants for promotion, and leaves highly capable individuals convinced, even though they take pains to hide it, that they are "losers" because a particular plum has eluded them.

For these reasons, a worthwhile undertaking is to bring into your awareness those irrational dilemmas that center on questions of success and promotion and then reframe them in terms that reflect the true nature of the situation. For example, "If Arnie gets the directorship, I will have lost, and that will mean that I'm a failure" might be reframed as "If Arnie gets this directorship, I will get another directorship" or, even better, "If Arnie gets the directorship and I do not, it is because of a particular combination of abilities and luck that favored him and not me. Therefore, my task is to understand the nature of that combination so I can change what is possible and accept what is not." (You'll find that your "reframings" are usually much longer than the childlike irrational beliefs they are substituting for.) Many of my clients are helped in this reframing task with a simple paper-and-pencil exercise. On the left-hand side of the page, they jot down their beliefs about what it takes to be, or to feel, successful. On the right-hand side of the page they successively reframe these statements until they become problem statements that fit the evidence, rather than irresolvable dilemmas.

Determine What the Selection Criteria Are

Once you've begun to see your situation more objectively, you're ready to take more active coping steps. Begin by determining as well as you can what the current criteria for selection are. For example, what kinds of people have been promoted to the level to which you're aspiring? Is there a "hero image" in your organization? There is in most. In Amos's organization, the board expected that anyone who was presidential material would be a "broad-gauged thinker" who could bring together divisions that were often in fierce competition for scarce resources. The board had selected the current CEO because he had clearly displayed those qualities. That he also hesitated endlessly over important acquisition decisions, so that the best were often lost, was accepted as an unfortunate fact of life. The point is not that it's better to be steady but slow, rather than strong and impulsive, as Amos was. It is that you must identify which criteria are in force in your situation, so that you can decide how to deal with them most effectively.

Selecting people for promotion poses some paradoxical problems for those doing the selection. Research and common experience clearly show that the best clue to proficiency in a higher-level job is effectiveness in the current job. Yet higher-level jobs often require talents, skills, and other personal attributes of a quite different order from those previously needed for success. Thus, aggressive, successful sales managers may not make effective marketing vice presidents, superscientists aren't necessarily efficient laboratory directors, and first-rate actors may not win awards as producers and directors. Those doing the selecting may play it safe and opt to hire from the outside rather than take the chance that they might be promoting someone to his or her level of incompetence. (While the same risk applies to beginning jobs as to those at higher levels, the risks to the organization seem less. Thus, the promotion of very able technicians to barely adequate first-line supervisors takes place all too frequently.)

In light of this reality, I have often suggested to ambitious clients that they compose a role that can be enacted in their present jobs that will demonstrate that they possess the qualities needed in the jobs to which they aspire. Amos, for instance, might have sketched out what qualities would characterize an executive VP for operations who had "a broader corporate view." Was it more knowledge of how the human resources and finance departments worked? That certainly was the way Amos interpreted the comment that he needed a broader perspective. Or would the key be greater concern for the success of his peers, the other vice presidents? How would his annual operating plan be changed if it were attuned to long-term corporate strategies?

Remember, we're dealing here with *perspectives*—the

criteria of selection are in the minds of other people. Consequently, in constructing this role for yourself you'll need to consider both the needs of the company and the qualities that those you wish to impress admire. Of course, you'll be the one to enact the role, and if it seems phony to you—that is, you don't understand or accept the value of what makes up that image—then your doubts will likely show through.

As a help in developing and enacting a new role for yourself, you might consider such broadening activities as enrolling in an executive development course. This kind of move will have a number of advantages. First, it draws attention to you in a positive way. Second, it provides an opportunity for you to report to the highest levels in your organization about what you've learned and how it might be used for developing the organization. (Don't wait to be asked to report; seize the opportunity.) Third, there is the simple psychological fact that if your organization has invested money in you, and those in the position to promote you know it, they are more likely to justify their decision by giving you the chance at a better job. Fourth, you might even learn something.

Identify and Change a Negative Image

Most of us manage to strike a reasonably comfortable bargain with ourselves by focusing on those of our attributes that we like and avoiding a too-close look at those that are less desirable. If we can't completely avoid being cognizant of our flaws, we explain them away, excuse ourselves, blame our misbehavior on others, and in other quite skillful ways, deflect seeing the full truth. Most of the time this is quite a handy arrangement, but at times it gets in the way. The plain fact is, if you aspire to continue along the fast track, you're well advised to

take a balanced look from time to time at what you bring
to the party so that you can (1) take full advantage of
your strengths, (2) eliminate or at least cosmeticize your
warts, and (3) find the best place for someone with your
particular mix of positives and negatives.

Here are some steps that will help you to identify any
negative images that others may have about you so that
you won't, like Amos, be the last to know.

Check with Friends. Your friends probably know more
about you than anyone else. How then, you might wonder, can they stand being with you? The answer is that
they like you—and while they really know that you are
not as wonderful as you sometimes think, neither are you
as reprehensible as you may imagine in moments of depression. In other words, they see you in balance, and
for them, the positive outweighs the negative. That
makes them an excellent source for finding out what your
perceived negatives are.

To get useful information from friends and close associates, you'll need to give them permission to be honest. (This is particularly important with those kindly
individuals who assure themselves and everyone else that
they firmly believe in being honest and open with other
people. These folks will care so much about your comfort that it will be very difficult for them to tell you
anything that they think would upset you.) In particular, you'll need to make it plain why you're asking for
honesty: that you're interested in developing yourself as
a manager, or a professional, or a performer, and that
it's not your intention, after hearing starkly painful
things about yourself, to end it all.

The real key to getting honesty is this: whatever your
friends say to you during the first few minutes, nod your

head and thank them. If they haven't been sufficiently forthcoming, suggest that you're also interested in smaller, relatively insignificant aspects of your behavior. That should help get them started. Follow up vague or general observations with a request that they be specific: ask for examples, look behind labels and indirect statements. For example, if your friend says that you are "usually" willing to listen, ask to know about those situations in which you did *not* seem to listen well.

Make a List. The human ability to forget unpleasant things is phenomenal. For this reason, you will find it useful, if disagreeable, to jot down all of the negatives you will hear, or have heard, about yourself. Include those heard during performance reviews and those shouted by sarcastic bosses, sullen subordinates, or jealous peers. The point is not whether you really are everything that you've ever been accused of being, but rather that these particular others have seen you a certain way, and when you subtract the 75 percent that is due to their spleen, envy, or ulcers, there are probably some kernels of truth in their perceptions. Think of this information as a collection of snapshots of your behavior as filtered through, and distorted by, your friends' and associates' biases, wishes, and fears. You're the one who has to decide how much of what you hear is really you and how much is a function of other people's quirks; but don't let yourself slide into total denial.

In making your list, try to stay away from labels, such as "abrasive," "indecisive," or "not very well organized." Instead, describe the specific things that others believe you are doing or not doing that have led them to label you with those disagreeable qualities. Expect bouts of disbelief, a conviction that you have not done the things you feel accused of, and even a certainty that this list could not possibly be an accurate depiction of someone as wonderful and successful as you. Expect, too, bouts of blue funk and whichever other symptoms of tension and anxiety have become your favorites. Then, after you've finished explaining to yourself or others the "real" reasons why you behaved in the ways that led them to see you in a negative light (or concluding that your pushiness or hot temper are entirely the fault of dumb or recalcitrant people who drove you to it), take a deep breath and hunt for a better perspective. Understand that your reactions are merely signs that you are on your way to being able to change, as long as your skillful denials or blaming tactics don't completely throw you off course. If reading your list makes you feel like you've been hit in the face with a wet fish, know that you're on the right track. Your objective is that clear but kindly idea of yourself that psychologists call acknowledgment. As painful as it might be—and if there is no pain at all, you're doing an even better job of denial than most—by acknowledging that you are not living up to your own idealized image of yourself, you've embarked on a developmental course that can produce the polish you need both to get the most out of yourself and to smooth the way for whatever promotional opportunities are possible for you.

Check It Out. Because much of what both your friends and enemies have told you results from their own twisty perspectives, it's important to seek further before setting yourself to the work that self-development requires. Think of yourself as a crack behavioral scientist studying that most interesting person in the world, you. Observe yourself in meetings and while giving instructions to your subordinates. Is it true that when someone asks a question, you are always the first to answer? And is your answer pushed in the face of the questioner in that superior tone that says "My way is the only way." Or, when commenting to a subordinate on a recent presentation, do you find yourself tossing out such lukewarm pap as "You handled that reasonably well" when you know that you *should* have said "Sally, you didn't sound prepared"? Sometimes it helps to quantify. Count the number of times during a week that you speak with a derogatory edge in your voice. Ignore as irrelevant whether or not your victims deserved to be held in contempt, because that isn't the point. The point is twofold. First, if you are seen as someone who frequently puts others down, and if the executive image in your organization is antithetical to that behavior, you will be reducing your chances of moving upward. Second, people who feel demeaned seldom perform at their best, and the performance of those at the receiving end of your scathing comments will be a poor advertisement for "good interpersonal skills." Remember, every study of the reasons why executives are sidetracked has shown "lack of interpersonal skills" as a leading cause.

Minimize, Contain, Control

Paul was referred to me by his boss, the division general manager, because his "poor communication skills" were reducing the performance of his department. The department human resources manager had mentioned to her divisional counterpart that in a number of exit interviews, Paul was described as being insensitive, a "confirmed know-it-all" who frequently lost his temper at meetings and cut down staff members regardless of their rank. Why was the company willing to pay for individual consultation for Paul? Because he was technically brilliant, a man of "rare scientific vision," an intense, enthusiastic whirlwind who personally made sure that every product that went out the door was done right and done on time. They didn't expect miracles from my work with Paul; as Paul's boss put it, "This guy's got so much on the ball that we'll be happy if you just polish him up a little bit and, especially, stop him from rolling his eyes when someone makes a comment that he doesn't agree with. When he does that, everyone is sure that what he's thinking is 'What a stupid jerk.' Paul works almost eighteen hours a day, every weekend, and he never takes a vacation because most of his staff, including his supervisors, are angry and demoralized and rarely productive. He's complained to me that he can't hire people who can work quickly—and it's true that his department is in the 'Find out what's needed and get it out quickly' business. But I know that they're slow because they are paralyzed by the notion that no matter what they do, he's going to yell at them about it."

As Paul's boss implied, a *small* behavior change on your part can make the *big* difference between the perception of you as a "sharp guy with a few rough edges" and "a talented fellow, but just too abrasive (indecisive, hardheaded, shortsighted, aggressive—you fill in the blanks) to move up any further.

Here are the steps to help you manage your difficult behavior enough so that it won't interfere with your promotional chances.

1. Limited Goals. Pick one or two of the behaviors from your "ugly list" that you believe might be impeding your progress the most. One useful criterion is the number of times the behaviors are mentioned by a variety of people. (Paul selected "criticizing employees in public" and "not listening" as the two most important failings for him to work on.) As you work on your target behaviors, keep in mind that human liabilities are most often strengths that have been excessively or inappropriately applied. As I suggested to Paul, the same quick mind and confidence that led to his appointment as department head could also make him sound like an impatient know-it-all who believed himself superior to everyone else.

2. Put on the Brakes. At the instant you become aware that you're doing just what you've decided you want to do less of, stop. In practice, this means finding some socially acceptable way to break off the behavior—in mid-sentence, if necessary. While this is not initially easy to do, it does get easier with practice.

For example, during his initial efforts, Paul twice became aware that he was publicly calling a subordinate supervisor on the carpet during a staff meeting. The first time it happened, he felt emotionally overwhelmed and yet found himself continuing his reprimand, but with a dry throat and a vein throbbing at his temple. What amazed him was that the recognition that he had done just what he had determined not to do had not stopped him from repeating it ten minutes later with a different supervisor. As Paul described it to me, "I could not believe that I had just screamed at Nate for having let the M30 project fall behind. I mean, there I was, having screwed up once, doing the same thing again! You know, in the past it had never even occurred to me that there was anything the matter with letting people know what they've done wrong, regardless of who else was there. But it was better the second time. I stopped myself in midsentence and said 'think about it, Nate' and moved on to the next agenda item."

3. Select Substitute Behavior. Behaviors like Paul's, tending to scold subordinates in public, shaming or ridiculing them in a way that prevents better performance in the future, arise from a complex of causes. Therefore, it's very handy that you don't need to fully understand all the reasons behind your self-limiting behavior to keep it from becoming a major interference. Self-knowledge *can* free you from old, deeply programmed ideas that inhibit your effectiveness and your capacity to enjoy what life has brought you—but you can do a good deal to modify your *behavior* even before you fully understand why you do all those foolish things.

Like Paul, you should expect to find the behavior that you most want to stop often bursting from you as if it were out of your control. Instead of merely saying to yourself, "I shouldn't be that way" or even—and this is far better—"I don't *want* to be that way," think of some substitute behaviors that you can throw into the breach. Paul chose these two: "I want to hear your side of it, but let's talk about it later," and "Wait a minute, tell me more." The first one he brought into play when he found himself castigating a subordinate or accusing a peer. The second worked well for him when he suddenly realized that he had interrupted, or had leaped to answer a question too quickly, before he knew the full story.

4. Learn to Repair. It's unlikely that you will gain immediate control over behavior patterns that have served you well (and ill) for many years. For that reason, learning to repair any damage that occurs when you slip can act as a fire control measure, preventing the problem from spreading. In addition, taking some repairing action, since it calls attention to your concern for others, can help to feed their perception that you are indeed a changed person.

Repair has three steps: acknowledging that your behavior was not productive, stating your regret that the other person was on the receiving end of that behavior, and returning more objectively to the issues that led to your own inappropriate behavior. Here is Paul's report of how he handled the repair with his subordinate, Dick.

PAUL [sticking his head into Dick's office]: Can you give me five minutes, Dick?

DICK [not looking up]: I suppose.

PAUL [sitting down]: What I did in the meeting this afternoon was absolutely inappropriate. Losing my temper is something I've done all my life, but I know that I can't afford to do it as a manager, and I've set myself to stop, but I sure didn't that time.

DICK: You sure didn't!

PAUL: Well, if it gave you some bad moments since then, I'm really sorry.

DICK [slowly turning to look at Paul]: As a matter of fact, Paul, I was just sitting here, thinking about trying to transfer out of the department. I don't really care what you say to me about my work—but right there in front of my own people!

PAUL: You know, it's funny, Dick, but until a little while ago I never really thought about how losing my temper made other people feel. I guess I always thought they deserved it. Anyway, I've been thinking about what it was that set me off, and I believe it was this. I had assumed that the F38 project was about ready to go out the door, and when you mentioned that you were still fooling around with the software, I blew. It strikes me that we need some better way to keep me up to date about where these projects are.

DICK: Well, you know, Paul, we still have four days to go before F38 was scheduled to be completed.

PAUL: Sure, I know that, but Del Clark has been after me about it, and from a conversation I had with Joe [one of Dick's crew] I thought it was practically finished. The point is, Dick, you and I need a more regular way to review what's happening so that I don't assume all kinds of stupid things. What if we meet on Fridays, from eleven to twelve to run through the project list and talk about anything else that you or I want to talk about.

DICK: Sounds like a great idea. I've been wanting to ask your advice on some personnel problems, but you always seem so busy with your own stuff that I haven't. Besides, I've told myself that I'm getting paid to solve the problems, not to bug you about them.

PAUL: And I'm getting paid to give you all the help I can. Now I'm doubly glad that we've set up these meetings.

Monitor Yourself. As with every other learning endeavor, feedback is essential to enable you to modify and correct behavior that contributes to an undesirable image. We have already discussed some techniques for getting corrective feedback from others. In addition, you can obtain useful information on how you're doing by paying close attention to the reactions of others to what you say and do. For example, Paul was alert to the defensive sound in Dick's voice when he reminded Paul that the due date on his project had not yet arrived. His attention to Dick's tone enabled Paul to reemphasize that his intention was not to further accuse Dick, but to find a way to avoid similar problems in the future.

Three monitoring questions to ask yourself are:

1. *Am I actually doing what I intended to do?* How do I sound? Have I succeeded in getting the main things said?

2. *How well am I doing it?* Where could I be more skillful?

3. *How is the other person reacting?* Does she sound defensive? Does his demeanor—reddening face, leg beginning to bounce, frozen body posture—betray an emotional reaction?

Review for Progress. At sensible intervals—once a week to begin with, once a month after you've seen progress— look back on how your efforts have gone. Review the specific objectives that you initially set for yourself. Have you made progress? Have you lost your temper only once in the last two weeks, when you used to lose it four times a week? Have you had positive comments from subordinates, peers, or superiors that you're easier to get along with, or less moody? A pat on the back, whether delivered by an associate or by yourself, will not only make you feel good, but will help you persist in your effort to change.

Build a Support Group. Unless there are specific reasons not to do it, I suggest that you tell your subordinates and especially your boss about your efforts to better manage your liabilities. There are several advantages to doing so. First, it makes your colleagues ready sources of feedback. While monitoring yourself is essential, other opinions reduce the temptation to engage in plain or fancy denial by explaining away your slips, forgiving yourself for outbursts because others are to blame, or otherwise indulging in skillful self-deceptions. Second, you might be able to engage your boss as a coach. I believe that all employees have a right to expect coaching from their bosses, though, admittedly, not all bosses see it that way. If you have one who is willing to observe you in action and give you clear and direct feedback on how you are doing, take advantage of your good fortune. Third, your changed behavior will lead more quickly to changed perceptions about you if the people who count are alerted to what they ought to be looking for. If you have shared with your subordinates that you intend to listen better to them and to work with them in a less emotional way, they will be on the lookout for signs that you are actually changing.

Changing a Negative Image

Even when you have learned to manage your own difficult behavior, it will take a while for others, including those whom you most want to influence, to know that you've changed. While it would be no more than simple justice if acting differently were enough, it usually is not. Frequently you have to take some positive steps to break a negative image that others may hold about you.

Three factors contribute to this frustrating delay. First, we human beings are by nature stereotypical thinkers. That is, we tend to categorize what we see based upon past experience. Situations that are somewhat different in actuality may seem identical to us, perhaps because the two situations share some particularly salient features. While this sort of thinking process is useful for making quick assessments of what's going on, it often gets in the way of our seeing genuine but relatively small changes, a not inconsiderable handicap when one needs to do fancy footwork in a rapidly changing environment. In practical terms, this tendency means that if company executives have learned to think of Paul as "hot-tempered," "abrasive," and "not very good with people," they will tend to overlook moderate changes in his behavior or to explain them away as aberrations or flukes. In short, we're stuck with the fact that those we want to impress will tend to see in us, for a lot longer than we'd like, what their experience has led them to expect.

As if that were not problem enough, most people have a second and equally strong inclination to see things as they would *like* them to be. But, you might ask, why should Paul's associates or his subordinates want to see him as a poor manager? The answer lies in another nearly universal human quality, one that most of us will own up to when we're honest with ourselves: the iniquities of others confirm our own superiority. After all, is any potion more potent for quelling those fleeting doubts about ourselves than watching another's fall?

Finally, negative images can hang on long after the irksome behavior has changed simply because no one is perfect; mistakes and slips are bound to occur. Every time Paul glares at a subordinate it reinforces the original picture of him as abrasive and amplifies the inertia that slows down perceptual change.

What these sobering facts mean is that changing another's image of you requires both a specific counteracting plan and persistence in putting your plan into effect. The basic method for breaking an old stereotype so that a new one can take its place involves three steps: (1)

identify what those who hold the negative image would expect you to do; (2) do the opposite; and (3) verbally affirm the change.

Identify What They Expect. Let's say you have concluded that influential others see you as one who "gets along well, but can't make quick, hard decisions." (Remember, what matters is not whether their picture of you is accurate; it's how they conceive of you that you're trying to change.) Ask yourself what specific behaviors would follow from that perception. For example, would they expect you to postpone making budget-cutting decisions until your boss or the controller forces you to take action?

Do the Opposite. To break others' stereotype, you must confront them with evidence that cannot be stretched to fit the stereotype—no small order, given most people's skill in seeing what they expect to see. The first step is to identify situations in which you can behave in a manner quite the opposite of what is expected.

For example, you might think immediately of the decision to close several field offices, which you are supposed to implement. You know that for some employees, the closings will result in lost rank, and for others, an unpalatable choice between quitting and enduring long and arduous commutes. Deciding which offices to close is just the kind of situation in which the stereotype calls for you to dawdle, dodge the issue, or wax maudlin about the human costs. But you've been working on your reluctance to make unpleasant decisions, and next Monday's executive staff meeting is exactly the place to start your image-breaking program.

On Monday morning, while shaving or putting on

makeup or brushing your hair—anything that calls for you to stare at yourself in the mirror—acknowledge that in the past your genuine interest in people, your ability to listen to others' viewpoints, your belief in high-quality decisions—virtues of which you are justifiably proud— at times have caused you to put off important decisions. Also remind yourself that for six months you've made progress in stopping yourself just when you felt the impulse to procrastinate. Now you have the chance to exhibit the new you. So, as soon as the meeting has convened, you stand up (to get everyone's attention), announce that prolonging the decision will only make things worse, outline the criteria that you've developed—of course, you've done your homework and have decided on the fairest way to close the offices—and urge that the decision be confirmed before the meeting adjourns.

Verbally Affirm the Change. As soon as possible after acting to shake the old stereotype, talk to as many people as you can about the incident. For example, after your demonstration of tough and rapid-fire decision making in the Monday meeting, make it a point to talk over what happened with your boss. Tell him or her what your intentions were and get feedback on how well you did. Do the same with your subordinates and, if possible, with peers and anyone else who will listen. "I just felt that this was a decision that had to be made quickly and fairly, and I pushed as hard as I could to get it done in one meeting." Of course, you would say this only if that is exactly what you did feel. Your purpose here is not to fool anyone, but to furnish them with a new image of you that encompasses your changed way of doing things.

Why not let them come up with their own revised stereotype? Simply to avoid the possibility that they might shrug off your forthrightness as merely a fluke— uncharacteristic behavior from an indecisive "softy." As most astute courtroom lawyers have discovered, some- times to the detriment of truth and justice, while people are usually aware that something has happened to them, they only know precisely what it is when someone has given it a name.

Identify Senior Staff Opposition to Your Promotion
A particularly disheartening experience when you are trying hard to rise in the ranks is the discovery, or sus- picion, that senior executives with the confidence of those in seats of power oppose your promotion. Their resis- tance to you may have a basis in fact: you may indeed have flubbed an assignment or shown a lack of skill at some time in the past. That you have learned from un- pleasant experience and are now capable of handling a higher-level job often escapes their attention simply be- cause they are not informed about how able you've now become. Regretfully, their negative opinions of you may also be simple prejudice toward people of your ethnic group, profession, part of the country, sex, height, weight, age, or accent. Either way, it's well worth con- siderable effort to bring into play the technique of changing a negative image to counteract their misguided view of your potential. Your objective is *not* to turn someone who's against you into an avid supporter, or even a lukewarm one. Rather, in most cases all you need to do is to reduce that person's negativity enough that the forces moving you upward will have a freer play.

Almost four months after Paul had embarked on his "contain my liabilities program," I was stopped by a corporate human resources manager who rather gleefully suggested that Paul was going to be one of my "failures." Passing through Paul's division, he had heard Paul's voice "ramming some choice words down somebody's throat." Knowing of the incident, I acknowledged that Paul had slipped, but I pointed out that it had been the first and only time in a month that he had done so. It was hard not to chuckle at the look of mingled disbelief and disappointment on my informant's face. He might not now be a fan of Paul's, but neither would he proclaim quite the same negative view of him.

Use a Small Wins Strategy

Even the most successful plan to neutralize opposition to your advancement will take time. Nor should you expect that you'll necessarily reach your objective in one long leap. Like a good mountain climber, you may need to scale the peak in a series of smaller, carefully chosen moves—what has been called the "Small Wins Strategy." The following example provides an illustration.

Virginia, whom we met briefly at the start of chapter 1, was an extraordinarily competent financial analyst who rose rapidly in the office of the treasurer in a Fortune 500 company. She acquired expertise in a variety of investments and developed a program for moving funds throughout a network of banks that generated half a million dollars of income not anticipated by the company. Within five years, she had become manager of international investments and had set as a target for herself an appointment as assistant treasurer. In short, she was speeding along merrily on the fast track—and she was about to hit a wall.

I was asked by Virginia's boss, the corporate treasurer, to work with her after several peers and two of her most competent subordinates complained that Virginia was abrasive and "too ambitious." Shocked that she should be found so wanting that she "needed to be therapized," Virginia was in tears at our first meeting. (Note how neatly she had boxed herself in with an irrational belief. "If my boss thinks I need consultation he must think I'm a terrible person." To her, the game was up before it had started. When, with a little help, she had reframed her reaction to "They must think I'm really something to be willing to pay all that money to smooth out a few rough edges," she was ready to begin work.)

Indeed, Virginia made rapid progress in her efforts to deal with her superior tone and impatient order giving—behavior that stemmed from her (not inaccurate) view that many of those with whom she was working were slow to grasp points that she saw in an instant. She began to see that her strong drive to move upward as soon as possible was beginning to interfere with the very thing she was striving for. Her boss, Ted, a moody sort to begin with, responded to the push and shove of his own job by occasionally rewriting—and presenting himself as the author of—reports that would eventually cross the CEO's desk. Each time one of these instances would occur, Virginia would march into his office and inquire when she was going to be named assistant treasurer. To her, Ted's evasive and indirect answers were confirmation that the company was not about to let a woman into the executive suite. In fact, she had misidentified the problem: there *was* resistance at higher levels to Virginia's appointment, but it stemmed primarily from word that had leaked upward about her abrasive behavior.

Virginia's first step, then, was to identify and begin to counteract the negative image she had developed. As she became more confident of her ability to handle the troublesome aspects of her behavior, I suggested that she try a Small Wins Strategy instead of identifying success with an appointment to an officer position that continued to elude her. Ironically, the all-or-nothing approach had left her stuck instead of moving her forward. In contrast, a Small Wins Strategy would provide a practical channel for "wanting to get ahead" by focusing attention on achievable, short-term goals. It would also serve as an antidote for the side effects of too much "wanting." Remember that too strong an emotional investment can interfere with your ability to judge and distinguish nuances in situations, and it impedes your creativity in finding ways to get around barriers. "Blind ambition" is indeed an apt expression.

Choosing a Small Wins Strategy is not tantamount to accepting failure or even less than the best. "Small" does not mean trivial or unimportant, but rather real and achievable. Nor does it mean giving up on the large wins you're hoping for. Instead, the strategy is designed to get you as far as your ability and your good fortune will allow, while making life as much fun as possible along the way.

Here are the essential characteristics of a Small Wins Strategy as I outlined them to Virginia:

1. *Small Wins are targets that move you in the direction that you want to go.* In Virginia's case, the target of opportunity was presented by Ted, who (a) could see that she had indeed tuned up her management skills and (b) was eager to get her off his back. He obtained approval to set up a higher-level managerial position that considerably broadened Virginia's responsibilities and, more importantly,

made her the technical person who would accompany the chief financial officer and the CEO on their frequent trips to see members of the financial investment community. Interestingly, before she accepted the Small Wins' approach, Virginia's first response was to emphatically turn down this job as a "sop to affirmative action"!

2. *A Small Wins Strategy should involve more than just "bite-sizing" a large task: small wins need to increase your leverage in the system.* The job that was offered Virginia—"Senior Manager of Worldwide Investments"—seemed to fit the bill: her constant contact with the CEO would make it possible to win his acceptance of her appointment as assistant treasurer; the job would allow her to develop contacts within the financial community in which she had not previously dealt; and her new title would increase her prestige in the organization. If the job had merely increased her supervisorial range and brought her a higher salary, it would not have been a suitable target for a Small Wins Strategy. A bigger empire and a fat paycheck may be nice in themselves, but they lack the "prying things open" attribute that makes the small win a genuine move forward.

3. *It must be doable.* If there's no way for you to get started on it, any stratagem, however brilliant, is likely to be more a source of frustration than of satisfaction. There must be some feasible way for you to make progress with the resources of time, power, and access you have at your fingertips. Since Virginia's small win was handed to her on a platter, this

criterion was satisfied as soon as the offer was made. While that was fortuitous for her, most often the ideas for a small win will have to come from you. If Virginia had thought of the senior manager position herself, her next step would have been to probe its feasibility: "When and how should I ask Ted about it? Would our human resources manager object because I would be leaping too many levels in the hierarchy? Would Ted be likely to support me, even if his superiors aren't enthusiastic? If not, what can I do to make the circumstances more favorable?"

4. *It must be satisfying.* Your Small Wins targets, if attained, should leave you fulfilled, uplifted, and feeling good about what has happened, whether or not they move you ahead on a long-range plan.

At first it was quite difficult for Virginia to see how she could be expected to feel good about settling for a plum that was "dried up and shriveled" at best. In her eyes, she was completely ready to step into the executive suite; she had ability of a higher order than any of her associates; and she was personable, attractive, well dressed, and fully capable of hobnobbing with the senior managers "who, by the way, aren't any fantastic shakes themselves." Actually, there was considerable truth in each of these beliefs—but focusing on them was impeding both her progress and her enjoyment. After a time, Virginia was able to see that she had been caught in one of her own favorite irrational dilemmas: "If I don't win (as I define 'winning'), I lose (which means that other people are taking advantage of me, and that's not fair)." Boosted as well by some positive responses from nonwork friends on whom she tried out the idea of the promotion, she recalled a "silly, but maybe true" homily taught her by her parents: "You can either see a glass as half-empty and hate it, or see it as half-full and enjoy it." And she began to see her new job as worthwhile and enjoyable in its own right.

Play It Smart: Dealing with the Competition

Wherever you work, small hierarchy or large, small business milieu or the entertainment world, you will likely have competitors for the same places in the sun that you've set your sights on. There are several advantages to identifying those with the best chances for success and doing your best to look them over with as unprejudiced an eye as you can.

First of all, an objective survey of the competition will help you to identify what is currently wanted by the market you wish to penetrate, whether your "market" consists of the powers that be in your organization or the audiences you're hoping to capture. If you pay attention to comments made by key decision makers about your competitors, you may pick up clues about desirable skills and knowledge that you yourself can work on developing. Those tidbits of information can help you to avoid being blindsided by expectations that work against all of the candidates.

For example, recall the case of Tess, the industrial chemist who had set her sights on a directorship within a government agency. Even though most of the executives in Tess's agency thoroughly understood that administrative and managerial capability were not acquired through attaining a Ph.D., it was clear even to a layperson such as myself that without what one administrator called "a respectable degree," neither Tess nor anyone else could hope to be a real somebody in the agency. Any viable strategy would need to acknowledge that reality. That this informal requirement was unfair, irrelevant to the demands of the position, and questioned by thoughtful people at all levels in the agency did not eliminate the need to address it directly.

While it's easy enough to advise someone to "coolly and clearly assess the competition," it's not always easy for the recipients of that advice to carry it out. Three common judgment biases seem to interfere the most with an accurate appraisal of the competition: downplaying their competence, exaggerating their strengths, and interpreting their efforts to advance themselves as malevolently planned moves designed to eliminate anyone else in contention (which means you). As understandable and common as these perceptual errors are, they make useful planning almost impossible.

Let's take a closer look.

"My Competitors Are All Idiots." During periods of emotional high—and particularly after an effort has gone especially well—the enjoyment of the moment may put your sense of your own weaknesses to sleep and lead you to contrast your assets with the all-too-obvious liabilities of others. When I asked Tess to tell me why top management favored her chief competitor for the next division director opening, she found herself unable to talk about him except in negative or patronizing ways. As I pushed her to explain why seasoned executives would even consider incompetents or nonentities for promotion, she began explaining away his strengths as quickly as she enumerated them: "Hollis is technically brilliant but that's not really important for a general manager's job." While both of those statements were quite accurate, they were out of touch with another fact: that Hollis's reputation as a scientific star could easily push such "minor" liabilities as the lack of administrative ability out of mind. Focused as she was on her own strengths, Tess could see only where Hollis fell short as compared with herself.

One of the striking things that has emerged from our studies of managerial thinking styles is the propensity to judge as somehow defective those who think about things in a different way.* For example, steady and structured people we call "Analyst" thinkers frequently see the rapid-fire mentality of "Pragmatists" and "Realists" as signs of careless incompetence, while to the latter, the "Analyst's" emphasis on order and painstaking examination of data seem to be nothing more than the rigidity of "bean counters." Yet each style of thinking has its own strengths and its own liabilities. The pitfall you need to be wary of is seeing others only in terms of your own strengths.

"My Competitors Are Nine Feet Tall." We all have times of feeling down, discouraged, and deenergized. Particularly during these periods, obstacles can seem overwhelmingly difficult and competitors impossible to beat. In our study of thinking-style differences, we have seen just the reverse of the "competitors are all idiots" bias: competent managers focusing exclusively on the achievements that stem from others' effective use of their partic-

*Those who would like more information on styles of thinking and their relation to managerial effectiveness are referred to *The Art of Thinking* by Harrison and Bramson (see chapter 3 reference list) or can write or call INQ Educational Materials, Inc., P.O. Box 10213, Berkeley, CA 94709; telephone: (415) 891-9984, outside California (800) 338-2462.

ular mental capacities. Suddenly one's own strengths seem to shrink in importance: "What they really like around here are aggressive people who charge out after something. If they get it, they are heroes, and if they don't get it, it's all chalked up to bad luck. It seems as if careful planning doesn't count for anything."

When I find my clients either overly concerned with their competitors' strengths, or ignoring them, I suggest that they jot down for each individual the strengths and liabilities that seem most appropriate to the particular job in contention. It can do wonders for a more balanced perspective.

"They're All Out to Get Me." When others interfere with your attainment of your goals, it can be difficult not to see their actions as motivated by a wish to hurt you. While occasionally that might be the case, it is equally likely that they are simply acting from a belief that your goal is not in the organization's best interests. Even more likely, they are simply pursuing their own self-interest and may not even be aware of the damage that is being done to *your* ambitions.

The Art of Playing the "Statesmanlike" Role

Seeing your competitors as they are—neither better nor worse, neither out to get you nor irrelevant nonentities— can help you adopt a role that I have found to be of great help to those who are in the running for significant promotions: becoming as "statesmanlike" as possible.

Here's an example.

Norma and Mark are both contenders for promotion to marketing manager. At every meeting, they scrap over whose ideas are the best and over who should get additional funds that become available. They tear down each other's ideas, resorting to criticism and sarcasm as they let all concerned know how great their own achievements are and how much they might do if only they had greater leverage and resources. Susan, meanwhile, is also under consideration for promotion, but she shows herself to be above the fray, going out of her way to bring the discussion back to what's best for the organization, whether or not her own ideas prevail or her own section gets additional funding. Rather than being one of the "bickering children," she demonstrates a loftier and longer-range view. Reality, rather than rhetoric, she implies, should determine who gets what, and she is willing to place her own program on the line. Susan offers help to other managers, including her competitors, when they're overloaded and sometimes privately suggests to senior management that available resources can be directed to units other than her own.

Who do you suppose will get promoted in this scenario? Although it may strain your credulity, my observation has been, without exception, that it is the statesmanlike Susans who end up with the most resources and who are chosen for the most important jobs in the organization. There are several plausible reasons why playing the statesman has such salutary effects.

1. It is obviously genuinely beneficial for the organization; in other words, it's an example of how one can do well by doing good.

2. Since you will not undertake this role secretly—on the contrary, you want everyone to be quite aware of what you are doing—it creates the perception of a mature, "nonproblem" person who is committed

to excellence. (Can you help it if the competition acts and looks childish by comparison?)

3. Evidence from a number of studies suggests that most people are skeptical of self-praise and are far more impressed by the positive comments of others. The statesmanlike role is almost invariably noticed and discussed in private conversations, not only by superiors, but by peers (who are frequently puzzled by behavior that is not self-seeking and who may be at least vaguely aware that somehow they have been one-upped, or, more accurately, allowed to put themselves in a onedown position). All this is not to suggest that there is anything perverse or unethical about playing the statesman. It would be hard to characterize as immoral an approach that is based on an objective analysis of the situation, that focuses on what is best for the larger organization and on what is fair and equitable. Playing this role so as to demonstrate the maturity of your outlook would be unethical only if you were surreptitiously undermining the role through secret conversations with powerful people. What makes the role authentic is that in your private conversations you continue to make the case for what's good for the organization as a whole, letting others with more influence and power than yourself look out for your own interests. The fact that they will is a fascinating by-product.

Continue with Your Own Development

Since 1978, almost a third of my consulting time has been spent with talented but flawed senior managers who were referred to me by their superiors (on occasion the referral has come from the chairman of the board and my client was the CEO). Whether promotion to higher level was contemplated or had already been accomplished, the request was the same: to do something, anything, that might mitigate the manager's abrasiveness or "sheer inability to see anyone else's viewpoint but his own." Thus, the initial problem is always how to show confident, successful individuals that further development is still worth pursuing, and perhaps even necessary if they do not want to become one of those of whom it is said, as it was of Winston Churchill, that their brilliant careers are behind them.

When Professor Laurence Peter suggested that organizations often promote people past their level of competence and leave them there, he clearly captured the feelings of many people who are impatient with the behavior of higher-ups in their own organizations. Over the years I have come to realize that, in truth, most senior managers perform most effectively just *before* they are moved into the executive suite. When the reason for this apparent paradox struck me, it seemed quite obvious—all of us need feedback to perform our best, but the higher up you go in any sort of hierarchy, the less personal feedback you receive.

There are several reasons why essential feedback dries up as you move higher. First, the more power you have, the more difficult it is to get those who are most immediately affected by your managerial behavior—your subordinates—to tell you how and where you've goofed. Of course, any good executive will seek and usually obtain rigorous argument from subordinates about policy decisions, but a strongly worded "That's not the right way to go, Boss," is not the same as "Say, Boss, did you know that when you make presentations, you're pretty boring?" Second, even superiors seem reluctant to give honest and specific feedback to those who have been judged to have the "right stuff." Problems with your bottom-line performance, surely, will be called to your attention, you might be scolded for embarrassments, and perhaps patiently hinted to—as was Amos in our earlier example—but you're fortunate indeed if, as a vice president, you are given the gift of an open discussion about how well you personally are doing.

The third aspect of this myth of executive perfection is put in place by the incumbents themselves. It's a special kind of arrogance that comes from past success, the Greeks called it *hubris*. It was that self-deluding pride, they said, that was inevitably followed by Nemesis, that dark emissary of the gods who dealt unkindly with those who credited themselves with godlike powers. Not that there is anything wrong with having confidence in your abilities or feeling satisfaction because your quality has been recognized and rewarded. Rather, modern-day hubris means thinking and acting as if your victories are achieved totally through your own attributes, without the help of luck and the support of others—and starting to feel that you have nothing more to learn. (When clients say to me in our initial meeting, "The way I manage must be OK because it's gotten me where I am today," I always figure it's going to be a long day.)

If you lose perspective on your own behavior, your development will slow or cease, probably without your knowing it. In short, you'll make yourself a candidate for Professor Peter's Principle if you mistake the greatly reduced feedback that accompanies success for infallibility or a state of grace.

The Importance of Keeping Current

As Srully Blotnick, a psychologist who has studied individual business careers, has pointed out, senior managers often are reluctant to keep current about new technical developments and advances in methodology. In part this is because technical matters are properly delegated to technically trained subordinates. However, when department directors or vice presidents admit in a complaining tone that someday they'll "have to understand better how the management information system works," they are not simply affirming the rationale that "I can always hire technical people." These grudging acknowledgments reveal an understandable resistance to a world that changes faster than human beings are constitutionally designed to absorb. Blotnick has pointed out that middle-management executives, while longing for an appreciation of their wisdom and experience, are often seen by younger subordinates as resistant to new ideas and techniques. As you move up through the hierarchy and acquire that commendable and valuable wisdom, don't forget that complaining about the complexity of the MIS system will make you look out of date and past your prime to more technically current subordinates and to hotshot staff people who can bad-mouth you, or worse, patronize you, to powers that be. To put the point more positively, ensuring that you learn about new tools of the trade—especially about how they might be used to understand or solve problems—will give you the appearance of someone who "keeps up" as well as provide the knowledge you need to effectively utilize those who report to you.

Here are a few signs that you might not be staying up to date:

1. Feeling suddenly tired or bored when a new technology is discussed.

2. Skipping pages when an unfamiliar area shows up in a professional article that you are reading.

3. Downplaying the value of a new approach because "the old way has worked well enough."

If you catch yourself indulging in any of these behaviors, pause and take stock. You may be about to cross the line between being valued for your experience and dismissed as out of touch.

Do Some Team Building

Many of the requests for me to work with middle managers have been prompted by complaints to senior management from subordinates of the person in question. Surefire generators of equivocation about promoting someone out of the ranks of technical supervision are unhappy complaints made by able workers.

In addition to helping those clients correct the particular behaviors that have made them ineffective with, or offensive to, their subordinates, I often urge them to engage in a special kind of team-building process that allows grievances to surface and transforms them from unproductive complaints into solvable problems. The process consists of two interlocking steps: (1) using a confidential method to elicit team members' comments about both what is going well and what is interfering with the team's effectiveness, and (2) setting aside sufficient time for understanding and resolving issues that show up in the data (to provide the needed aura of confidentiality, and as an aid to facilitating the problem-solving process, third-party consultation is often valuable, either from outside paid consultants or from human resources department staff).

If the process is carried out responsibly and professionally, you can expect these results: your staff will work better together, enjoy working more, and complain about you less; you'll function more effectively as a manager because you'll know what is on the minds of your staff; your subordinates will demonstrate a level of responsibility that may surprise you if indeed your own communication or delegation has not been the best; your plans or decisions will be better balanced, that is, more in touch with more of what's going on around you (those who are so confident of their perspicacity that they ignore sources of feedback, usually learn about their blind spots only after they have fallen into a hole); and, not least, your superiors will begin to see you as someone who works well with people and therefore as ready to advance up the next step.

WHEN POSITIONING YOURSELF ISN'T ENOUGH

So far, we've assumed that you will probably run into some common obstacles on your way to the top—many of them partly self-created—and that with the proper perspective and a dash of ingenuity, you can eventually surmount them. Of course, it would be unrealistic to imply that this is always the case. Sometimes, in other words, the squeeze at the top is immutable—and you will be squeezed out. How will you know when your best efforts to change a negative image, keep up to date, and so on haven't paid off? Is it time to move on to a new organization and, if so, how will you know that the newer pasture you're contemplating is really greener? These are the questions we will consider in this section.

Signs that You've Been, or Are About to Be, Sidetracked

What signs that you are about to be sidetracked should you be alert to? Here are fairly common indications that you may be in trouble:

1. Your subordinates are openly complaining about you to your boss or to the human resources department. Since you may or may not be told directly about complaints, be wary of questions about how well you're getting on with your staff or whether you're having "communication problems," as well as any suggestions that you "spend more time getting to know your subordinates."

2. Your boss shows irritation or even anger over slips that used to be overlooked. Previously, he or she had softened questions about your late reports with a joke or even a bit of evenhanded criticism, but now the sounds are short, angry, or sarcastic. Either the annoyance was there all along and is just now surfacing, or you may not now be meeting your boss's expectations in some other way. Don't wait for an explicit account about the nature of your shortcomings. Take it that something is causing disappointment in you, and review past conversations for clues. Keep in mind that much criticism is veiled or indirect.

3. If other people are chosen for two or three vacant positions for which you believe you were the best

candidate, review the suggestions made previously in this chapter for pertinence to your own situation. Switch from yellow alert (keeping an eye on things) to red alert (action stations) when, in addition to being passed over, you are assured and reassured of your value to the company and are given general, as opposed to specific, reasons why you were passed over. Ask what the selection criteria were, which of them were deemed most and least important. Then check them out against your own notion of how well you are doing, and how important competitors rate on each of the important criteria. If you get specific answers to your questions, use them as a basis for designing your own development plan. If you continue to get vague assurances and general replies, watch out.

4. Your subordinates seem impertinent, disrespectful, or overly solicitous. In the Blotnick study, managers who had fallen off the promotional track were often patronized or privately ridiculed by their subordinates, who could see the handwriting on the wall even when their bosses were bent on looking the other way. When the brightest (if perhaps not the most loyal) of your subordinates begin to eat lunch with other executives instead of with you or their peers, start wondering.

Be warned that it can be tempting to dismiss or explain away signs that the pyramidal squeeze is including you out. It's particularly understandable that Fast Trackers have difficulty letting go of the belief that competence and "results" will always outweigh shortcomings in the "softer" side of management. After all, it's "results" that got them where they are. But, as we've seen, the higher you go, the more important the "softer" side becomes.

The setting was a super-large wood and wood products company with international holdings in timber, lumber and paper mills, and paper products manufacturing plants, as well as extensive marketing and sales components. Harry Strong had been promoted a year earlier from Manager of Forest Technology to Regional Manager for the Pacific Rim. He had earned that promotion by standing out, in a year of low profits, rising costs, and loss of market share, as a manager who was able to bring in projects under budget and on time. Harry was a tough, bright, creative problem solver, and he knew it. When his human resources manager summoned enough nerve to tell him that she was hearing many gripes from some of the subordinate managers he had inherited, he became furious with her, dismissing the complaints as coming from "the incompetents that my predecessor nurtured," and proceeded to carry on as usual. When his boss suggested that, as part of his own development plan, Harry ought to work with me on "better communication," he complied with obvious reluctance.

Two months later, he concluded that he had learned all he needed to know about being nice to people. He also continued to authoritatively argue those who disagreed with him into fuming silence, and publicly take junior staff members to task for being stupid when they disagreed with him. During this period, Harry also brought two important projects to successful conclusion and developed a marketing strategy that was accepted, albeit reluctantly, by the corporate marketing department.

When, six months later, Harry was abruptly fired, he was dumbfounded. His boss, the area vice president, had this to say when he asked me to meet with Harry, at the company's expense, to help him understand what had happened: "Sue Brite, the HR manager, had met with Harry four times about the complaints she'd received. And I sat down with Harry twice during performance reviews and gave him chapter and verse on how disruptive he was and how he couldn't storm into the MIS manager's office and cuss him out, or humiliate a supervisor with twenty years' experience as he did Red O'Brien, and still expect to be rewarded by the company." Like Amos, whom we met earlier in the chapter, Harry had shaken off all the signs that things were not going well, hypnotized by his successes into assuming that accomplishment was all that counted.

Knowing When to Go, and Going Only When You Know

We have already discussed ways of changing your behavior—and letting others know you've changed—to position yourself as best you can when you begin to feel the effects of the squeeze at the top. At times, though, there are sound reasons for seeking a future outside of your present organization. For example, what you have to offer simply may not fit with what those in charge of promotions think is needed. And the problem may not be your personal qualifications: in most companies, and often in industries as a whole, various occupational groupings rise and fall in the degree of influence they have on policy and promotions. In the film industry during the 1930s and 1940s, studio heads controlled the conditions of employment and possessed most of the power to reward or punish. As glorified as the motion picture stars were in the minds of the public, with very few exceptions their working conditions were highly restrictive and their contractual arrangements amounted to a kind of serfdom. By the 1970s, however, movie stars (and their agents) had moved into more powerful positions, demanding, and getting, great sums of money and often substantial ownership in the films themselves; many used this enhanced influence to become producers themselves.

In technologically oriented organizations, a "guiding coalition" of engineers and financial executives often work together to drive the organization to produce products of high technical quality brought into the market at the lowest possible cost. When market conditions become tight, however, and competitors begin stealing customers, a new "guiding coalition" of marketers may come into ascendency. If you happen to be an aspiring marketing manager in the first case, or an engineering or financial manager in the second, you may find that promotion to higher levels simply is not possible. Then too, organizations in some industries seem to be in love with the rather wasteful practice of hiring managers and key professionals from each other, producing what the electronics industry calls the Silicon Shuffle. Beyond the beginning levels of supervision, managers find that promotional openings are consistently filled from the outside. Their frustration is mitigated only by the knowledge that if they attend enough conferences and conventions and learn to present themselves properly, they too will be courted by a competitor.

There are other potential stumbling blocks as well. At times you may find yourself competing against too many superstars. While no slouch yourself, you may recognize that your chances of advancement in that particular setting are not very good. Or you may be employed in a family company or similarly closely held organization and find yourself running into a caste barrier: no matter how sincerely they appreciate your contributions and want you to stick around, you're not going any farther up the ladder, because being good isn't good enough if you're not a member of the family.

All right, you've taken stock as objectively as you can and decided that the wisest thing is to move on. Before you do, here are some rules of thumb to keep in mind.

Watch Your Motivation. Are you simply moving away from an unpromising job or are you, instead, feeling unappreciated because of an uncomplimentary performance review? Are you temporarily feeling second-rate because a friend, your child, or that nudnick from another department is already making more money than you are? These are the sorts of questions to which you need to attend seriously and with as much objectivity as you can summon. Remember that those critics who have pointed out to you that you are doing something that is robbing you of the best performance you're capable of are helping you to grow, even if that isn't what they intend. If your intention is to show "those unappreciative slobs" that they can't get away with giving you the kind of negative performance review you've received, you may simply be taking your own personal millstone along with you. The point is not that it's a virtue to keep your hand on a hot stove, but rather that you shouldn't let the anticipated relief from removing your hand prevent you from wondering how it got there in the first place.

Listing what you most value in your present job may help you get a fresh perspective about what you will be leaving. (The effect is not unlike the experience of people who, having put their homes up for sale, often find that they've gained a renewed appreciation of what had become quite ordinary as they hear the admiring comments made by prospective buyers.) You may not change your mind about going, but you'll have a handy checklist against which to match any new offers that come your way. Keep in mind what psychologists call the "contrast effect." The worse you feel about the job you're leaving, the better a new job will look. What's more, there is a tricky reiterative effect: your unrealistic fantasies about a good-looking job you're contemplating will make the job you have now seem that much worse, which in turn will make the new job look even better, and so on.

Stuffy as they seem, devices like pro-con lists done for both old and new jobs can help to minimize the degree to which your imagination sets you up for a fall.

Mapping the Terrain. Srully Blotnick has suggested criteria for judging prospective jobs. I believe they are particularly useful for those in midcareer who, for whatever reasons, may be looking for greener pastures. Here are my versions of Blotnick's criteria embellished and illustrated by my own experience:

1. How healthy is the new company, and how healthy is the industry in which it is embedded? Although he had the knowledge and brains to know better, George Taylor, feeling both his oats and an urgent impatience to get to the top, left the general managership of a division in a major corporation to become CEO of a start-up electronics firm. Although the pay was excellent and he was given a free hand, the initial capital available proved to be insufficient to keep the company afloat during one of the pre-

dictable down cycles that befall that industry. Blotnick suggests that such moves are not uncommon. I believe they result from that overly optimistic, rose-colored view of the world that, as we've seen, is both a strength and a liability for ambitious and competent people.

2. If you are contemplating a move to a very large company or agency of government, *specifically* where will you be going? All units in large organizations are not equally safe or equally fertile ground for your own growth and development. Don't become so enthralled by the enticing prospects of a new position that you neglect to ask the safety question as it relates to the particular setting into which you're moving.

3. Are they expecting miracles of you? Watch out for a reverse contrast effect: you look terrific because you're replacing a turkey. When you turn out to be merely first-rate, will they be disappointed and will you be blamed for misleading them?

4. How much influence does your prospective boss have? Useful clues are the relative size of the unit's budget; who the boss reports to; how many layers down in the organizational structure the unit is. Pay attention too to the flavor of others' comments, as seasoned by their grimaces or smiles, when you mention your prospective boss's name.

When a former client, Don Gold, asked me to work with him and his new department, he started off the meeting with a long and mournful discussion of the mistake he had made in leaving a comfortable divisional director job in one of our larger state governments for a regional directorship in a huge federal agency. "How could I know," he complained (actually it was more of a whine) "that the Assistant Deputy Under Secretary to whom I report was put in that job because he'd been promoted upstairs so many times, no one knew any place suitable for him? It's not that he's dumb or incompetent, it's that he has a knack for rubbing important people the wrong way. We don't get the money we need; we don't have the policy influence we need. I should have stayed with the state."

5. Will you be able to take your present customers, clients, or team with you to your new position? Successful professionals who have built a following of satisfied customers or clients, or managers who have assembled particularly able and effective staffs, often believe that they can build on their previous achievements by taking these valued assets with them. Their prospective employers may also believe it. Before either party counts on the transportability of these assets, however, a hard and realistic assessment is in order. It's tempting to let casual assurances lull you into believing that the warm loyalty you feel from clients or staff is fastened to you and not to the role you presently inhabit. Your best bet is to try to look at the situation from the perspective of the people you want to bring along. Their protestations that you've "helped them out a lot" doesn't mean they will go to any trouble to follow you if it doesn't make sense to them. (After all, would you?)

Charming Gerald Harley parlayed his sixteen years as a human resources manager and his demonstrated competence as an organizer into an offer from a successful management consulting firm. Gerald had planned, set up, and managed a major training facility for a nationally known indemnity insurance company. While it was never written into his employment agreement, both he and his new employer expected that he would bring thousands of dollars in client contracts with him. They both should have realized that those "sounds like a good idea" murmurs from his former colleagues did not indicate a strong willingness to undergo the difficulty involved in gaining approval for external contracts from the insurance company's financial executives. The new employer's disappointment did not surface at the time, but three years later, some difficulties arose, and Gerald was accused of having oversold himself. The fact that his old connections had brought in the grand total of two small contracts worth three thousand dollars, instead of the many thousands everyone had assumed, was mentioned as a prime reason for believing that Gerald had not lived up to his promise.

6. Do you have a contingency plan if the new job blows up? For example, could you, or would you, return to your old job? What is the current market for your kind of skills? What is the state of the industry in which you work? Is the industry stable enough that you can expect job openings to be available if you need them? Could you stand the loss of income if you had to for a time? (Take a pessimistic view of how long that might be.) Do you and your family have the stamina to weather whatever storms might

come up? (Take an optimistic view here; external crises usually bring out strengths in most families.)

What About Loyalty? Organizations do not like to lose high performers, especially those who have been consistently rewarded and moved up the ladder. So it's not unusual for appeals to be made to "loyalty to those who have helped you" when one of these valuable individuals talks about leaving.

While there are surely instances in which these appeals are fair and reasonable, in general I believe that loyalty to a work organization—as distinct from loyalty to an individual or a cause—is a seemingly mutual transaction that in reality goes only one way. I suggest to my clients that they consider the fate of "loyalty" when an organization is forced by diminishing revenues to lay off employees. Although management may sincerely regret the hardship to workers and may even delay the layoffs past the most prudent point, the layoffs will occur because they must. The point is not that the organization is being disloyal to its employees, but rather that "loyalty" is not the relevant notion. I believe that these are the questions to ask yourself when trying to examine what, if anything, you owe an employer you're planning to leave:

1. What are the costs to myself if I stay?

2. Are there benefits to staying that outweigh the costs to me?

3. Can I adjust the timing of my departure so as to ease the transition for both myself and my employer?

4. Have I fulfilled any promises that I've made? If not, can I honorably leave them unfulfilled? (Be especially sensitive to commitments you are legally required to fulfill, including oral as well as written contracts.)

Keep in mind that commitment to an employer's goals—which is a part of your "contract"—is not the same as "loyalty" to an entity that only wants you when it can afford you.

THE SPECIAL TRAUMA OF MERGERS AND ACQUISITIONS

From time to time I have consulted with organizations which were in the process of acquiring, or being acquired by, another organization. For the consultant, the experience is not an easy one, akin to that of a Red Cross staff worker at a natural disaster. That there will be casualties is accepted as inevitable; but that much of the carnage could have been prevented or minimized is sad and frustrating.

For those who have invested much of themselves in moving toward the top of whatever pyramid they are inhabiting, the experience of being "merged" is always unsettling, frequently devastating, and at times disastrous. Consider the following account.

Cindy Weiser first learned that the breakfast cereal company for which she was director of advertising had merged with a former competitor several times its size when she read about it as she ate her daily portion of her company's product. She wasn't too disturbed, because she simply didn't believe that it was true. She had had lunch with the CEO the previous day, and he had said not a word. Nor had he looked particularly anxious or fussed about anything; in fact, he had spoken encouragingly about the possibility of beefing up the advertising budget in the coming year. But the moment she walked into the building, she knew, with a sinking feeling in her stomach, that something big had happened. "It was the pits at the office today," she told her roommate that evening. "I'm not worried, though. I've built the department from ten people to forty, we have great statistics, and everyone in the advertising community knows it. I'm going to make out OK."

Three and a half months later, I faced an angry, tearful Cindy. "Shall I quit?" she asked me. "I feel so humiliated, ignored, and betrayed that I just want to get out of here. I spent nine years working my way from copy assistant to director of advertising, and now they want me to go back to a crummy manager-level job. For two months I've been making the rounds of the senior management people at 'the shark' [Cindy's label for her new employer]. Their advertising director is a fathead—everyone knows he 'fixes' problems by throwing money at them—but for some reason or another they decided to leave him in the power position. And, as one of their absolutely insensitive and stupid senior vice presidents said to me, 'Since you're not quite ready for a vice presidency, my dear, we'll just have to find a suitable managership for you.' [In Cindy's company, as is quite common, the director rank she had held put one within sniffing distance of the executive suite and carried with it significant financial benefits.] I tried to hang on to my directorship by proposing a new job in marketing, but it just didn't fly. It's hard to think of tossing away all the years that I spent in this crummy company, but I've got too much to offer to be stuck back into being a glorified account manager."

Do things always work out poorly for everyone when mergers occur? Not at all. Cindy's old boss, for instance, stepped into a newly created vice presidential position (the job had been under discussion for six months prior to the merger). However, those who have studied the effects of mergers have identified several common and troublesome reactions on the part of affected employees.

After the first disbelief has worn off, there is usually a period of relatively calm acceptance, a sense that all will work out well in the end. Gradually, fear for the future and rumors of wholesale firings at the managerial and executive levels reverberate and become the subject of worried conversations that can drive other matters into the background. Interest in the tasks at hand is overwhelmed by helpless anger at the old organization for not "taking care of" its own, often driving formerly competent and able individuals into a kind of lassitude that lasts until reassignments are made or people are indeed asked to accept the "generous severance plan."

Clearly, if you're on the fast track and the organization you work for suffers this kind of seismic shift, you may be in for tough times. Here are some tips for making the transition period less stressful and, just as important, keeping your career on track.

Position Yourself Mentally

What you want, of course, is to remain clear-headed, objective, able to discriminate real dangers from fears born of rumors and fed by whatever dark premonitions of disaster are part of the emotional baggage we all carry with us. The problem is, when your familiar and steady surroundings turn strange and wavery, calm objectivity can soon give way to fury or panic. The cure will not be found in enjoining yourself to "stop worrying!" You'll do better to set yourself to some specific tasks, such as the following:

1. Build yourself what is sometimes called a "horror floor." Take a mental journey through all the potential disasters you can envision. Summon up visions of humiliating encounters—money going out but none coming in, your friends sympathizing with you because of your loss of status while secretly being glad that it's you and not them. As you confront each one, ask yourself, "And then what would I do?" As you answer that question after each of these awful eventualities, it is highly likely that you will discover that no matter how serious the tragedy, at length the sun will rise on a new day. Building a horror floor will not change what happens to you, but it can help you respond to events as competently as possible.

2. Describe in writing what it feels like to live through the difficult period of the merger. Almost invariably, those who do this feel relieved of tension. Equally important, as you externalize your feelings you will become less likely to turn them back against yourself. Remember that depression is frequently anger turned inward, boredom is often anger not directly expressed, and that feeling like an "unappreciated victim" can sap you of confidence just when you need it the most. Clear your head of unrealistic notions of organizational loyalty (review the discussion earlier in this chapter). Assuming your company or agency has been paying you regularly

does it really owe you anything more than a fair chance to find another job? After all, would you not have accepted a job with another organization if the rewards and working conditions had tickled your fancy?

3. Avoid "ain't it awful" conversations with peers and, more importantly, with subordinates. Sharing your feelings with others can be useful if you end the conversation with a realistic but optimistic comment such as "Well, whatever happens, ten years from now, this will all be a vague memory." But conversations that place you in a victimized role tend to tap the dependent feelings that are left over from childhood in each of us. It's understandable to feel lost and unsupported when those you formerly saw as strong, authoritative, and in charge, seem concerned only with their own survival. But such feelings may prevent you from carrying out the next very important step.

Keep Competent

It is sad to see managers and their units respond to "merger trauma" by falling from the high levels of competence they had previously maintained, allowing project deadlines to pass unheeded and waste and inefficiency to go uncorrected. As difficult as it might be, it's well worth making the effort to maintain or even improve your normal level of performance. First of all, you prevent yourself from sliding further into the despair that can engulf you when you've lost your external supports. All you really have left to fall back on is your knowledge of your own ability to get things done, and when you see your performance slipping, an important emotional prop begins to erode. Second, an evident lack of productivity might cost you dearly when the decisions are made about which people from the merging companies should be retained in the executive or managerial ranks.

Develop a Plan

One of the most valuable stress preventers in an unstable situation is anticipating and planning for surprises. Rather than being taken unaware, try to assess your chances of surviving the managerial melding. Is your counterpart in the other organization a person of greater experience or reputation? Are you being merged into a much larger organization? Regardless of pompous statements to the contrary, when big sharks are eating little sharks, almost all the power stays with the big shark. Possession of an executive position is usually more important than sheer ability or even bottom-line performance.

Actively explore the other alternatives open to you. Would it be possible to develop a new position to meet the needs of the merged organization so that you are not in direct competition for the position you previously held? If you anticipate being forced to consider accepting a demotion—from director to manager, for example—which managerial positions would leave you strategically in the best place? That is, which job might have the most visibility to those who will be reviewing future promotions? (Recall our discussion of the Small Wins Strategy.) Finally, if your plan includes searching for jobs outside the new company, review the criteria presented in the previous section.

Capitalize on Guilt

Whether or not you think you will leave the organization, it's wise to negotiate a severance plan as early as possible. My observation has been that after a while a kind of emotional numbness overcomes those who have the awful responsibility of turning out former friends and they fall back on rules, policies, and procedures to make what should be individualized decisions. At that point, an initial and rather wholesome guilt stops driving the organization's severance decisions, and you might find yourself with a plan that will provide you with less support than you would like, if indeed you do strike out on your own.

A number of writers have pointed to the squeeze at the top as the toughest of career hurdles. In his intriguing study of two thousand careers, Srully Blotnick found that the self-defeating reactions of those who had risen rapidly not only prevented further movement, but robbed their organizations of the full benefits of their hard-won knowledge and experience. But, forewarned is indeed forearmed. If you expect fear, envy, and even some paranoia to cloud your judgment, you will be less panicked, you will be able to maintain a calmer perspective, and you will be able to stay on the trail as far as realities will allow.

4

Keeping Your Distance from Unhealthy Organizational Practices

For some, life on the fast track is a constant confrontation with powerful pressures—and opportunities—to engage in a variety of practices that are unhealthy. I don't mean unhealthy for the Fast Tracker's bank balance, nor for the immediate profitability of the organization, but unhealthy in the sense of setting the stage for illness of the mind, and even of the body. Among the most common that I've seen during my years as a consultant are:

- guileful presentation or outright falsification of data to give the appearance of success, to hide mistakes, or to evade community responsibility;

- stealing, embezzling, or taking bribes;

- participating in the unfair treatment of employees by concealing information they needed for an informed career choice, by going along with an unjust firing, or by condoning unsafe working conditions.

However, this brief list is only intended to suggest the range of unhealthy practices, from the "slightly" dishonest to the downright immoral, in which you may be—or more likely, have been—inveigled, invited, or virtually commanded to engage. For a credible, if depressing, catalogue of the possibilities for wrongdoing that one can encounter in the fast track, I commend to you the daily and weekly news media. My purpose in this chapter is not to decry the present state of public morality, and still less to prescribe a code of behavior, for we each must come to terms with our own ethical selves. It is, rather, to point out the circumstances that make you, as a Fast Tracker, especially vulnerable to being drawn into sticky practices, to offer guidelines that can help you determine when to be particularly wary, and to suggest steps for evading the traps without necessarily giving up an otherwise good job. The ethical decisions you make are between you and your conscience—and it's precisely for that reason that dabbling in messy situations can exact a unique form of personal toll on your well-being. Here is an example of two executives who found themselves caught in a not unfamiliar trap.

I had heard that Felix had been fired for "price gouging," and I was not particularly anticipating my final consultation with him. He would, I expected, be full of the sort of angry grieving that most of us feel when we've gotten ourselves in trouble. While my noble intention would be to guide him toward a realistic perspective about whatever had happened and perhaps to bolster him in plotting a future course, I suspected that he might have little inclination for that sort of self-edification.

I could not have been more wrong. Felix told me that he had looked forward to our meeting and to getting my impression of what had happened. He was in surprisingly good shape emotionally. Yes, he was sore at a company that he felt had betrayed him, but he had an excellent reputation in the industry, and he knew that he was innocent of any wrongdoing. He had repeatedly told his superiors that the prices charged against his department's largest government contract far exceeded actual costs. "But I also knew that there was no way we could hit the dollar goals that they'd set for us if we readjusted the prices to where they should be, and I made sure that Harry [his boss and the division president] knew it too. I said there was nothing to do but bite the bullet and adjust our profit goals downward. But Harry was certain—at least that's what he said—that I must be wrong, because that pricing formula had been in effect for years and it must have been OK or someone would have said something. Well, it was clear that he was not about to tell the Group Head that we weren't going to make quota, so I asked him to talk to Fritz [the corporate CEO], because if things went wrong, I didn't want to get stuck. I mean, we were maybe even criminally liable, especially if we looked like we were trying to keep everything quiet. You've heard Fritz, haven't you, Bob, always talking about how he wants this to be an above-board and ethical company? If he really meant it, then he'd swallow a few quarters of red ink and find some way to mollify the investment people so our stock wouldn't take too bad a beating. At least that's what I told Harry. But I think it was just too much for him. Harry had been given the division, the largest in the company, only nine months ago and he knew that everyone was depending on him to keep bringing in triple-digit profits. He told me to let the matter ride until he decided what to do, and that's exactly what I did. I figured I had done all that was right for *me* to do, so I just

:ept things running and tried to avoid everybody. Now
've been dumped so the company can say to the Feds
hat they *had* a little pricing problem but they've 'taken
care of it.' I can't do a damn thing about it, because I
lidn't put anything in writing. I probably wouldn't do
nything, anyway, even if I could. The fact is, I'd never
;et a decent job if I did."

Felix, it was apparent, was handling his firing well. It
vas Harry who was the basket case. I met with him
hree weeks later—he had taken two weeks leave after
10tifying Felix that he would be "allowed" to resign. He
vas ashamed, he said, that such a thing had happened
n his division and that he had been forced to fire Felix
as a damage-control measure." Four months earlier, a
ew division controller had shocked him with figures that
eemed to point to enormously inflated profits. Although
he high prices charged against the government contract
1ad originally been justified, they did not reflect the sig-
ificant cost-saving measures that Felix's department had
1stituted. While it was this price/cost differential that
vas contributing so heavily to the division's outstanding
rofitability, eventually federal auditors would catch on.
.t best, the company would lose its favored contractor
.atus.

"Well," Harry said, "I was devastated. Why hadn't
e known about this before? I was sure the controller
1ad made a mistake, or that he was just an old lady who
vas scared of the really great money we were making.
elix had once mentioned to me that he thought we
1ght to review the whole pricing structure, but we'd
ever gotten around to it, and frankly, it didn't seem
ery important to me because things were going so well.
ow there's nothing to do but to try to negotiate with
1e Feds for a profit level that compensates us for becom-

ing more efficient. Unfortunately, Corporate believe
that Felix knew what was going on all the time and wa
using it to make himself and his department look good
I don't really think so, but I felt I had to let him g
anyway. After all, he *should* have known and come t
me sooner. It's true that I wouldn't have been very happ
about having to tell the boys at Corporate that we n
longer had the golden touch, but what the hell, that'
what managers are paid to do."

While Harry's words were brave enough, his de
meanor wasn't. Although we had agreed on an hour'
consultation, he kept glancing at his watch, and h
moved to the window to adjust the blinds twice—for n
reason that I could see. More obvious was his scratching
During this entire recital his left hand moved back an
forth on his right knee, rubbing, scratching, rubbing
Harry may have thought that he had only done wha
circumstances and logic had mandated. But a part c
him was not yet convinced. While I have found Fas
Trackers no more immoral or, for that matter, mor
than the general run of people, they are often at greate
risk of behaving unethically precisely because of the m
tivation, energy, and ambition that contribute so muc
to their success. Let's examine some of the reasons fo
this heightened vulnerability.

The Higher You Go, the Higher the Stakes
For one thing, the stakes are higher for Fast Tracke
than they are for most people. The areas of responsibilit
over which managers and executives hold sway are larg
and the profit and loss potentials for them and their o
ganizations can be huge. The sales volume for Harry
division, for example, exceeded $300 million annuall
While it's true that, after a time, these amounts becom

disassociated in an executive's mind from the kind of "real" dollars that he or she spends for family expenses, they do represent enormous assets and the fates of thousands of individuals. Against the perspective of such huge sums, amounts that might otherwise be impressive seem unimportant—as one executive put it, $200,000 is mere "slippage" when you have a $200-million budget. For some Fast Trackers, immense personal gains can seem available at the stroke of a pen or the dropping of a word or two into the right ear.

But it's not only a question of money. In a number of ways, the emotional stakes can be even higher. Whether they are the heads of small businesses or hierarchical executives like Harry, Fast Trackers deeply and sometimes desperately want to hear only about wins, never about losses. Not only are they professionally committed to the success of their organizations, but they see their own success and, perhaps more important, their self-esteem as depending on a constant stream of good news. In this respect they and their superiors often reinforce each other. Paradoxically, the more that those involved like and respect each other, the more potent the wish to avoid disappointing cherished, yet unrealistic, hopes. At best, the result is likely to be a constant watering down of information, abetted by both the sender and receiver. We'll never know exactly what Felix told Harry about the inflated prices, but from having sat in on similar conversations, I suspect that Felix used words like "probably," and "perhaps," which Harry heard as "possibly," and "there's some chance that." Felix was left feeling that he had satisfied his responsibility, while Harry registered just enough doubt to avoid taking the step with his boss that Felix had managed to avoid taking with him.

As if the desire to please were not enough pressure to dissemble, a rather common concern, prevalent amazingly enough, even in the highest organizational ranks, adds a potent pressure of its own: the fear of being fired. Several twisty kinds of realities often give substance to this apprehension. Although it is commonplace in organizations to ask subordinate staff members to indicate the level of performance they believe they can attain, it is almost as common for superiors to assume that the proposed targets could be raised if only the motivational stakes were increased—a step they proceed to take by tacitly adding a substantial increment to the subordinates' performance goals. This practice is particularly common when the subordinate has been bold enough to estimate a loss rather than a profit for a given year. Superiors may verbally acknowledge that a loss must be sustained in order to build market share or increase essential research and development, but the wrinkled foreheads of executive committee members communicate the truth: if you were any good you'd show a profit anyway.

Interestingly enough, the management-by-objective process, initially developed as a way of allowing employees to participate in goal setting, has often been distorted by the demand for consistently increasing profit into something quite different. As Harry put it when questioned his assumption that a loss in his division's remarkable profitability would mean the sidetracking of his career, "Around here, you are judged solely on whether or not you make your numbers, not how well you carry out your job. No matter what they say to your face, Fritz and his boys believe that a good executive can bring home the bacon no matter what the circumstances are."

Long Live the Organization—Whatever It Takes

Often the personal pressures we've been discussing are exacerbated by some beliefs—partly true, partly untrue, and usually untested—that frequently find their way into the minds of organizational leaders. Here are some of the most common:

- When it comes to a choice between our survival as an organization and the needs of our employees, clients, customers, or the public, the organization comes first.

- The only real objective of a profit-making organization is increasing profit. Everything else serves this goal.

- What's good for the organization is good for whoever is associated with it.

I'm not suggesting that all or even most organizational leaders would subscribe to these statements without qualification—although I have met many who recited them as a kind of business catechism. (In contrast, studies of the most effective executives have repeatedly shown that most of them see the attainment of performance goals as the hoped-for end result of service, quality, operational efficiency, and the development of useful products.) What matters is that people lower on the ladder often *believe* that these are the bottom-line values held by those higher up. Thus, for anyone embedded in that organization, putting individual or social needs above those of the company or government agency can seem like heresy—and we all know what closed societies do with heretics. For many people, the organization is that sort of separate society in which people can be induced by such shared beliefs to do things they would not have considered doing in their "private" lives. This is not dissimilar to the kind of phenomenon often described in connection with the antisocial behavior of soldiers stationed outside their own countries, or the reprehensible acts that can occur when ordinarily law-abiding individuals are aggregated into a mob.

The Burden of Being Free

Finally, generally, the higher up you move in any sort of organization, the more freedom of action you have. To some extent, this is simply the result of the way the delegation process works. While every management authority emphasizes that each delegation ought to be accompanied by an explicit plan for monitoring how well the delegated responsibility is being carried out, that is seldom the way it works out. Instead, some version of "this is your baby, now run with it" constitutes the delegation order, without a clear understanding that monitoring is not the same as interfering and that it is a duty as well as a right. Thus, many senior managers believe that they are relegated to the status of worried observers until a catastrophe or repeatedly unattained objectives move them to take the delegation back. This mistaken notion—amazingly widespread especially at the highest levels—has a double effect. First, if you have been successful in reaching your objectives, it is unlikely that anyone will look too closely at how you did it. Second, because the delegator is seldom monitoring very well, you're mostly left to your own devices. With rich prizes up for grabs, with a multitude of organizational pressures pushing and pulling you from a narrow moral and ethical path, the primary stabilizing forces you have are your own inner values and your ability to maintain an objective and long-range view. In these circumstances, a number of factors can make it difficult to maintain your integrity, two of the most important being the deceptive assumption that you can believe what you see and the tendency to take one's cue from what other people are apparently doing.

Perceptual Plasticity. First there is the phenomenon an associate of mine calls "memory magic." No matter how objective we may wish to be, the evidence is overwhelming that our emotional states, including our desires and fears, strongly affect how we remember and interpret experiences. "Just the facts, ma'am" is an ideal, not a reality, for memory is a creative process. What you remember of prior discussions, including commitments made, will be severely affected by what you wish had occurred, just as your own emotionality about a decision or set of circumstances will change the way you interpret the "facts."

Did Felix *explicitly* point out to Harry the difference between the current costs of producing his department's products and the prices being charged for them? Or did he remember the conversation that way to fit his image of how a strong and valiant executive behaves? Or perhaps it was Harry's memory that subtly twisted the facts. After all, if boldly dealing with tough times is what "managers are paid to do," and if Felix *had* unequivocally hit him with the bad news, Harry should have acted long before he did.

The important point is that, as far as I could determine, neither Harry nor Felix was deliberately distorting what had happened. Rather, they were reporting what seemed to them to be quite clear memories of what they said and did. If most varnishing of facts was the result of deliberate lying, our moral lives would be much simpler. Either we would resolve to be ethical or we would decide that self-gain was justification for misrepresentation. The trouble is that the complexity of our minds gets in the way. Even when we decide to act ethically, that crafty, unconscious part of us, whose principal job is indeed to look out for number one, can decide something quite different.

Such was the situation with Burt, the managing partner of ABC Partnership. In my presence, he had verbally committed himself to relinquish the leadership of the firm to another partner if the gross income failed to reach a certain specified amount within a year and a half. Six months later it had become apparent that his plans for developing the business would take longer to bear fruit than he had expected. When I suggested that he renegotiate his agreement, he cheerily informed me that it was lucky that he had two and a half more years to go before he had to worry about meeting his income target. Because of my status as a neutral in the affair and the trust he had in our relationship, I am certain that he was not trying to mislead me—he believed that his recollection of the specifics of the agreement was entirely correct. Is it merely a play on words to say that Burt was not dishonestly self-seeking, although his memory was? I don't believe so. In part, I'm convinced by the results of many studies that demonstrate the mutability of human memory. But even more compelling to me are instances of my own innocent— meaning that I was unaware of any shady intentions— self-serving recollections.

Everybody's Doing It. Chicanery in the workplace is nothing new, and given the pressures toward dishonesty that we've already reviewed, it's unlikely that the situation will improve much in the future. It is not a very encouraging picture, for the knowledge that others are behaving immorally with considerably enriched purses, and often without censure, can undermine whatever resolution we have to behave ethically. After all, when sleight of hand on Wall Street appears commonplace and old-line manufacturers of breakfast cereals lace their cholesterol-reducing products with cholesterol-producing ingredients, are rigorous moral standards worth risking promotion and other prizes to maintain? In a world in which our highest elected officials lack credibility and are reelected anyway, where are the reasons to refuse to take advantage of a privileged position? To complicate matters, even though public morality still leans—if waveringly—toward "honesty is the best policy," there are a number of other factors that make individual ethical dilemmas much less clear-cut.

Honesty Is in the Eye of the Beholder. For one thing, some people who are not necessarily "bad" are seldom troubled by ethical questions. For example, our studies of managerial thinking styles have suggested that those who strongly favor one particular style of thinking—we call them Realists because they construct reality from what they see, hear, smell, and touch at the moment— tend to lose patience with anything that keeps them from moving as swiftly as possible to the targets they have set for themselves. With that perspective, whatever cannot be directly sensed—ethical notions and *others'* feelings, for example—hardly enter into the picture, especially if they stand in the way of capturing the prize.

Because they assume that others see things as they do, these fast-moving, confident people often violate conventional morality without believing they are doing anything wrong.* I have often cautioned them not to underestimate the degree to which others can be put off by clever maneuvers or a careless application of force that dismisses the importance of others' distress. "It's not fair," as those with deeply imprinted moral values have insisted when I have pointed out that some of their fellows may not suffer at all when committing transgressions that would leave them naggingly guilty.

Does that mean that Realist thinkers never suffer pangs of conscience? Not at all. However, the point at which they begin to be troubled may be much farther over the line than others believe is appropriate.

A Realist's behavior will be "ethical" when it is shaped by an assortment of rewards and punishments that make honesty pay off better than dishonesty. Therefore, clearly stated expectations of those who are in a position to reward or punish them will guide Realist behavior more than nebulous ethical considerations. So, here some of us are, burdened with powerful injunctions to be good, while some of our office mates can cheerfully transact their tricky deals, as guiltless as a weasel in a henhouse. Yet they did not choose their own styles of thinking, nor did we; in fact, many authorities believe that such tendencies are at least partly inherited. Nor did we or they choose our families and the nature of our upbringing.

Innocent Decisions Can Lead to Evil Consequences. As we'll see in later chapters, organizational hierarchies tend

*The staffs of regulatory agencies are loaded with individuals whose mental equipment inclines them to trust those they are supposed to regulate. When they discover that some of those "good people" are not much concerned with the social goals that underlie the rules they enforce, they are deeply offended and often revert to implacable over-regulation.

to obscure the view of top decision makers to the full consequences of their decisions. Feedback about unplanned-for effects of decisions that seemed sound when made is filtered out at each level. Employees believe that senior management "must have known that this would happen" and, those worthies, in turn, often interpret warnings from below as the usual resistance that follows any change. The scenario goes something like this:

— CEO of a major airline at an annual all-management meeting: As I've stated in the last annual report, the first priority of this airline is, and will always be, safety.

— Same CEO at an executive committee budget meeting: I'll expect a 10 percent reduction in operating costs from each of your divisions.

— Vice president for operations, one month later, speaking to maintenance facility superintendents: It's going to be tight, but we need to come up with a 10 percent cost reduction at each repair and maintenance facility; the boss won't listen to any argument.

— Maintenance superintendent to shop foremen a week later: You're each going to have to cut one person from your work crews. I know you're already short-handed and it will come out of your hides, but you'll just have to make do.

— Repair shop foreman, at 4:30 in the afternoon to a tired mechanic who still has another job to finish before he can go home: Did you check out that loose latch on the outside cargo hold, Charlie?

— Charlie, hurriedly, while on his way to his next job: Yeah, Mac—I think it's probably safe enough!

— CEO at a regular executive committee meeting: I think you all know that I'm determined that safety will always be our highest priority, regardless of cost.

HOW TO COPE WITH UNHEALTHY ORGANIZATIONAL PRACTICES

Given these complexities, keeping your distance from questionable activities can require thought, effort, and more than a modicum of self-searching. Not surprisingly, an inward look is the first, and most important, step to take if you are to deal effectively with unhealthy organizational practices.

Discover What *You* Must Do

In his most important book, *Man for Himself*, psychologist and social philosopher Erich Fromm set forth his belief that those who violate deeply held personal standards will in some fashion make themselves pay for it. Nothing that I have seen in twenty years of delving deeply into the lives of others, and in living with myself and those closest to me, has led me to doubt the fundamental truth of that belief. Here are some of the ways that you can expect to exact payment from yourself more or less proportionate to the heinousness of your sins, as your inner self sees them:

- *By getting yourself in trouble.* Newspapers are full of tales of very smart people with very clever schemes who then do stupid things that get themselves caught and publicly punished.

- *By getting sick.* We used to call it conscience, until such unpsychological terms became unfashionable. But recent findings about the mechanisms by which the mind affects the body reveal that your conscience—or whatever you want to call it—can indeed kill you.

- *By making yourself miserable.* If getting thrown into jail or giving yourself arthritis or ulcers seems too extreme to the inner you, there are always the old standbys: anxiety, tension, depression, sleeplessness, and all the other highly efficient self-punishments that can interfere with the enjoyment of your work or your life.

The trouble is, by the time you've exacted these penalties from yourself, you've already transgressed. What you want, of course, is to prevent the transgression from happening in the first place. The major task, which most people find paradoxically difficult and easy, is to pay serious attention to the nudges of your conscience.

Recognize the Problem

For most of us, feelings of guilt or shame are old acquaintances that tend to intrude whether we want them or not. But frequently, we are inundated with so many sources of tension— especially if we're facing a difficult (or tempting) situation with high stakes involved—that these softer, minor-key messages that we're heading in a direction we might regret later are submerged in the racket of a hundred other anxieties. Is that peculiar tightness between your shoulder blades the result of being tempted to do something wrong? Or is it simply the result of pressures to produce? Yet when pressed, my clients have professed to know when they felt guilty or ashamed; the larger problem seemed to be using such feelings as guides to behavior. Here are some tips for dealing with both sides of this paradox.

Describe the Facts. In seminars and with individual clients, I have suggested that managers identify in writing the specific conflicts and contradictory expectations they believed themselves caught in. This is helpful for at least three reasons. First, most ethical dilemmas are not unique to particular situations; they show up in slightly different guises across many settings and circumstances. Often, it's possible to see a pattern across situations, a clue that you might be, at least in part, setting yourself up. Are you, for instance, nodding your head noncommittally when subordinates suggest a marginal maneuver, thinking that you'll say no later, but "later" always turns up after the deed is done. Second, writing a thought down seems to bring it farther forward into consciousness. Part of you may not really want it there, but keep in mind that a conscious choice is always less productive of deeper anxiety or depression. Third, there is good evidence that something written down and discussed with another person will be more likely to be acted upon.

Your first task, then, is to jot down the salient facts of your troubling situation. If you were Harry, your statements might look like this:

Fritz has asked me [Harry] to fire Felix because he put the company into a potentially disastrous situation.

Felix says that he believes he did everything that was proper for him to do, and I believe that he believes what he said.

Fritz believes that we should show everyone that we do not condone dishonesty.

I think that while Felix may have been dumb, he was not dishonest.

Or this:

My division has been offered for sale to a rival company with headquarters across the country.

To avoid the danger of the best people leaving, I've been told not to inform my employees.

It is a fact that they constitute a major asset of the division, and if substantial numbers resigned, the purchaser's offer might be considerably less.

I've been told that whatever happens, I'll be protected.

Identify the Issues at Stake. Next, using simple words, capture those thoughts or feelings, however vague, that have made this matter more than just an exercise in good judgment about costs or revenues or engineering practicality. Try to keep the underlying issues of honesty or fairness separate from the consequences that might result from any particular decision—not because those consequences are irrelevant, but because it's healthier to knowingly compromise your values than to shove them out of awareness, where they will certainly work their black art into the future. (I am not endorsing compromising your values; here, I am merely assessing the relative dangers to your health and peace of mind.) Your statements may look something like this:

On the one hand, I feel some loyalty to the company, and I'd like it to get as good a price as possible from selling this division. As a manager, I'm supposed to support the legitimate decisions of my bosses, even if I disagree with them. The question is: is this legitimate? On the other hand, my staff trusts me, and it feels lousy to hold back information that could significantly affect their lives.

Clarify the Consequences of Doing What You Think Is Right. Your third job is to set down consequences: what might befall if you stay with what your inner thoughts tell you is right? You'll note that I'm *not* suggesting that you weigh all of the facts and consequences to determine the proper course of action, as if this were merely an exercise in rational decision making. In part, that is because of the ease with which rational decision making can slip into rationalization, that elegant form of denial in which you cite seven excellent reasons for doing something while ignoring the one negative that would outweigh them all. More important, the issue for you is not whether the wrongs "objectively" outweigh the rights or vice versa, but what your private voice, the one that speaks for the best in you, tells you when you force yourself to pay attention to it.

Some further distinctions are important here. First, not every decision that involves inflicting pain is an ethical problem. Many decisions do indeed involve balancing costs against benefits, and often some of the costs involve disappointing or distressing fellow human beings. An obvious example is the decision to lay off competent and loyal employees because of a drop in company income. As difficult and painful as that decision can be—especially for those of an altruistic turn of mind—it is not an ethical dilemma unless it is self-serving. It would become a moral issue if, for example, you were to use the money saved from the firings to increase your own compensation without a proportionate increase in your value to the organization.

A second important distinction is between your own deep, if sometimes quiet, intuitions about how humans ought to treat one another, and the many social expectations that were poured into you early in life. Were you taught as a child that when you are invited to a social affair that does not directly conflict with other plans, it's good manners to accept? Do you, consequently, feel compelled to say "I'll be there" when you would rather spend the evening with a book? Or, if you opt for staying home, do you feel as rotten as you would if you had done something truly wrong, rather than concluding that pleasing yourself is no more morally reprehensible than pleasing another. Reevaluating for yourself the validity of such early messages is a part of the continuing process of maturing. Indeed, the discovery that others' expectations need not be a ruling force in one's life is often a significant milestone in personal counseling. The problem is that the line between carefully taught beliefs about customary social proprieties and those values that are an integral part of you is not at all sharp. Difficult as it sometimes is, there seems to be no alternative but to question the validity of each of those expectations thoughtfully, matching it against your experience and judging whether it deserves to be part of your personal set of standards. Your thoughts might sound something like this:

As a kid, I was taught always to be truthful. However, there are many times when I don't say everything that might be said because I don't want to create a hassle or rile someone else without purpose. Yet I haven't found myself dwelling much on any of these events, so I guess it's not bending the truth in itself that's bothering me. Management doesn't tell employees about every pending decision that might affect them, and given the amount of time available, it couldn't. So, I guess how honest I am depends on a lot of things in the situation. On the other hand, I've given my gang a lot of reasons to believe that I have their interests, as well as the company's interest, at heart. In fact, I've told them as much, and this decision won't be a trivial one for them, since for some it might mean moving across the country. Sure, the sale might not go through, so if I'm going to tell them, I ought to hold off until I'm as sure as I can be. Wait a minute! All this ruminating is beside the point, because I really know that *I've* got to tell them what's going to happen to them or I'll feel like a heel.

As in this case, it's often in the midst of testing out the currency of a belief and its relevance to the puzzlement you're trying to resolve, that—sometimes as a sudden insight—you will know what you require of yourself if you are to maintain your integrity. When that voice speaks to you, obey it.

Develop an Action Plan

Having decided how you must act, your next step is the very practical one of determining how to take that action with the least adverse consequences for yourself. In effect, you must have an action plan that will help you do what you've decided you must do. Here are some useful steps to take in developing that plan.

Reframe the Question. Most of us, particularly when we feel strongly about something, tend to frame questions in an either/or format; "Either I fire Felix or I lose my job"; "Either I keep quiet, as I've been asked to do, or I tell my staff that the division might be sold." Framed in this way, complex questions usually get answers that are—to paraphrase H. L. Mencken—simple, straightforward, and wrong. It can take time to escape the faulty thinking this sort of restricted perception brings with it. (At times, I have spent the better part of two hours with clients facing similar dilemmas, but it's worth it.) Your goal will be to find a series of statements that not only fits all of the facts as you've determined them, but also reduces the areas of conflict and contradiction by surfacing the assumptions and foregone conclusions. Since you will link short phrases with "and" (never "or"), your new product will probably lack the terseness and economy of "Either I fire Felix or I lose my job." To compensate, however, it will provide a sounder basis for an effective plan. This is how Harry's reframing of the "fire Felix" decision looked in its third draft.

If, after I've checked out the facts and reviewed the evidence, I believe that Felix did not fully realize that his prices were indeed dishonestly and unlawfully inflated (he might have known they were dishonest, but not that they were unlawful) because he did a lousy job of monitoring price/cost data (not unreasonable to expect from a Ph.D. in engineering), then it will be clear to me that he deserves a punishment short of firing—an official, in-the-file reprimand, or even a demotion. I can bring all this to Fritz as the outcome of my investigation and try to get him to acknowledge the facts and maybe even the way I have interpreted them. (Whether or not he agrees with me, I'll look like a strong manager who knows what he's doing, and right now I could really use that.) If Fritz insists that Felix be fired (wait a minute, maybe he only *believes* he should be fired—that's not the same as insisting), I'll point out that Felix is my responsibility and that, even though I'm aware of Fritz's anger, I've chosen not to terminate. If Fritz himself fires Felix in spite of the case I've made, I'll know that at least I have not been coerced, seduced, or frightened into being a party to it.

As you can see, reframing not only provides a sounder basis for your own action plan, but provides the basis for helping others to see the situation as it is rather than as they expect or want it to be. As it turned out, Fritz's anger at Felix did stem from his assumption that "Felix must have known about the inflated price structure when he agreed to the profit goals set for his department. No one with his experience and education could have overlooked a discrepancy that large." While that assumption was plausible, in fact, Felix's innovative experimentation and tinkering left little time for the mundane monitoring and control activities that, to quote Fritz once again, "any experienced manager would see to."

Pin Yourself Down. While any thoughtfulness about decisions such as these is useful in itself, you will accrue several specific benefits by sketching out your plan in some detail. At the least, a summary of important points, and even better, some bits of actual dialogue, will help you tread carefully, with both tact and the degree of honesty that you've decided upon. It's always risky to trust your skill at impromptu conversation to find just the right words to describe delicate, emotionally sensitive situations. In addition, a few notes will help you to get the most from a preconfrontational discussion with a mentor. In cases such as these, that person should be someone not affected by the results of your actions. A candid conversation with an outsider you trust will help you retain perspective and keep you from sliding into rationalization or retreat. If you suspect that your stand might put your job in jeopardy, you'll also need to gain as much support as you can from those who would share any hardships with you. (This does not mean shifting the burden of decision to them. Only you can know what it is that your better self is telling you to do.) Keeping one's nerve when drawing personal ethical lines is difficult enough even when you know that those whose opinion you value are behind you. Without that assurance, the inner conflict can be overwhelming, and it can rob you of the sureness that will get you through unscathed. Sharing your plan in some detail will also help involved others rest somewhat easier by assuring them that you know what you're doing—that you will not, for example, take an exaggeratedly confrontational stand.

Talk It Over with Someone You Care About. Keep in mind that it is not only the wicked who commit wicked acts. As we have seen, temptations and situational pressures alike can be enormous for those who move into and up the fast track. For that reason, it's important not to underestimate the allure of richly rewarded, if illegal, opportunities. Sudden visions of previously unhoped-for wealth or the excitement of instant celebrity have had a demonstratively hypnotic effect on individuals who up to that point had seemed solid and generally sensible people. An almost sure test of whether or not you may be stepping over an important moral or legal boundary is your ability, or inability to be more exact, to discuss what you're considering doing with someone who is close to you, a spouse, child, parent, or dear friend.

In a recent case, as reported in *The Wall Street Journal*, Jose Gomez, a thirty-one-year-old auditor, in return for rapid promotion and some two hundred thousand dollars in "loans," went along with his company's efforts to cover up illegally spent client funds. Interviewed while serving a twelve-year prison sentence, he described this phenomenon succinctly. When asked what led up to his stepping over the line, he said:

"It was a professional decision, a judgment decision. I had a terrific argument with myself. It just came out that way. If I had sought some counsel from someone that I had some respect for, if I had . . . talked to my wife. It's interesting. We've been married for years now, and it's the only item that I never discussed with her or shared with her in any way."

Interestingly, after Gomez finally decided to cooperate with authorities, he had no trouble talking over the whole situation with his family, and, in fact, gaining their support.

Do a Worst-Case Analysis. An often helpful panic preventer, when faced with a potentially risky situation, is that form of worst-case analysis we covered in chapter 3—"building a horror floor." The process applied to this situation is similar: visualize yourself taking each of the steps listed in your plan; imagine the worst that might happen, and then force yourself to ask and answer the question—"And what might happen then?" For example, a worst-case analysis of a projected conversation between Harry and Fritz about Felix's firing might look like this:

- I give Fritz the results of my investigation and recommend that Felix not be fired. (And what might happen then?)

- Fritz is absolutely furious and accuses me of insubordination. (And what might happen then?)

- I try to make him see that a good executive lives up to his own values and that in the long run this is good for the organization. (And what might happen then?)

- Fritz gets even angrier and fires me. (And what might happen then?)

- I give him a chance to cool off and then check whether he really meant it. (And what might happen then?)

- He confirms the fact that I'm fired. (And what might happen then?)

- I have to find another job. (And what might happen then?)

- Given the times, I might have to take a job at a lower level. (And what might happen then?)

- I'd probably feel lousy being a general manager again after having tasted the fruits of Mount Olympus, but I'd live through it—and anyway, in this job there's been a lot of bitter with the sweet. Plus, I could live with my conscience.

Before You Need It, Build a Foundation for Refusing to Go Along. While it doesn't always work, there are a few positioning steps that can help you survive those times when you must take a stand on an ethical issue.

As we have seen, organizations that measure individual success solely on the basis of quarterly or annual profits, production figures, or sales revenues can foster a cheating mentality—or considerable guilt—in managerial staff. (I've seen firsthand some of the dysfunctional fruits of this "realistic" approach. In fact, a frequent goal of mine has been to influence the CEO to develop and give weight to long-range and qualitative executive-performance standards.)

Yet, in organizations such as these, I've heard senior executives privately puzzle over the possible value of longer-range considerations, although they seldom mention them in public. Even executives who feel uncomfortable discussing "softheaded," nontangible goals often believe in their importance. They may wish they had the "luxury" of pursuing such goals, and complain that their subordinates seem to show little insight into the importance of a broader vision. Thus, it's worth trying to gain the sort of stature that will help you to weather a variety of storms by projecting yourself as a manager who is not only a strong individual contributor, but also a far-sighted team player, one who puts legitimate organizational needs ahead of his or her own personal goals.

In this connection recall the advantages mentioned in chapter 3 of taking a "statesmanlike" role, and the specific steps that show you to be just that sort of broad-gauged person.

Similarly, try proposing long-range, developmental goals for yourself as part of your annual performance package even if—perhaps especially if—you are not able to tie the achievement of these goals into the compensation plan. In short, the more you can position yourself so the "numbers" are seen as only a part of your success—albeit an important part—the better able you will be to show, without seeming irresolute or weak, that an honest handling of an ethical issue is the way to create an innovative, high-producing organization.

THE BOTTOM LINE: MAINTAINING YOUR INTEGRITY—AND YOUR HEALTH

It's painful to be in a situation in which your commitment to the health of your organization, your concern for your own advancement, and your highest expectations for yourself are in conflict. Unfortunately, this fast track hazard is often hard to avoid. True, you can possibly sidestep it by starting your own business. Even then, the pressures of the marketplace often can nudge you into cutting moral corners in order to stay in the fray. Another possibility might be to find employment in a smallish organization under leaders whose ethics agree with your own. While not-for-profit organizations would seem to offer a haven for those who want to escape ethical dilemmas, even there the temptations can be present and sharp. Government agencies are large purchasers of goods and services, with attendant possibilities for bribes of one sort or another. Even in modestly budgeted, voluntary agency settings, the push for success is still high. I have seen a number of instances in which performance goals were fudged to gain glory and government grants.

As a high achiever, then, sooner or later you're bound to face the choice of going along with—or keeping your distance from what you believe to be—unhealthy organizational practices. What I am certain of is this: whatever the cost in money or position, do whatever you must to avoid acting in a way that contravenes your own values, especially when you feel powerless to prevent it. Even in hardheaded physical and psychological terms— leaving aside considerations of morality—what will your gains profit you, if you lose your own self?

5

Power Pathologies

Anyone who has had close acquaintance with the inhabitants of the upper reaches of organizations knows that jockeying for power, openly or deviously, is the rule rather than the exception. The not-very-surprising reason for this pervasive phenomenon is motivation. Or perhaps it would be more precise to say it is an *excess* of the very motivation that sets Fast Trackers on the road to the top in the first place—the need to be ascendant, influential, and powerful.

To get a feel for power in high places, let's listen to Rick, a much-respected chief financial officer, as he describes Jim, the chairman and CEO of his organization. Two days before, Jim had announced that Herb, not Rick, would be the next president.

"Do you know what really drives that double-dealing son of a bitch?" Rick tossed out before I even had a chance to sit down. "What makes that bastard tick is power—nothing but unvarnished, 'I'm the head bull around here' power. I may be nothing but an overeducated farm boy, but I know a pissing contest when I see one. He's purely addicted to showing everyone—and me in particular—that he, and only he, is in charge. Sure, he's probably handed you a hundred reasons for giving the job to Herb instead of me. But the real reason is something else.

"Seven months ago I told him that I couldn't go along with his pet acquisition project and that I thought he was jumping the gun again. At that moment I could see in his face that he was going to show me who the hell was boss. Jesus, I knew that all the time. But being CEO does not—I say again, does *not*—make his decisions infallible. That dumb outfit we—I mean *he*—acquired has already cost us a bundle, and we haven't even finished installing new management.

"I know you're here to hold my hand during this 'emotional crisis,' Dr. B, and I appreciate it even if that bastard probably put you up to it—OK, OK, no insult intended. I'm just still pretty sore. But I'll get mine back. You wait and see what happens to Herb in six months. If he's gone along with whatever Jim wants, he'll feel like shit and he'll have lost everyone's respect, and I include Jim in that. If he speaks up like I did, he'll be out on his ass. Then, when Jim is forced to put *me* in next time, he won't dare pull anything funny. A CEO who loses three top people in a row is not likely to last long himself."

Rick's predictions were almost all correct. The acquisition was sold at a loss two years later, Herb angrily quit after being asked by Jim to "stay on as my special assistant, because you're just not the kind of president we need at this time," and influential members of the board did, indeed, begin to have "informal discussions about Jim. Rick was wrong only on one point: Jim never did ask him to take over the presidency.

What are we to make of Jim? Was he simply a born authoritarian who could not tolerate any difference of opinion? Or was he a basically sound person whose judgment was corrupted by the power and position he had attained? The answers I found were somewhat more complex than these black-or-white questions suggest, as you will see when we return to this case a little later. First, let's examine some of the ways in which those same inner drives that have moved you to your present rung on the ladder can interfere with your coming to terms with the increasing power that accrues to anyone who moves up the fast track.

Power comes in many shapes and sizes, but whatever form it takes, the Fast Trackers I've known want more of it. In their study of what motivates managers, Harvard psychologist David McClelland and his associates found that a need for power and influence was the most striking factor that differentiated managers from the general populace. If you're in a managerial position, the odds are two to one that feeling in charge is of above-average importance to you. My own data show that if you're already ensconced on the executive floor, the odds are even greater that your need to be dominant will be unusually high.

These findings are certainly not unexpected. Surely part of the inner push to undertake a supervisory job is the wish to be closer to the top of the pecking order than the bottom. If you did not enjoy or at least gain some satisfaction from feeling powerful, then having the authority to impose sanctions on others would be at best unsettling and at worst a source of continuing and stressful inner conflict. From almost any perspective, a preference for being the hammer rather than the nail is a prerequisite for relishing a leadership role; indeed, applied to an executive the term "power lover" would seem to be less an epithet than a job qualification.

Nonetheless, an affinity for power will not in itself guarantee that you will be a happy executive—nor a good one. Jim, Rick, and Herb all wanted control over each other and over the company, yet they were equally miserable and equally guilty of using their considerable energies to their own detriment. Like every other human attribute, an appetite for power can be both a strength and a liability. If unconstrained or ineffectually applied, eventually it will diminish accomplishment and show itself as personal weakness. (Unfortunately, "eventually" can seem like forever to those suffering under poorly used authority.)

Of course, this is not to say that all problem managers have a misguided love affair with power. Some simply found themselves thrust into positions of authority with little wish to be on top. Their modest need for control is pitted against other, equally strong internal pushes: to be personally competent, to be accepted and liked by others, or simply to be left alone. As we'll see, in their struggle to resolve these conflicting desires, they can end up confusing not only those they lead but themselves as well.

The story of power pathologies, then, is a tale of motivations—motivations running wild, motivations in conflict, motivations that push their owners in directions dissonant with the aims of their organizations. To understand and cope with the hazards that come with power, you need to know something about how human motivation works—and more especially, what motivations drive your own behavior. Accordingly, the first part of this chapter provides a brief refresher on human motivation and a self-quiz that will give you an approximate fix on your own motivational preferences. Next, we'll review what research has shown about the effects of some key motivational factors on executive satisfaction and the kinds of power problems that follow from different motivational patterns. Finally, we'll consider suggestions for making the best of your own set of work-related needs as your journey up the fast track inevitably brings you greater and greater power.

THE MOTIVATIONAL MIX

While as human beings we all have similar needs, we do have them in varying degrees, and we seek to satisfy them in different ways. To see what that really means, let's look at four competent, hardworking people working side by side in the same office, Sally, Jane, Bill, and Eric.

Sally is known to her friends as a take-charge person. She often tells others what to do, and when she can't do that, she'll invariably try to advise them (her friend Jane would say "argue with them") on the best way to proceed. Jane, who also takes up a good deal of the available conversation space, hardly ever tries to influence others. She spends most of her talking time chatting about interesting work problems or plans for the weekend. Bill (whom Jane privately calls a grump) finds her a nuisance. "She's always yakking about something," he says, "and it spoils my concentration. I wish I had an office—even a cubbyhole—so I could work alone." Eric, on the other hand, doesn't really mind Jane's socializing as long as the focus is on a project they're working on together. He enjoys the job they're jointly responsible for and gets great pleasure from working out solutions to thorny problems. Unlike Bill, who reacts testily every time he feels Sally is looking over his shoulder, Eric shrugs off Sally's bossiness. As he sees it, her willingness to push other people has helped get projects out the door on schedule, and, even more important, her aggressiveness about getting the group more resources has frequently paid off.

As human beings, Sally, Jane, Bill, and Eric are pushed by a complex of inner forces, but much of their dissimilarity can best be ascribed to differences in their motivations. In order to feel satisfied and fulfilled, Sally is driven to feel dominant and influential in relation to the others with whom she works. Her need for dominance is so powerful that if she were denied a legitimate opportunity to be dominant, she would feel frustrated and keenly dissatisfied. She might leave the group, or, more likely, divert her needs for power into less constructive channels, becoming what others might call a "troublemaker." Jane, on the other hand, cares much less about influencing others than she does about maintaining friendly relationships with them. People like Jane, who get their primary satisfaction from maintaining congenial relationships, have a high need for affiliation. Bill may look misanthropic to Jane, but he's more accurately seen as a good example of someone with a strong need for autonomy, a wish to be left alone to do his own work without interference. Unlike Sally, Bill doesn't need to boss others. What he most wants is the chance to be his own boss, uncontrolled and unimpeded by anyone else's behavior. Eric is one of those personally effective people for whom the chance to tackle a challenging job is satisfaction enough. Since he also enjoys working with others, he doesn't share Bill's antipathy to being tied to a group, and he seems to have little need to resist Sally's take-charge behavior.

Clearly, dominance over others, having rewarding social relations, a wish for autonomy, and the satisfaction of real achievement are not the only satisfactions that people strive for. But these motivations seem particularly relevant to the world of work and, as we'll see, when conditions are right, each can induce Fast Trackers to mishandle the power that comes their way. For that reason, obtaining as clear a picture as you can of the relative strength of these needs in your own motivational mix can help you to stay on course. Here's a questionnaire for doing just that.

A Self-Assessment Instrument for Motivation*

Instructions. Below are listed twenty statements that describe various things people do or try to do on the job. Each statement is followed by a set of numbers that indicate the relative frequency with which the statement describes individual behavior. Beside each statement, please circle the number that most accurately describes the frequency of your own actions.

	NEVER	ALMOST NEVER	SELDOM	SOMETIMES	USUALLY	ALMOST ALWAYS	ALWAYS
1. I do my best work when my job assignments are fairly difficult	1	2	3	4	5	6	7

Adapted, with permission, from the Manifest Needs Questionnaire developed by Richard M. Steers and Daniel N. Braunstein, 1976.

2. When I have a choice, I try to work in a group rather than by myself 1 2 3 4 5 6 7

3. In my work assignments, I try to be my own boss 1 2 3 4 5 6 7

4. I seek an active role in the leadership of a group 1 2 3 4 5 6 7

5. I pay a good deal of attention to the feelings of others at work 1 2 3 4 5 6 7

6. I go my own way at work, regardless of the opinions of others 1 2 3 4 5 6 7

7. I try to influence those around me to see things my way 1 2 3 4 5 6 7

8. I try hard to improve on my past performance at work 1 2 3 4 5 6 7

9. I tend to disregard rules and regulations that hamper my personal freedom 1 2 3 4 5 6 7

10. I find myself organizing and directing the activities of others 1 2 3 4 5 6 7

11. I take moderate risks and stick my neck out to get ahead at work 1 2 3 4 5 6 7

12. I prefer to work interactively with others, rather than alone 1 2 3 4 5 6 7

13. I strive to gain more control over events around me at work 1 2 3 4 5 6 7

14. I tend to seek out added responsibilities on my job 1 2 3 4 5 6 7

15. I try to be agreeable with my coworkers as a matter of course 1 2 3 4 5 6 7

16. I generally consider myself a "loner" at work 1 2 3 4 5 6 7

17. I try to perform better than my coworkers .. 1 2 3 4 5 6 7

18. I find myself talking to those around me
about nonbusiness matters 1 2 3 4 5 6 7

19. I try my best to work independently on a
job 1 2 3 4 5 6 7

20. I prefer to be "in command" when I am
working with others 1 2 3 4 5 6 7

Scoring Procedure. Transfer your scores from the questionnaire items to the appropriate boxes below. Then add each column of figures to arrive at your total scores.

1 ☐	2 ☐	3 ☐	4 ☐
8 ☐	5 ☐	6 ☐	7 ☐
11 ☐	12 ☐	9 ☐	10 ☐
14 ☐	15 ☐	16 ☐	13 ☐
17 ☐	18 ☐	19 ☐	20 ☐
Totals I ☐	II ☐	III ☐	IV ☐

Scoring Scale. After you've completed the questions and done the scoring, transfer the totals that appear in the boxes alongside the Roman numerals I, II, III, and IV to the boxes underneath the profile matrix you'll find just below.

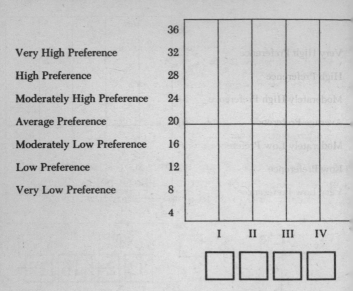

	36
Very High Preference	32
High Preference	28
Moderately High Preference	24
Average Preference	20
Moderately Low Preference	16
Low Preference	12
Very Low Preference	8
	4

I   II   III   IV

I = The Need for Achievement
II = The Need for Affiliation
III = The Need for Autonomy
IV = The Need for Power

For the final scoring step, find that place on the lin
above Roman numeral I that represents your score i
need for achievement and place a dot there. Do the sam
for each of the other motivational needs, and connec
the dots by straight lines. The resulting graph will giv
you a profile of your work-related motivational prefer
ences. As an example, I've shown Eric's profile below
As you can see, his total scores were 32 for need fo
achievement, 24 for need for affiliation, 16 for need fo
autonomy, and 12 for the need for power.

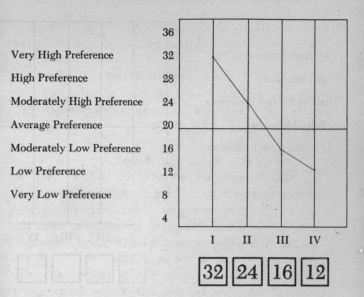

The shape of your profile is probably the best way to interpret your scores, because it shows their relative strengths as determiners of what moves you. While there is certainly no "ideal" profile, you can roughly compare your scores with those of others by using the following benchmarks.

- If your score is under 20, you show below average preference for that motivation

- If it is around 24, you show a modest preference

- If your score is around 28, you show a high preference

● If your score is 32 and above, you have a very high preference for that motivation*

What the Quiz Measures: A Closer Look at the Four Key Motivations. Before I explain how to interpret your scores, let me describe a bit more precisely what characterizes these four motivations.

1. *The need for achievement.* People with a high need for achievement derive satisfaction from personal accomplishment itself, largely disregarding external rewards such as money or power. High pay, status, and celebrity are welcomed primarily as signs that others whom they respect recognize and value their accomplishments. They may strive hard to outperform others for the same reason—not because they want to win, but because they enjoy the challenge to their abilities. Achievers feel best when they are making a unique contribution, have overcome personal or environmental obstacles, and are meeting their self-imposed standards of excellence. Their emotional "highs" come from that exhilarating feeling that arises when they use their personal abilities to some worthwhile purpose. On the other hand, they feel thwarted when forced to work at tasks that are too easy or repetitious, and when they receive little feedback from others who are important to them.

---

*Those ranges center around an *overall* average score of 20 and are based upon a standard deviation of 4. However, if you are already in an executive suite, and in a highly technical field, you'll find that the "average" loading among your peers in both needs for achievement and power will be much higher.

2. *The need for affiliation.* Those with a high need for affiliation like people and like to be with them. For example, they enjoy feeling that they are a part of a group, especially that sort of closely connected group we call a team. They are most content when they are liked and accepted, and know that they're getting on well with the others with whom their lot has been thrown. Open conflict, an indication that a relationship might not be harmonious, is disturbing, so high affiliators often strive to smooth over any signs of conflict.

3. *The need for autonomy.* People who have high needs for autonomy are most content when they feel self-directed, personally plotting their own courses without interference—or, for that matter, help—from others. They like private work space, free from distractions caused by others. When they are forced to work as part of an interactive team—that is, when the completion of their own work depends upon satisfactory performance by others—these loners are likely to feel acutely distressed.

4. *The need for power and dominance.* Those with a high need for power are most fulfilled when they believe they are controlling or strongly influencing others' behavior. They feel most alive when they are arousing strong emotions, positive or otherwise, and are uncomfortable, even demoralized, when they feel inconsequential or without control. Status, reputation, and position are valued mostly as ways to add to their store of power. Holding the center of attention or gaining the admiration of others are not, in themselves, of much interest to "power" individ-

uals, unless, of course, they *also* have high needs for affiliation or achievement.

Interpreting Your Scores. The best way to interpret your motivational scores is to see them as a profile of peaks and valleys. Think of the peaks as indicating those motivational areas that are most important to you. The midpoints represent needs that, while still part of your overall makeup, have relatively less power to drive or pull you along in your work life. The valleys point to motivations that are of much less weight for you. As we move ahead, you'll see that there are both boons and banes associated with each peak and valley.

You may, however, have no dramatic peaks or valleys. It's entirely possible to be motivated in all four areas to about the same extent. Moreover, your scores may all be high, low, or in the middle. The fact is that some people are fuller of burgeoning needs than others. The good and bad news is that a relatively flat profile has its own benefits: a more "well-rounded" approach to life—and its own hazards: an internal battle among motivations that nudge you in different directions with about equal strength.

A caution: your scores on this short test provide a general picture of the relative strength of each of four important needs. But no paper-and-pencil measure can describe anything so complex as human motivation. Questionnaires like this only provide a structure that enables you to organize your own perceptions about yourself. Moreover, after you've read through the balance of this chapter, you may decide that your scores missed the mark in adequately characterizing you. In that case, I suggest that you review your responses to the items to make sure that you weren't unduly influenced by how you believe you *ought* to feel, rather than by a more candid assessment of yourself. If a second perusal still leaves you wondering whether your ratings were accurate, try to get some feedback from a few people who know you reasonably well and who will be honest. Ask them to respond to the items as if they were you, and be ready for some surprises.

At any rate, use this test *only* as a guide. Before you make a career decision based upon motivational preferences, discuss your decision and the reasons behind it with a counselor or a friend with no personal investment in your decision.

MOTIVATIONAL PATTERNS AND THE HAZARDS OF POWER

Your own mix of the four key motivations can help you both to use, and to misuse, the opportunities for power that come your way. We cannot here go into the fascinating topic of human motivation in the detail it deserves. I simply want to suggest the power pitfalls most deserving of your careful attention as you move along in your career.

The Perfect Match? High Power Position and High Power Needs

Let's start with a look at what would seem to be a perfect match for Fast Trackers on the rise: high power motivation fitted to high positions of power. If feeling dominant is necessary for your contentment, moving up in the world will bring you just what you need—increasing opportunities for influence and control. As a supervisor, you will have the right to impose sanctions on others, both formally through salary and promotion recommendations, and informally by your choice of who gets interesting, dull, or nasty assignments. When you rise still further, you will have the right to ponder and grant final approval to the decisions made by those who report to you. Even better, as your status grows, people will begin to act toward you with those little signs of respect— even a bit of subtle subservience wouldn't hurt—due one of your recognized power.* This, in turn, increases your ability to influence their opinions and actions, just what those with high power motivation find so gratifying. Certainly a satisfied relish for power helps to balance the onus of responsibility for scarce and valuable human and material resources that Fast Trackers must often bear.

Given the beauty of this arrangement—people who want power having it by filling positions best occupied by those willing to exercise power—how can intelligent executives find themselves led astray?

To get more intimate insight into the nature of this hazard, let's listen in on Jim, the CEO in the example that opened this chapter. In one of our consultation sessions, he ventured into a justification of his very high compensation package (I had not raised the question myself; Jim was, rather, venting his anger at an article in a news magazine that questioned "the excessive compensation of the new nobility—corporate CEOs").

"Do they realize," Jim demanded, "what it's like to

---

*Employees are often disappointed in the performance of their bosses because—as most people do—they tend to attribute more authority and power to those of higher rank than the higher-ups themselves believe they have. When those in power seem to willfully choose not to make desired changes, it's difficult to believe that they really care about those below.

know that when I finally OK a decision, I've committed this company to a course of action that could make or break it? Everyone else has an opinion about what's right to do, but opinions are cheap. I have to be sure that I'm right and then make the commitment, but I can never forget that it's me and me alone that is responsible."

At this point, I broke in and asked "Why do you do it?"

Jim replied: "Because it needs to be done, for one thing. I guess I really believe that I can do it as well or better than anyone else around here. I've been trying to groom a successor, but I'm discouraged about that. Rick is sharp and tough enough, but he's a black-and-white thinker. Once he makes up his mind, he stops listening. Herb is flexible, and as sharp as they come. Even better, he has the kind of long-range vision that's needed. But somehow he doesn't seem tough enough. He's not willing to stand up and say 'I'm the boss and we'll do it my way because it's right.' "

If I had any doubts about why Jim was still struggling with the burdens of high office well past his sixtieth birthday, I lost them at that moment. One did not need much sensitivity to discern the pride and satisfaction he felt at being one of those intrepid human beings confident enough to insist that his way was the only way to go. Yet, as we've seen, Rick predicted accurately enough that Jim's headstrong approach would continue to cause trouble for him. So, which perception of Jim was correct? Was he the power-mad autocrat that Rick described, or the noble warrior he saw himself to be?

My conclusion, reluctantly acknowledged after eight months of rather inconclusive consultations, was that he was both. Or, more accurately, he had been moved into the presidency eight years earlier principally because he had the courage to act boldly, but at some point he had crossed the line that distinguishes the productive and skillful exercise of the power motivation from the state we touched upon in chapter 3—the arrogant pride that the Greeks called hubris. The result was all too predictable: instead of firm leadership, a stubborn clinging to his own "infallible" decisions; instead of an evenhanded evaluation of his subordinates' strengths and liabilities, erratic judgments impelled by a need to have his power confirmed by those subject to it.

It is a dismal truth that success is a fertile ground for hubris. When I first began consulting with top-level executives, from time to time I would encounter a frustrating kind of bland rejection of my suggestion that an alternative approach might be worth trying. It took the form of "The way I've always done things must be OK—look where I am now." Perhaps they were right, I thought. Perhaps their apparent flaws were simply part of the charisma and confidence that had propelled them up the ranks. And in fact it is often difficult to see the difference between justifiable pride in accomplishment and the inordinate pride that takes personal credit for the gifts of good fortune or the clever work of others. But the distinction is critical. Confident pride is the foundation for the bold decision making in the face of sparse information that is often required of the senior manager; hubris, as it did with Jim, is the sort of pride that makes power so corruptive. Unfortunately, success tends to breed them both.

It is not difficult to find a number of reasons for the slide from a strong sense of self-efficacy to hubris. For one thing, most of us have, as leftover baggage from our early childhoods, fluctuating feelings of omnipotence and powerlessness. If you've spent any time with a two-year-old (not the least of the reasons this period of life has been called "the terrible twos"), you will have seen ample evidence of both the confident expectation that a demand for ice cream before dinner will produce the desired result—and the disappointed rage when it doesn't. While it's usually outside the circle of our present mature awareness, most of us feel secret glee when, as authoritative adults, others move briskly off to do what we've told them to do, and not-so-secret rage when they seem to resist.

This psychic reinforcement of leftover feelings of omnipotence is strengthened by that other concomitant of success, lessened personal feedback. Constant kudos from subordinates who then scramble to minimize whatever damage has resulted from our personal failings have never been a great promoter of humility in anyone.

Then too, there are the trappings of status: boxes around our names in the organization chart, larger and larger offices—not to mention windows with a view. While these accoutrements are usually couched in terms of special requirements of the job—their primary purpose is to signify our importance. It's easy to forget that while such messages are intended for others, they also go inward. I can still remember sitting in the grand new office that was awarded to me just after my promotion into the executive ranks. It was filled with light from the three large windows on one wall—as large, I remember noting, as anyone's other than the CEO's.

Alone, after the head of plant maintenance had finished bustling around seeing to the arrangement of the furniture in this wonder of offices, I walked slowly around the room, straightening pictures that needed no straightening, fingering the pen-and-pencil set I'd received as a promotional gift from staff I had just left. I am sure that if I had been able to put words to the delight I felt they would have been "with an office this big, I must really be important."

Finally, let's not forget the chief and necessary ingredient of the shift from confidence to arrogance—whether you are an executive, a manager, an artist, or an independent professional—a whopping load of power motivation. Almost all of the executives that we have tested have shown "need for power" scores of at least 26 on the motivational test you've just taken (or roughly equivalent scores on similar tests).

Whether or not it concerns you that arrogance makes you a less pleasant human being to be around, are there not other, more serious outcomes? As the example of Jim suggests, the answer is yes. Like most human attributes, when pushed too far, confidence and motivation for power become self-defeating. Here are some of the most frequently seen symptoms of executive hubris. As you'll see, most of them are the result of the complex interaction between the image that you project and the reaction to that image from subordinates.

Distorted Projections. There is an appealing logic in the line of thinking that says, "If I'm an executive (or otherwise a person of status), it must be because of my superior perspicacity." Up to a point, there's some truth in that proposition. Certainly, the ability to see, grasp, and analyze complex problems is an important criterion for promotion to higher management levels. However, past success and present position don't *necessarily* mean you will always be a smart, clear thinker, and knowing when you are, or are not, can sometimes be quite difficult. As we have seen, most executives are optimists by nature who need to learn a little pessimistic self-discipline as the resources over which they have sway become more sizable. If you are such a superconfident optimist, it's critical, for example, that you force yourself to pay attention to the ill tidings of negativists on your staff and to require worst-case analyses before carrying out important decisions. Most of all, remember that if your sense of personal competence becomes inflated, you may find yourself powerfully tempted to explain away or simply disregard realistic appraisals that aren't what you want to hear.

Anger at Being Questioned. As someone who has moved up the fast track, you've learned to trust your judgment—and your success seems to certify that trust. Consequently, a measure of impatience and even irritation when others persist in bringing up opposing viewpoints is understandable, if not constructive. On several occasions, I witnessed Jim's uncensored outbursts at Rick and others of his staff. While he accused them of not being team players and of being "obstructive," it seemed to me that he was equating unqualified agreement with teamwork. The net result was a reduction of useful palaver. As one of Jim's oldest friends put it, "Jim was the smartest one among us, and I felt really good when he was picked to be CEO. I thought that we were in good hands and that the company was really going to shine. But he changed, and now you just can't talk to him. Don't get me wrong—he's still a very smart man, and I always listen hard to anything he has to say. But once he's decided on something, he doesn't seem to want to hear any argument at all."

To Be One Up You Must Put Others One Down. It's long been the general consensus of students of human nature that all of us like to keep our relationships in balance.

For example, we are only comfortable in our relations with others when, at least in our perception, the respect we give and that which we get back are about equal. Thus, while we seldom think of it that way, when we feel denigrated, it's because, on the respect dimension, our relationship is out of balance. That balance is inevitably upset in relationships between the more and less powerful. While the powerful party may find giving an order a reassuring confirmation of his or her competence and authority, the receiver of that order—whether it is reasonable or not—is likely to experience a feeling best described by the term "one down." It's all too easy to leave people feeling one down even when you don't wish to. For example, when you offer to help someone, the very offer implies that you know more, or are more skillful, than they. In addition, it's always tempting to add to your own store of self-esteem by demonstrating how strong, able, or attractive you are in relation to others. While you may indeed have more of these qualities, that reality will not often reduce the hurt of the "you're inferior" message that comes through loud and clear in your demeanor. Your tone of voice, the words you use, may imply that you are the more knowledgeable, brighter, more powerful, and otherwise superior person. If others could be honest with themselves, and you, they would probably admit to a complex, if modest, feeling of anger at you and at themselves. Whether or not their feelings are justified, people who feel one down will try to redress the balance one way or another. If you're fortunate, they may do it with a snappy comeback, an argument, or a fit of temper. If you're not so fortunate— if, for example, they see you as too powerful to deal with openly—they'll strive to equalize things by withholding whatever it is that you want from them. Worst of all, neither of you is likely to know exactly what is going on. The fact that, by withholding their best efforts, they also do themselves in is simply a tribute to the strength of that marvelous balance mechanism.

Rick "chose" an interesting way to regain his equilibrium with Herb. Although it was Jim who ordained Herb's promotion to president, it was in relation to Herb that Rick believed he had lost face. On the surface he continued to perform his duties as chief financial officer, but there is little doubt that he also deserved more than a modicum of credit for Herb's eventual fall from grace.

Among his more effective moves were these. First, he appointed third- or fourth-level managers to committees and task forces that previously received his personal attention. Since other executives took this to mean that the groups were to serve as "committees" rather than as action-generating groups, many of Herb's ideas were bogged down in endless discussions by competent but confused people. Second, although I almost believed him when he claimed that this was not his intention, Rick clearly communicated his negative attitude toward Herb to his subordinates, who then felt torn between their loyalty to him and their commitment to the organization. As might be expected, this difficult ambivalence was often resolved at the cost of the full support that Herb needed to make his own imprint on the organization. For example, the corporate controller, one of Rick's direct-report subordinates, "notified" Herb of a discouraging cost trend in one of his most promising new ventures by means of a single paragraph buried in an otherwise unremarkable report on general administrative costs. This is just the sort of negative compromise that conscientious but conflicted individuals feel driven to when caught up in a leadership battle. The controller did his job, but in a way that nullified one of its basic purposes—alerting top management when something has gotten out of hand.

"Perhaps Herb should have read *every* report with care," said Rick, with not the hint of a smile, as we talked over Herb's angry astonishment at discovering that one of his projected profit centers had instead come in at a loss. "But you know, Bob, if he did, he'd never do anything else." One thing that Rick wanted me to be completely clear about was that he would never condone purposely harpooning Herb. "I might not think he's the right person for the job," he said, "but now that he's got it, he deserves his chance."*

To sum up all of these dismal possibilities, where one has a strong power motivation that is tainted with hubris, a well-balanced relationship can easily become an exercise in one-upmanship. If this should happen to you, don't be surprised to find your path blocked by those of your fellows who somewhere along the way felt one-downed.

A Mini-Quiz on Power Motivation and Hubris. Here is a short quiz that will help you to recognize whether you have yet succumbed to an incipient sense of omniscient omnipotence. If the questions seem a little overdrawn, they are purposely so; my experience has been that those who have already been infected with the hubris disease

---

*You may be wondering why we all don't stop one-upping each other and work together as equals. In fact, the most productive and rewarding human relationships have that quality. If, occasionally, they slip out of balance, both parties work hard by pointedly handing to each other the affection, consideration, or courtesy that will restore the balance, simply because it feels so good.

often need bitter-tasting medicine before they'll pay attention—the major ingredient of the cure.

1. Do you frequently feel smarter than those around you?

2. Which criterion do you use to test your decisions against: "How can I build my empire?" or "What's best for my organization?"

3. Do you sometimes feel an almost manic sense of potency, certain that your ideas are the right ones, and impatient with those whose minds move so slowly?

4. Do you tend to brag about how confident and cool you are even when you're not interviewing for a job?

5. When sitting with other strong and powerful people, do you find yourself glowing inwardly at the thought of being a member of such an elite group?

If you have answered "yes," or "occasionally," or "sort of" to these questions and you had a score of 28 or higher on the need for power dimension, be forewarned that a full-blown case of hubris may be developing. As you read the rest of this chapter, keep in mind that while hubris feels good, it sets you up for a fall—over your own feet.

Less than Perfect Matches:
Other Motivational Needs and Positions of High Power
To be sure, a Fast Tracker with an overdose of the need for power is something like a sweet-toothed kid with connections in the candy store. There are, however, other power difficulties that can fall out of other motivational

mixes. They include: refusal to accept the power vested in your position, an excessive concern for making sure that the work is done right, and the unskillful use of appropriate redirected power.

"I'm Just One of the Gang": Managers with High Affiliation Needs. To say that someone has high affiliative needs means that they like people and want to be liked by them. If you have been so blessed, and especially if you also possess a quality of mind—my associates and I call it the Idealistic thinking style for obvious reasons— that channels your thinking toward helping others, you may be caught in a rather obvious dilemma when power and responsibility come your way. You will invariably be required by circumstances, or your own superiors, to assign tasks that your people don't favor, inform them of work that does not meet your standards, or sidetrack them into jobs that may set back their careers. Most people don't like receiving negative feedback or being demoted, transferred, or fired, and even if they intellectually understand that you are merely doing what your job calls for, they will probably be angry at you as the bearer of bad news. If you heed your inner motivations to be nice, you will slack your job. If you act like a responsible manager, you risk losing their acceptance of you—bad news all the way for the likable and nurturing person you are and want to be.

In these circumstances the mature choice is to take the proper action and bear the strain of being stretched two ways at once. But there is another and subtler way out that can help you to duck the problem altogether. You can, at least for a while, pretend that you do not in actuality have authority over your subordinates because you are "just one of the gang."

Dave Woodley was one such case. Dave was founder and senior partner in a medium-sized law firm. A first-rate lawyer, he had parlayed a talent for insightful case analysis and a down-to-earth, sincere, and open manner into a practice so successful that when I met him he was the head of a firm of fifteen.

Dave insisted that both his partners and associates consider themselves his equals because, as he said, "Lots of years in practice do not great minds make." Weekly staff meetings were held during which junior members were asked to "sign up" for cases that interested them, and all were encouraged to make suggestions that would improve the functioning of the office.

When I entered the picture, there were only two major problems: the firm was losing money, and many of the most talented of the younger partners were leaving to try their luck elsewhere.

While there were a number of issues that needed to be resolved in the firm, two common themes came out in my interviews: "We don't get enough direction," and "Dave is so busy we never get a chance to talk to him." And Dave was indeed busy, since much of his time was taken up preparing for the uninteresting cases that no one else wanted. Privately, he lamented his disappointment in people who were willing to sign their names to work that was poorly done, citing some lawyers who had left the firm and some who were still on staff. I asked him whether he had laid out his concerns as plainly to them as he had just described them to me. I was not too surprised that he had not, although he pointed out that he had often thought of doing so. As you might guess, on the motivational test Dave showed high scores in both need for affiliation and need for achievement and a below average score in need for power.

Certainly informality and a manner that communicates to subordinates that differences in authority and status do not imply superiority of either mind or character are assets to anyone who works with others. On the other hand, authority relationships imply a contract between individuals in which one grants and the other accepts an unequal distribution of power—power to reward, power to punish by withholding rewards or privileges, power to unilaterally sever the relationship. Dave genuinely wished he did not have that power and even admitted to a belief that it was wrong to have it. He soon intellectually accepted the fact that he either would have to learn to do what was distasteful to him—at times, impose his will on others—or choose someone else to be a managing partner.

Many words later, most of them spent exorcising an early learned, but mostly untrue, belief that people always hated those who had authority over them, Dave found a productive way out of at least one of his dilemmas. During a day-long off-site meeting, he and his staff developed a set of criteria by which cases would be assigned. With that accomplished, he was willing to accept the role of final arbiter who would make sure that the system was functioning well.

When Wanting to Do Well Can Mean Actually Doing Worse: Executives with Too-High Achievement Needs. One of David McClelland and his associates' most surprising findings was that while the most effective executives had a need to exercise power, many of them did not have high needs for achievement. When I came across this interesting fact, it suddenly made sense of a phenomenon I had observed for years but not understood.

In consulting with executives in high-tech industries, I found that most had both a high need for power and a high need for achievement. These intelligent men and women recognized clearly the advantages of consistent delegation, that pushing decisions down to the technical level would help keep the scientists and engineers upon whom they depended content and involved. They even suspected that such delegations would reduce the number of crucial decisions made in ignorance because they were three or four levels removed from where the actual work is being done. Despite this intellectual clarity, it was apparent to me, and to their impatient subordinates, that their delegations were sporadic at best and that substantive contacts between senior managers and busy project staff were far more frequent than made any sense. (In one organization, for example, I counted eleven signatures that were required to authorize the expenditure of $400,000 for a new technical development—in a corporation with sales revenues of over $1 billion.)

The basis for this disparity between intention and behavior was easy to see when the McClelland group pointed it out. Executives with high needs for achievement had difficulty giving up the challenge of the work itself and the satisfactions that came with hands-on accomplishment. Thus, like my technically trained executives, McClelland's high power, high achievement executives' attempts at delegating their power to others were equivocal and easily brushed aside by the appearance of any of the thousand difficulties that can spring up when complex decisions are implemented. Hard as it is to believe, a need to do things right can stand in the way of your taking a chance that others can also learn to do them right if given an opportunity to make mistakes.

COPING WITH POTENTIAL POWER PROBLEMS

The research is clear: if you intend to be a star in a high-level leadership position, it would be to your advantage to be one who gets satisfaction from being personally influential and in charge. Further, you should be motivated only moderately by the fun of the work itself and by a need to have others recognize and admire your achievements; you should be a person who cares little for whether you're liked or accepted by others. Further, you should feel driven by either ethical or practical considerations, or both, to satisfy your power needs by meeting organizational goals rather than enhancing your personal fortunes.*

But studies of identical twins raised in different families have persuaded most authorities that there is more of a genetic determinant in many aspects of human personality than was previously suspected. Thus, the odds are that nature started you well on the way to becoming the sort of person you are.

While it certainly seems quite true that nature has predisposed us to hear some siren calls more than others, the evidence is equally strong that human beings are very

---

*This point is an important one. In plain words, even if you check out with the ultimate motivational profile, you still must learn how to be dominant without being domineering, and to influence people without leaving them feeling one down. As I mentioned in chapter 3, surveys of senior management have invariably pointed to relationship problems as the greatest barrier to promotion beyond technical supervision. For every abrasive executive who, through sheer technical or intellectual merit, is an exception to this rule, there are many more who are fuming because they have been passed over (often by senior managers who feel it is futile to tell them why).

malleable creatures who, with attention and effort, can learn to enhance, control, or embellish that which nature has given us. So all is not lost if you wish to pursue the fast track but simply don't have a powerful push to dominate your fellows. Perhaps getting the work done properly is, at bottom, more important to you than who's in charge. Perhaps you simply have to concede that you are one who really likes most other people and cares about how they feel about themselves and about you. Or you may be the kind of very independent character who would just as soon work alone without interference, or help, from anyone. With the proviso that working against your dominant motivations is often somewhat onerous, there is much you can do to find a leadership career that is consonant with your personal attributes. But first, it's important to face the question of whether the rewards are worth the cost.

Are the Rewards Worth the Costs?

Becoming a successful executive if you have only a moderate need for power is indeed possible, but it's seldom completely comfortable, simply because you are constantly in the position of engaging in activities that give you little satisfaction. If you are such a person, you might find it wise to think carefully and hard about whether the rewards of the fast track are worth years spent in an occupation that is not truly fulfilling. When you knowingly *choose* to accept a difficulty as the price of attaining a goal you value, you'll substantially reduce the toll it will take on both your mind and body.

For example, Amy Winston concluded that, for her, the price was too high. After eight productive and satisfying years as senior accountant for a local department store chain, Amy Winston accepted a promotion to accounting supervisor. She had doubted all along that she would enjoy having charge of other people and, in fact, had refused two other promotion offers. Finally, however, the wish for a higher salary, and a fear that she was timidly running from advancement and responsibility, tipped the scales for her. She accepted the next offer that came up.

Two years later, she was referred to me by the controller. Although she was a manager of outstanding technical competence, in two years as a supervisor she had doubled the rate of personnel turnover in her unit. She had been repeatedly accused in exit interviews of the same sins that I had noted in others who had acquired authority with little relish for using it, even less understanding of how it ought to be used. She scolded employees in public, they said, she was often impatient, she refused to listen, and she had frequent outbursts of temper. In fact, she was showing the classic signs of someone frustrated past the tolerance point.

When I first spoke with her, Amy was very clear that she had wanted out shortly after accepting the promotion, but she fought the impulse because she did not want to be a quitter who couldn't stand up to the challenges of new responsibilities. When Amy saw that her greatest assets—a good mind and an unrelenting need to do quality work—made it hard for her to understand, let alone accept, the "slipshod" (her word) work of her subordinates, and that the kind of frustrated anger that she saved up was not at all uncommon in managers who don't matter-of-factly confront employees at the time mistakes are made, she felt free to search for an employment arrangement that better suited her personality. Nor was she the only one who was relieved when she requested a transfer. In fact, the controller, valuing Amy's technical ability and loyalty to the company, quickly made a place for her as an assistant to him, with complex technical responsibilities, but no direct-report subordinates.

Amy, who by that time had recovered her sense of humor, alleged that the speed with which he acted was due primarily to his worry that she might change her mind.

Amy's decision was right for her, but arriving at it required that she look candidly at herself—her qualities of mind and motivation, and her reasons for moving into managerial ranks, rational and irrational. Here are the questions to think through when you are faced with a similar decision:

1. What are the costs to you if you stay in a leadership position? For example: do you feel a lack of satisfaction with, or comfort in, your daily tasks? Have you noticed angry or withdrawing behavior in yourself that results from job-related conflicts between your responsibilities and your natural proclivities?

2. How much do you really value the rewards you are receiving; for example, higher status and position, greater compensation, broader responsibility?

3. What would be the consequences in loss of pay or prestige of moving to a nonmanagement job? Would any of these be recoverable in a non–fast track job? (Amy actually gained in status from her move.)

As you mull over your answers to these questions, pay attention to any intuitive responses. They are probably the best clues to the resolution that will benefit you most in the long run. If a small voice says to you, as it did to

Amy, "I don't really *want* this," heed that voice. It most probably knows best.

Suppose, however, that your conclusion is that, uncomfortable or not, you want to ride the fast track as far as you can. With that decision thoughtfully made, here are some suggestions for finding the best fit between yourself and the employment vehicles available to you.

Find a Place You Fit

If you are not power motivated but opt to stay in the fast track, it simply makes good sense to search for a career path that will both take advantage of your talents and provide opportunities to satisfy the needs you do have. Here are some possibilities from my own experience and observations.

- If your affiliative needs are high, there are organizations that, because of the personal inclinations of the founder, support an egalitarian style of management, group decision making, and a friendly, "family" atmosphere. Your chances of building a satisfying career in those organizations are likely to be much better than in, say, a hard-driving government agency with a quasi-military orientation.

- Companies or government agencies that are organized with a tightly controlled pyramidal structure often downgrade the value of team supervision. They depend much more on written or person-to-person communication and thus are less dissonant to managers with high needs for autonomy.

- Within a given business or industry, certain departments—sales, advertising, employee development—

provide a social atmosphere that can make even management fun for high affiliators.

● Highly technical organizations are often amenable to a flat organizational structure with little hierarchy. The work is done by autonomous teams who jointly decide on work plans. This sort of structure fits well with those who have high needs for both achievement and affiliation.

Coping with Conflicting Motivations

Most people with little wish to be dominant never find their way onto the leadership ladder, and, if they do, often move quietly off. The case is much more troublesome for those who have high power needs and also high needs for achievement, affiliation, or autonomy. If you are one of those, you have already found that being pulled in two or more directions at once can be stressful and confusing, but you are probably less aware that your ambivalence may be leaving those you manage on similarly shaky ground. It can be disconcerting for them to be scolded by a disappointed boss who then trys to be especially friendly when what is really needed is clear feedback and firm pressure to improve. The following actions on your part will help.

Stay Aware. Keep reminding yourself of the dysfunctional behaviors to which your cherished but confounding motivations may drive you. (Don't be put off by the nonsensical belief that "you shouldn't be that way," because, in fact, there is no other way you can be.) Take whatever ridiculous measure you need to. If you are a high affiliator, a note in large letters taped to the bottom of your desk's center drawer may help. For example, "I am not responsible for everyone's happiness" in bold letters will remind you that your genuine liking for people can sometimes nudge you to indirection and hinting instead of effective confrontation. Remember to look at it every day, or at least before the next time you must take corrective action with an employee or say no to a fellow manager who needs a favor that you ought not grant.

If, instead, you're a high-achievement type, "Let go of the task" can serve as a simple reminder that no executive should take the time to ensure that *all* work is done to the highest standard—and that most enterprises will move along quite well in spite of that fact. (Recall from chapter 3 that most successful executives focus their attention on a few key tasks and work hard to see that they are done excellently while letting the remaining jobs fend for themselves.) The mental balancing act you're striving for might be paraphrased something like this. "My present position requires that I let subordinates and peers do their work as seems fitting to them. I'm not going to like letting go, but it's my intention to do so."

Create a Role for Yourself and Rehearse It
Learning to distrust, and then contain, your "natural" behavioral impulses is a useful first step but, having created a vacuum, you need to fill it with a regimen that is tough enough to withstand the battering it will get from your urges to do what you really want to do. That means creating an executive role for yourself that will guide you in the areas in which your own motivations might lead you astray.

Here's what this prescription would mean if you were one of those juicy individuals with both a high need to be dominant and an equally high need for affiliation. (We might express this combination as "I want them to do what I tell them to do, but I want them to be happy about it.")

Your initial chore will be to select two or three important leadership tasks in which your conflicting motivations might interfere with a realistic performance of your duties. For instance, the necessity to finalize a decision that runs counter to the wishes of a key subordinate. In developing this role configuration, ask yourself these questions:

- What can I do in advance that would help me carry through with implementing this decision without equivocation or explosive anger (the two most common symptoms of conflict)? For example, I might tell my staff in advance that having heard their opinions, I will privately arrive at a decision.

- What clues will tell me that I'm losing control of my intended response? For example, hearing myself equivocate.

- What can I do to get back on track? For example, learn to use phrases such as "It's simply not possible to change it at this point."

Advance Work. Among the best preventives of boss-subordinate collisions are clarifications—as specific as possible—of who has the authority to do what when nonroutine decisions are to be made. Your part of such conversation might sound like this:

"Here's the way I'd like to handle things when it turns out we really disagree about an important decision. In my opinion, our jobs call for us to be completely candid with each other. I'll always want to hear your view of the situation and I expect that you will never tell me only what you think I want to hear. What I hope we'll both be striving for is a way to encompass both of our notions of what's important.

"But when we can't agree on the most appropriate solutions, I believe that my job as manager calls for me to use my best judgment to choose the course of action we'll take. I'll give you my reasons insofar as I can, so that you'll understand why I acted as I did. After I finalize that decision, I'll expect us both to execute it as well as we can, to evaluate how well we're executing it and to assess how well it's producing results."

Your goal is to make it as easy as possible for you to maintain control without jarring the sensibilities of either you, or your valued employees. You will be in charge—important to you—yet they will feel neither patronized nor placed in a one down position, also important to you. You have, after all, not claimed that superiority of judgment was conferred upon you by your promotion. Merely that it's your job to be the final decider.

Watching for Signs of Slippage. Use the signs of whatever kinds of distress you feel as clues that your motivations may be interfering with your best intentions.

Here's how Sidney, a successful stockbroker, put it: "On Tuesday, I had a long argument with Charlie, my lead bonds analyst, about whether we need an updated computer system. He'd gathered tons of data, and had documented six problem areas in our client follow-up system that I agreed were costing us money. But I felt pretty sure that with some less expensive fixing up, most of it could be handled reasonably well with our old system. My stomach began to ache, and I started to cough the way you know I do when I'm really getting upset. As soon as I realized what was happening, I knew I was getting angry. Actually, the nice thing about coughing when I'm pissed is that it gives me a good excuse to get up and get some water, and that gives me the time—what you call the break in the interaction—to come back and do what I know I need to do: make him feel good because of all the work he did, let him know I'm willing to take another look at it in six months, and then tell him what my final decision is. And that's what I did, which is good. But, you know, it still isn't easy."

Your signs of inner distress might not be quite as handy as Sidney's for pulling yourself together. But whatever your telltale symptoms are—that pressure behind the eyes that signals repressed tears of frustration or anger, or a spasm of your diaphragm, or a bouncing foot, or a tightening of muscles in your back or shoulders—they will serve the purpose of letting you know that you need to catch a breather in which to think through how best to resolve your internal conflict before moving on to the next step.

Acting Purposefully to Get Back in Touch. As Sidney had learned, the first thing to do when you've discovered that your motivations have taken over from your mind is to stop the interaction any way that you can. Some possibilities include a trip to the water cooler, a bathroom break, a fictitious appointment (but only if you can, in good conscience, lie a little), or a simple statement that you want to think about the problem alone for a while. The break will give you temporary relief from having to respond and a chance to think of exactly what you're going to say when the meeting reconvenes. Remember that when you feel blocked, yet powerless to get around the block without losing something you want very much, the result invariably will be a rush of emotion. So your own balked motivations can fool you into seeing things from a perspective that is more relevant to them than to the realities of the situation. For instance, as we've seen, power motivation will often make "Who's in charge?" the real issue in a discussion ostensibly focused on the problem-oriented question of "What actions will maximize our gains?" Strong affiliative motivations, similarly, will push you to suppress productive conflict over substantive issues in favor of friendly relations and good feelings.

During your interval alone, you can also think about how to present your decision to your subordinate so that it does not communicate "inferior," "unappreciated," or other threats to his or her self-esteem.

Debriefing others about the results of your decisions from time to time can also help you keep an eye on whether or not motivational issues have begun to erode the quality of your leadership. Similarly, a monitoring and review session with a mentor, consultant, or spouse can help you detect the difference between strong feelings about the best decision alternatives and strong feelings about your position vis-à-vis your peers or subordinates. Once again, this sort of discussion is not of much use unless your confidant believes you want a candid response, not reassurance that you acted wisely.

Whatever our motivational inclinations, we all face the same tasks. First, we ought to seek out those situations that promise the greatest satisfaction for people who are put together the way we are. Second, we need to understand as much as we can about our own particular mix of motivations, whatever these may be (in the last pages we have, in the main, focused only on the motivational combinations that tend to be the most distracting for Fast Trackers). Third, we need to accept the fact that our most powerful drives are constantly importuning us for satisfaction, that they may push us, often against our better judgment, to find ways to appease them. Finally, we need to learn how to skillfully manage or contain those very aspects of ourselves that provide us with our greatest joys, our needs to compete, or love, or achieve, so that we do not trade immediate highs for long-term lows.

6

Isolation and Lack of Support: How to Build and Maintain a Support and Communication Network, Even Though You're a High Flier and Everyone, Including You, Thinks You Don't Need One

I had gone to Terry's office on a Saturday morning, at his request, to interview two serious candidates for the job of national sales manager for his medium-sized publishing house. The interviews had followed their usual course—the candidates trying to find just the right path between sincerity and caution, not quite certain about the degree to which I might actually be able to penetrate the veneer they worked so hard to maintain. Afterward I mentioned that I hadn't been able to see as much past their surface selves as I'd like. That remark led to an hour's conversation with Terry (I listened mostly)—centered on how hard it was for him to feel close to anybody "because no matter how nice they are, everything they do or say is done to make some kind of impression.

"I have noticed," said Terry, "that since I became president—no, since I moved up to the third floor [where the executive offices were located]—I have not been able to have a relaxed, open, person-to-person talk with anyone in the company, except maybe with old Joe, who's been foreman in the mail room forever and doesn't give a damn about anyone. Sure, they all joke with me, but there's a stiffness about it—and it's not just them, it's me too. So I always leave feeling like I don't really know what they're thinking about. And it's not much better with my own staff. You know, when I'm sitting in on the budget sessions, listening to everyone's proposals and the fancy justifications that go along with them, I sit there and just wish that I could know what they really think about it. I've tried to ask them once in a while, but all it does is start them wondering what I'm accusing them of. Some close up and say they'll get back to me. Of course, what I get is ten more pages of justification. The others just get sore and ask me to get off their backs and let them do their jobs.

"Hell, it hasn't been that long since I was head of international business, and I sat right where they are now, trying to sell my programs to the guy who preceded me. Maybe that's what the problem is: when you get all this power over other people's lives, all they ever do is try to sell you. If this is what they mean by 'lonely at the top,' they've got the wrong word. I don't feel lonely; in fact, I wish I could get away from people for a while. The more conversations I have, the more I feel insulated from what's actually going on. What makes it really bad is that I'm the one who's responsible to the board and the stockholders for the success of this company. I can't delegate that. I can't share that with anybody."

Like Terry, most of my fast-tracking clients don't see themselves as lonely. Their working lives, they say, are overloaded with people, mostly in meetings, meetings, meetings, each of these interactions demanding more than superficial involvement—weighing proposals, paying attention to others' sensitivities and to the subtleties of the influencing process.

Yet, while they would deny being lonely in the midst of this plethora of people, most of these self-sufficient men and women do report feeling emotionally distant from, and consequently unsupported by, those with whom they so busily interact, bosses, colleagues, and subordinates. Isolation and lack of support are not as stormy as a blocked promotion or as disorienting as being overloaded beyond your tolerance level, but they are, after a time, emotionally wearing. They are also, as we'll see, a frequent cause of executives monkeying with matters they've delegated to others, a practice which invariably results in less communication upward and even greater isolation.

While I have seldom heard the words "isolation" or "lack of support" used in this sense by my clients ("lack of support" is commonly used as a synonym for disloyalty, meaning "they won't simply do what I tell them, without complaining"), much has been said in passing that has helped me to identify four aspects of executive life that largely make up the reality encompassed by these two terms. They are

- feeling out of touch with the work of subordinates,

- doubting that you are hearing the full story,

- realizing that you have no one with whom you can share your thoughts, and

- feeling alone at the forefront of the battle.

You might think of them as symptoms to be on the lookout for shortly after you've had your first two promotions.

It is interesting, if a little sad, that these feelings are so commonly felt by those in leadership positions that they have become normalized, even idealized. The strong, ethical, but detached leader who deals with the responsibility of command by maintaining emotional distance is enshrined in our literature and lore, from detective fiction to history texts. Little wonder that most Fast Trackers who experience these symptoms boast about them as if they were battle scars or, as Terry sees them, an inevitable, if mystifying, concomitant of executive status.

Like each of the other hazards we've explored, the isolation that successful people experience derives both from some fast track realities and from their own understandable, but not always constructive, reactions to those realities. Here again, knowledge of the dangers in the terrain, especially those that do not clearly announce themselves, will allow you to take preventive measures. Fortunately, in this case, prevention is well within your control and rather easy to accomplish, at that.

In this chapter we'll examine the factors that lead those who move into successively more responsible positions to feel estranged and unsupported and then focus on the coping steps that can prevent or ameliorate the effects of those feelings.

WHAT TO EXPECT

The effects of executive isolation accrue so slowly that its victims often are not aware of them until someone—a friendly consultant or a spouse, for example—asks them to talk about why they've been so moody lately. Here are some questions that can alert you to the effects of this vague but potentially debilitating condition and assist you in deciding to do something about it:

- Do you feel out of touch with what's happening in the lower levels of that part of the organization for which you are responsible? Do you find out that things have not gone according to plan only when disaster strikes or bottom-line results turn out to be less than you anticipated?

- Do you have difficulty fully trusting most of what you're told? Do others sound as if they are defending, justifying, or lobbying, rather than matter-of-factly describing their candid impressions to you?

- Do you often look for ways to go around your subordinates because you're vaguely suspicious about whether you're really being informed about what's going on?

- Do you find that you have no one in your organization with whom you can speak candidly and freely about your own reactions, worries, and fears without caring about how wild, hostile, or depressing they might sound?

- Do you frequently feel as if you are alone in the battle? (By "alone," I mean without colleagues or friends who wish you well for *your* sake rather than solely for their own.)

Becoming aware of your feelings of being alone, cut off, or unsupported can help you avoid some typical but maladaptive coping responses, such as these:

- Responding to the comfortable affinity that you feel for a few of your associates (it's worse if they are subordinates) by making them your special confidants and primary sources of information. Not only will this tend to give you more and more selective and biased perceptions of the state of affairs, but you might also be seen as someone who unfairly plays favorites among the staff. And "favorites" have never been known for jarring the sensitive ears of their benefactors with any but the most positive feedback. True, on the surface you will feel more "in the know." But your more sensitive inner ear will hear any sycophant quality, and the result will be an increased sense of isolation.

- Using a person who has an "assistant to" relationship to you as a sounding board and informant. Most people who accept these kinds of positions see service and protection as important parts of their jobs. You may be protected from just the information that would leave you feeling in touch.

- Establishing mechanisms for going around your subordinates in an effort to bring in less biased or static-free news about how things are really going. This move is usually prompted by a genuine dilemma: you don't want to bypass subordinates to whom you've delegated important work, but you wonder whether you can really be sure they're telling you all, especially when the actual implementation is done several layers below. While the impulse is understandable and the practice common enough, going around them invariably will be seen as an abrogation of your delegation of responsibility, widening the distance between you and your direct subordinates and increasing your sense of disconnectedness from them.

• Glorifying your isolation, thereby turning a necessity into a virtue. Picturing yourself as another Rick—the hero of the classic film *Casablanca*—bearing the burdens of the world on your own broad shoulders is a pleasant fantasy and perhaps a harmless way of assuring yourself of your success. Adopting the mantle of the lonely hero, however, may also keep you from taking the steps that might realistically provide some needed support.

By this time, you may be thinking, "Wait a minute, Dr. B., this all seems like a lot of bother to go to just because I feel a little isolated from the rest of the ants climbing on this anthill. And why do I have to go through these nip-ups just to find out what's going on, anyway? Isn't it the responsibility of my staff and my peers to keep me informed?" My answer is yes, but. . . . Yes, it's true that getting yourself connected is not easy. Yes, in all likelihood you would be able to survive even though you felt relatively alone and unsupported in carrying out your responsible job. And, yes, it is absolutely true that everyone should keep everyone else constantly informed. But, as always, it is a matter of balancing costs and benefits. Executives have made monumentally poor decisions because those who had unpleasant information didn't pass all of it along or weren't listened to when they did. Further, while feeling isolated and unsupported can add to the stress of anyone climbing any mountain, some people do feel more disconnected than others. If you are one of those, taking the time to understand why it has happened, and trying a few of the coping steps we'll get to later in the chapter, can pay off handsomely.

CAUSES OF ISOLATION AND LACK OF SUPPORT

The forces that tend to isolate anyone who undertakes a leadership position are many and strong. The more you understand which of these—both inside and outside of yourself—are pertinent to your own situation, the more you will be able to minimize their harmful effects. The most important of the forces are: lack of time, status and power differences, peer competitiveness, and unrealistic beliefs about support needs.

No Time for Closeness

The elemental fact is that building relationships takes time, a commodity that Fast Trackers seem to have little of, whether they're on the rise or already at the top. For one thing, the more successful you become, the more your time is valued. While there are many person-to-person contacts in organizational life, most of them are in settings that preclude the kind of conversation that builds closeness, such as talking about personal goals, wishes, and feelings. Both you and those who work with you may believe they should reserve your time together for efficient, businesslike conversations on heavyweight matters, at the expense of the chattier kind of informal interchanges that build reciprocal knowledge, comfort, and trust. Even recreational activities—golf, tennis, parties—become vehicles for dealing with business rather than deepening personal relationships.

A further complication is the concentration required

by most white-collar jobs. One of the pleasantest aspects of my own blue-collar working days was bantering with the others on the electrical repair crew of which I was a member, while simultaneously replacing hotel lighting fixtures. The fact that each hotel had to be worked "hot" added a fillip of interest, but didn't keep us from rehashing the sporting events of the weekend while our hands automatically did their required work. Many times since, I've noted the power of such communal work to build unusual intimacy. Unfortunately, such opportunities seldom occur in modern organizational life, especially for white-collar workers, whose time together is mostly spent talking about what they'll independently do after the meeting.

Status Differences

Status has to do with social structures and with informal rules that suggest how people of more or less importance should relate. Although customs have changed considerably in recent years and there is more surface informality in organizations, it does not take a discerning genius to detect differences in style and vocabulary when first-line supervisor converses with division general manager. The tilt of the heads, the lack of interruption on the part of one but not the other, a certain blankness of expression on the face of the subordinate, and most telltale of all, such phrases as "I know you're very busy, but can I have just a moment of your time?" clearly show that status is still alive and too well in most organizations. True, as differences in rank become smaller, behaviors that signal which is the more important party become less noticeable. However, when I have played the game of guessing who in a group of strangers having dinner or playing golf was the boss, I've seldom been wrong. The point is that differences in status tend to stylize conversations and to interfere with the egalitarian tone that promotes closeness between people.

Power Differences

No matter how you look at it—from above or below—a difference in power has an estranging effect on people. (It's even worse if either party pretends that the difference isn't there.) I do not mean to imply that this distancing effect is a totally negative thing; it has its uses, as we'll see shortly. Many hierarchical systems—the military is perhaps the best example—have codified it and supported it with mechanisms that make formalized relationships the norm, thereby removing some of the stigma from them. While such clear, authoritarian definitions of role is one way to handle a complex social situation, it conflicts with the more participative styles that have come into favor in recent years. The result is that managers such as Terry are left feeling the effects of the power differential but confused about why and unsure how to handle it. There are some interesting reasons for the confusion.

How Do I Use Thee—Let Me Count the Ways. There is an aspect of human relationships that, whether we like to admit it or not, seems to be a part of the darker side of our nature, often decried, but seldom overcome.

With rare and precious exceptions, most human interactions are instrumental; that is, both parties are hoping to get some personal benefit from the interchange. That is not to say that human beings are incapable of relating to each other without seeking some gain other than the experience of the relationship itself. However, the plain truth is that most relationships are of what philosopher

Martin Buber has labeled the "I-It" variety, in which I act, whether I'm fully aware of it or not, as if you were a thing to be used to meet my needs. (The other, rarer, type of encounter is the "I-Thou" relationship, in which both of us simply experience each other, neither wishing anything but the sheer joy of our connectedness. We are fortunate if we establish one or two such relationships during our lifetimes. Even then, the I-Thou islands are often surrounded by a sea of I-Its.) In everyday life, this general human propensity is heightened by power differences. If you have power over me, almost everything I do in relation to you, whether or not either of us is aware of it, is likely to be colored by my wish that you use your power for my benefit.* From this perspective, Terry's plaintive wish that others be as relaxed and open with him as his nostalgic view of the past inclines him to think they once were seems oddly out of touch, particularly in one of his wide experience. But he's not at all untypical: I have often encountered intelligent, and in other ways worldly-wise, managers who insist that, promotions or not, they were still just one of the gang, "good old Andy" or "just plain Mary Jones."

If you should at some point find yourself similarly inclined to play down differences in power or status, I would recommend caution for two reasons. First, because it will be disconcerting to your subordinates—who know full well that "good old Andy" has power to enhance or diminish their working lives. Although they will

---

*I don't believe that recognizing this reality implies a cynical view of our capacity for service to others or for working hard to further the interest of the organizations of which we are a part. It does, however, point up the fact that if organizational goals are not in some way aligned with the personal goals of the individuals within the organization, accomplishment will be minimal.

still continue to try to get you to see things their way, they will now have to pretend that it's really a conversation between equals when it is not and they know it. For example, they are fully aware that you can recommend them for promotion but they cannot do the same for you.

The second reason for open acknowledgment of differences in power and status is more germane to the problem of executive isolation. For the convoluted conversation you will get from those subordinates who will be trying to disguise the fact that they are lobbying for themselves and their units can leave you with the feeling that whatever else you're getting from them, it is not the kind of straightforward talk that is characteristic of easy, natural relationships. In other words, your efforts to stay close to them can result in an even greater psychological distance.

In organizations in which life-and-death decisions need to be made, such as in the military services, it has been accepted for centuries that friendship and authority do not mix well. After all, if you allow yourself to know me personally and, worse, like me, will you be able to bring yourself to order me to undertake a dangerous mission? While most of us are not often faced with such consequential decisions, the issue remains, for might not your friendly feelings interfere with your being direct with me about my poor performance? And even if you feel unambiguous about our relationship, will I be equally clear?

Many of my clients, upon being promoted, have chosen to adopt the same formality with their subordinates that in their early years they resented in their superiors. I asked Millie, a mid-level engineering manager, who had taken to calling her staff by their last names and who always answered the phone "This is Mrs. Tanner," about what seemed to be her overly formal manner, given the no-necktie atmosphere in her department. Had she changed since being promoted into the managerial ranks?

"I always thought that people should just be people, no matter where they were," she told me. "Then I found that a few of my employees mistook my being friendly with them at social get-togethers as meaning that I approved of what they were doing on the job. After being called a 'two-faced back stabber' by one of them, I understood why my bosses had often seemed kind of stuck-up to me."

When I suggested that she had perhaps overreacted and that there might be a useful middle ground to be explored, she replied, "Maybe so, but I can live with being referred to as 'Colonel Tanner'—oh yes, I know about that—as the price of being able to be straight with people when I have to. I'll admit that it's been hard on me, because I don't have many outside chances at socializing, and I actually have a lot of warm feelings about some of my staff here. But you know as well as I do that some people will take advantage of friendliness as a way of getting by with work that's not the best."

Whether Millie had found that best place on the formal-informal continuum would depend upon several factors, for example, the level of maturity of her staff, and their ability to differentiate between cordiality (a matter of manners) and friendliness (a matter of liking). But her dilemma—wishing both closeness and objectivity—is real and is the lot of anyone with authority.

Peer Relations

Thus far we have been talking primarily about factors that force distance upon superior-subordinate relationships. Can't we, then, look to organizational peers for support and candid conversation? This is a particularly appealing notion for people beginning their upward rise, since most first-line employees draw close friends from the ranks of those with whom they work every day. Certainly a good deal of socializing does take place among peers in the middle and above ranks. However, several factors can more or less inhibit the continued close relations with peers that might reduce a sense of isolation.

Few of a Kind at the Top. For one thing, as you move toward the top of any organization you'll find fewer people with jobs similar to yours. Take controllers, for instance. In smaller organizations there is usually only one such job. Even in giant corporations, or mammoth government agencies, with many controllers (or their government counterparts) at department, division, group, and corporate levels, they are usually housed in separate buildings, in different cities, and often in different countries. While they might actually meet as a group once a year, there is little time for the development of close or supportive relationships. And of course the corporate controller has no peers: he or she is one of a kind. It may on the surface seem trivial, but the lack of opportunity to share thoughts and commiserate on common problems with like-minded coworkers can add substantially to the isolation of anyone whose sense of importance derived from membership in a professional group.

But doesn't that one-of-a-kind controller have a new set of peers—the human resources vice president, the chief financial officer, the vice presidents for marketing, R&D, and operations? As a matter of fact, these fellow executives can be a potent support group for the controller. However, as we shall see later, supportiveness in these groups seldom grows naturally. It must be seeded and continually refertilized. Without that work, relationships between the controller and the other corporate officers must contend against the distancing effect of that most human of traits, sibling rivalry.

Peer Competition. In chapter 3 we saw that one of the consequences of narrowing opportunities at and near the top is keen competition among peers for the promotional plums that are available. What is not as obvious is the equally strong competition for appreciation, respect, and glory. It is commonplace to assume that proven leaders are so self-motivated that others' opinions of them or their accomplishments are of little concern. I have found that notion to be largely false, especially among executives with a technical background, for whom collegial respect and admiration is important.

In many ways, organizational relationships replicate those of the family. There is the boss as the traditional "father," frequently an assistant boss who takes a less formal, "motherly," role, and the often jealous siblings who compete not only for "goodies," but also for attention, praise, and even affection. I have heard more than a few tough-minded, successful businessmen put their wishes for these parental benedictions into words. Here are some phrases culled at random from my client notes.

"I've never heard a kind word from Tom, and I'd really like to have his respect."

"If he gave me half the time he gives Harry, I'd be satisfied."

"I really wonder what he thinks of me."

"I don't know what I'll have to do to get her attention. She spends all of her time with the money people and practically none with me. Hell, MIS is important too."

The point is not that these executives are behaving like children. It is that the hierarchical organizations we're members of, by defining relationships in superior and subordinate terms, tend to reach into our own individual histories and resonate with the feelings we had as junior members of our family groups. On the surface, we feel obliged to be pleasant with our colleagues, but there is a part of us that "knows" that there is a limited amount of parental caring and attention to go around and our "siblings" are our rivals for it. That this "knowledge" is largely untrue—time may be limited, but regard and consideration are not—it retains its potency for making us feel that those who might be our allies are also our enemies.

No Help Needed. Another block to building better peer support systems is the assumption that mature and capable people can and will easily integrate themselves into any group. Therefore, both old and newly assigned group members often do little to make sure that the new person will feel included.

When Reese William's boss briefed me about him before I started on my round of preliminary team-building interviews, he warned me that Reese, the newly appointed operations vice president, was unemotional, all business, and almost rabidly against any kind of team-building efforts. Since such antipathies often come from mistaken notions about the nature of what is really a straightforward practical process, I briefly described to Reese what was going to happen. He smiled a little and said that he thought he believed me, because Mitch, one of the few colleagues he trusted, had told him that I'd actually had lengthy experience as a manager and was not just an ivory tower Ph.D.-type. He had, he said, been through a "groupie" session in which the team members "practiced good communication and told each other how wonderful they were." (The quotation marks should be read as meaning "what rot!")

"I don't think the guys in this group are wonderful at all," he said. "You can talk all you want about teamwork, but when I could have used a little help in getting oriented to working for our esteemed president, not one of those guys even offered to buy me a cup of coffee. What I found out is that everyone on this executive staff is competing with everyone else for the boss's favor and money. In fact, for the first six months when I came into the meetings, all I would get was a nod and maybe a hello and a question about whether my family had got settled in. Then they would go right on talking with the other 'old boys' in the group. Most of them have been around this company for years. How could they believe that I—who had just arrived from the Southwest—could just pick up the reins and gallop off? When I saw how things were, I knew that I had to do this job on my own. I don't really like it that way. But that's the way it seems to be."

Reese's resigned acceptance of being shut out is, of course, part of the problem. If others did not enthusiastically invite him in and offer him an orientation, neither did he let them know what he wanted or even complain that he wasn't getting it. When all assume that becoming part of a new group ought to be easy, no one is likely to do much about integrating a newcomer. It is not surprising, therefore, that studies have shown that recently appointed executives frequently feel that they lack the support of their fellows.

COPING WITH ISOLATION AND LACK OF SUPPORT

Doing something to alleviate feelings of isolation or lack of support turns out not to be as easy as it ought to be. The major stumbling block is realizing that you have the problem in the first place. If it's true, to paraphrase an old song title, that "Everybody Needs Somebody Sometime," you'd have to scratch far beneath the surface of those in the upper ranks of most organizations to find much agreement with it. For example, when I have posed building mutual support as a goal for off-site executive team meetings, blank looks and even snickers have been the most common responses. Yet, at the end of three days of strengthening the bonds of their work group, almost all will have recognized that they indeed are, or would like to be, a "band of brothers" who need the rejuvenation and refreshment that they can best get from each other.

I have often wondered what accounts for this resistance to something that feels so good when you get it. I believe the answer lies in the assumption that people who are strong and successful don't (and shouldn't) need the support of others to fulfill their responsibilities. Certainly our cultural myths about leadership would lead us to believe that powerful people can take care of themselves and that, if they can't, they must be lacking in the fortitude that should accompany their exalted status. Although this assumption may seem ridiculous when stated in this exaggerated fashion, stay alert to fleeting doubts that you lack the proper fortitude when, as you are sitting wearily alone in your office one night, you realize that you would really like to have someone at work to whom you could fully open your mind—even better, your heart—without losing face, or risking your chance for advancement.

Start with Yourself

A useful first step is to acknowledge any personal qualities that make you particularly susceptible to feeling isolated. For example, recognize that you, like most successful managers, are most comfortable at the top of the pecking order. Suppose, further, that you're also a people-oriented person—you like people, enjoy being with them, and need to have them think well of you. Clearly, you are caught in that not-easy-to-resolve dilemma we've touched upon earlier. If, as my boss, you tell me to do something disagreeable, I might see you as a villain, if you don't, then you're slacking in your managerial job.

It would be surprising if, in that fix, you did not protect yourself in some fashion, possibly with increased formality as your remedy of choice. While you might regret feeling isolated, it would hurt less than an inner conflict that can't be resolved. "Colonel" Tanner, whom we met earlier in this chapter, is an example of a manager who dealt with the problem that way.

Whether you're stuck with that dilemma or with another, or even if you can't find any reasons other than the isolating nature of organizational life, the more you can acknowledge that you do feel cut off, and that you wish you didn't, the more likely you are to take positive steps to reduce your feelings of isolation. Let's take a look at what's available.

Make Time to Build Supportive Relationships

While most of us properly fault the reality behind the maxim "The urgent always drives out the important," we frequently find ourselves living by it. All of our time is absorbed by the tasks of today with none left for less-demanding, but equally vital, work that might ease our tomorrows. Because feelings of isolation seldom scream for attention (they tend to whimper in the background), you may not have made the time required for developing solid supportive relationships. This relationship building can take several forms.

Informal Conversations. By far the easiest way to make or renew connections is to spend "visiting" time with both peers and subordinates, initiating conversations that, while perhaps work related, do not dwell on an immediate problem at hand. To have the desired effect, it's essential that you do *not* broach these conversations when you want something from the other person. Whether you intend it or not, selling or importuning him or her will insert an instrumental quality into your relationship. Instead, talk about such topics as your mutual expectations for your units, a general discussion of the state of the business you're in, how the other person addresses mutual problems (if you feel comfortable enough, try the question of how to maintain balance in your busy lives).

Won't these conversations seem phony or artificial? Not necessarily. While it is true that they did not arise spontaneously, they are soundly based on your belief that there is a mutual benefit in your understanding each other better. At any rate, the exchange needn't be so formalized as to border on the ridiculous ("All right, Mary, it's time for us to discuss putting balance in our lives"). Ample opportunities for informal talk can occur over coffee, while sitting together at the end of a long meeting, or during recreational events such as golfing. The important point is that getting started on such exchanges is taking time for something valuable, not wasting it. Informal conversations, even very limited ones if they are free of persuasions and arguments, enhance an atmosphere of mutual support and open communication far beyond what one might expect given the apparent unimportance of what is discussed. Indeed, some leaders have used this simplistic sounding method with considerable success. (Some of the techniques and examples in this section show respect for employees and an interest in their ideas. While that is a valuable by-product, our focus here is on their value in minimizing your own feelings of disconnection from others.) For example:

Renn Zaphiropoulos, a cofounder, president and chief executive officer of Versatec, a highly successful electronics manufacturing company, is so well-known for creating a climate of open communication and trust within his company that he was the subject of an article in *Harvard Business Review*. When low-ranking staff in the company were queried about what, specifically, he did that engendered such a supportive climate, they said that he was often seen around the plant, that he always smiled and said hello.

While Zaphiropoulos instituted many other policies and mechanisms that contributed to the innovative atmosphere, the time he took to demonstrate his own belief that "when people think you care about them, they give you their best," had a special impact on employees who otherwise might never have had a chance to know him.

One important proviso: if you chat with employees supervised by people who report to you, under no circumstances make assignments while walking around.

This can be especially tempting when, as a way of showing your interest, you ask questions and then get answers that puzzle you. The people you question, especially if you're several levels above them in the hierarchy, may be either frightened or flattered into getting further information for you, but it will almost invariably make their bosses uneasy. That uneasiness about possible erosion of their authority, even if unfounded, will not only lessen their ability to manage well but will make them even more wary about filling you in on the details of their operations. The less you know, they'll think, the less likely you are to "interfere."

Open Channels from Below

Human beings differ in the degree to which they are sensitive to what is going on around them. These differences are present at birth and are maintained through life, producing at one extreme stalwarts who are oblivious to storms raging around them and, at the other, supersensitive people who react animatedly to even the slightest change in their environments. Given the value that is usually placed on the capacity to remain cool when others are frantic, it is not surprising that, by and large, most managers fall on the less sensitive end of the continuum.* In other words, to some extent it's true that, from the vantage point of the people who are being supervised, their bosses are more often than not a little dense.

While a certain thickness of skin is doubtlessly handy during turbulent times, it can result in missed messages,

*This conclusion is based on data drawn from a sample of over 300 managers from a wide variety of profit and not-for-profit organizations. The measuring instrument was the Mehrabian Screening and Arousal Measure.

especially if they have been delivered subtly or nonverbally. When you do not respond to problems that others see as obvious and urgent, they'll stop trying to communicate. Or worse for both, they'll complain, leaving you feeling annoyed, misunderstood, and even more isolated. When the crisis, the early signs to which you were oblivious, breaks, you wonder, suspiciously, why you were not kept fully informed, certain that you're the only one who really cares. To avoid this all-too-common scenario open communication channels from below and take the time to keep these channels free from obstruction. Here are some specific techniques for keeping channels open.

Monitor Each Important Delegation. It's difficult to think of an aspect of management that has been more written and lectured about than delegation. Whether the topic is nurturing organizational innovation or managing time more efficiently, every authority insists on delegation as a prerequisite to any progress. What is curious is why all of this emphasis on delegation should be needed, since almost every manager I've known understands that delegation is the key to productivity and managerial happiness. I believe the best answer is the obvious one: while all agree delegation is useful, there are a number of understandable reasons why most of us have trouble with it.

A good part of that difficulty is a false belief that when a task has been delegated, the delegator must have blind faith that it will be well done, at least until a catastrophe has occurred (at which time it is hard to resist the thought that delegating was perhaps not the wisest thing to have done). I'm afraid that much of this misplaced assumption has been the fault of those of us who have urged delegation without an equal emphasis on the necessity of monitoring that delegation. Every important delegation ought to have as a mandatory accompaniment an agreed-upon process for keeping the delegator informed about how things are going. Nothing has left my clients feeling more cut off than delegating an important undertaking and then feeling that responsible management required them to wait around anxiously until the execution is complete. In fact, it is this tense waiting around that pushes action-oriented executives into the poking around that does undermine their subordinates' authority.

Senior executives with discretionary funds at their disposal often pull together a more or less formalized staff of "analysts" to check on the implementation of important programs. These "flying squads" (often known by such fond names as "Ron's rangers" or "the director's spies") are often competently staffed and potentially a source of new ideas, but their primary purpose is to alleviate the executive's sense of being cut off. Since these intrusive efforts are more often than not interpreted as a sign of uncertain trust and confidence, they induce otherwise responsible managers to play a variety of hide-and-seek games. The result is a greater rather than lesser insulation from the true state of things.

A more satisfactory approach is to make it a habitual practice to require that each nonroutine delegation include a plan for monitoring how well the project is progressing. The plan, made explicit at the time of the delegation, ought to regularly keep you posted about whether there is a plan of action, whether that plan of action was actually put into effect, whether problems have occurred, whether there is a corrective plan, whether that plan was enacted, what happened when it was, and whether it was modified, if necessary. Note that the emphasis here is not on the production of more performance data, already overdocumented in most organizations, but rather on how well the *delegatee* is carrying out the steps appropriate to the task. As Ellen Langer has eloquently pointed out, being mindful of the *process*—how something is done—fosters far more creativity and learning than a focus on how well it was done, or the thing itself. Although it is common to enjoin managers to *only* keep their eyes on bottom-line results, I've found that a too-avid focus on objective performance data has bred generations of nervous executives who, out of touch with how well their subordinates are managing, grab for the reins as soon as a crisis occurs. In other words, poring over quarterly production and sales figures will do very little to relieve your sense of being isolated from the action. (Remember Harry's surprise—in chapter 4—over the illusory nature of his division's magnificent profits.)

Institute Interlocking Staff Meetings. Interlocking staff meetings are sequentially scheduled meetings at descending levels in the organization. For example, the president and vice presidents meet on Monday, the vice presidents and their division managers meet on Tuesday, division managers and department heads meet on Wednesday, and so on. This good old idea—a planned way of massaging information up and down the organization—has been bandied about the management literature since the late 1960s. In practice, it is grasped at, sometimes desperately, by senior executives who feel uninformed or uncertain that their immediate subordinates are doing what they should to move information. Interlocking meetings usually work quite well—for a while. Then, six months or so down the line, the schedule deteriorates, those managers who are not inclined toward any kind of meeting stop having them. The senior manager who started it all—having had his or her sense of isolation ameliorated to some extent—is less motivated to do the work of keeping the system going, and after all, there are always more urgent matters. Needless to say, within a year, the feeling of isolation is back, and the senior executive, having tried them once, is convinced that interlocking staff meetings are another of those ideas that are "good in theory, but don't work in practice." Like the other techniques we are discussing, this one will work for you only if you maintain it over time. Principally that means expecting it to falter, as all human systems must, and then reestablishing it with enough minor changes (the time of day or the days of the week, for instance) to keep it interesting. Even better, occasionally use the meetings as a device for getting staff opinion. For example, have "each group identify the three most onerous central office procedures."

Establish Diagnosis Groups. Another mechanism that works well and is easier for middle- and higher-level executives to keep in place is the diagnosis group. A diagnosis group is made up of ten to twenty individuals from all levels of the organization who are charged with gathering information about how well the organization is operating for analysis and action recommendations. Two key requirements for the success of these groups are (1) to the extent possible, no one in the group is a direct subordinate of any other group member and (2) one group member is drawn from an organizational level that has full authority to implement any recommendations. The first requirement is necessary if members of the group are to feel as free as possible to speak their minds.

The second saves the group from the fate of most committees—much talk but little impact—because it provides a means for reconnecting the group with the organizational hierarchy.

For example, if senior vice presidents are members of the group, they can bring the group's recommendations directly to the executive committee. In this way, objections to the group's proposals can be answered by someone who was a party to the original deliberations. Further, the products of the group will not, as often happens when committee reports ascend unaccompanied into the organizational stratosphere, be dismissed as unrealistic, out of touch with the overall needs of the organization, and probably just the complaints of a few troublemakers.

In addition, each member of the group should understand that she or he is responsible for keeping in touch with other interested individuals at his or her own level, communicating the group's deliberations and passing on to them the nature of its findings and recommendations, and the reasons behind them.

Set Up Problem-Solving and Team-Building Sessions with Your Own Group. In chapter 3, I suggested team building as a way of enhancing your own reputation as an effective manager. Another, almost invariable, benefit from a well-conducted team development process will be a significant increase in the trust and confidence with which the team members perceive each other and you. And why not? When issues that have been annoying and frustrating are raised in confidence and worked through to mutually agreed-upon solutions, everyone, including you, will feel relieved. The unspeakable has finally been spoken. Whatever your staff might have thought of you previously—misconceptions all, of course—after the team-building session, since in it you were neither defensive nor vindictive, they will see you as a person who is concerned about people as well as performance.

It's not difficult to grasp why resolving annoying problems results in less tension and renewed commitment to the group. Less easily understood in purely rational terms is the increased closeness often felt by team members, even when there have been long-standing grievances among individuals. I have found this to be particularly true of groups that have been tasked, or have tasked themselves, with delivering high performance in a stressful environment. When I first encountered this effect, it awoke memories of the extraordinary sense of connection that formed within the combat infantry squad of which I was a part.

That depth of relationship may be impossible for most work groups, but it sometimes can be approached with the help of a well-trained organizational consultant who has had specific experience in team building. At a minimum, the process should include a technique for confidentially ascertaining what team members think is going well, and what issues, problems, or nuisances are interfering with their own, or with the team's, effectiveness. Enough time must be allocated to work through all the issues and to allow team members to begin to see one another as colleagues who, though they may not always act in accordance with their own best intentions, do have the good of the team and their teammates at heart.

Find and Cultivate Third-Party Listeners

If, as I have suggested, power and status complicate relationships, how and when can you be sure that you're getting candid straightforward opinions? If the weight of psychological research can be trusted at all, the correct answer to that question must be "seldom." Even when *we* fully intend to be open, our secret wishes both to feel and to be seen as a competent, likable somebody will select the facts to which we'll pay attention, and make us less than completely objective perceivers. Even if we saw matters without distortion, would others be unaffected by their knowledge of the benefits to be gained by pleasing someone whose goodwill they need? In other words, as a boss, or a competitor, or a fast-tracking upstart, you will be unlikely to hear an uncensored version of what those who want to gratify you believe to be true.

What this gloomy picture suggests is the value of calling on people whose viewpoint is *minimally* biased as an aid to keeping better in touch with what's happening around you, especially the effects of your own actions, and thus feeling less insulated from reality. Management consultants can be useful in this way if they meet these criteria: (1) they are fully booked and thus are not desperately worried about keeping you as a client; (2) they have shown a willingness to tell you what you don't want to hear, and the skill to say it in a way that makes hearing it possible. Internal consultants—human resource development staff, for example—can sometimes take this role, if they have been granted immunity by their bosses from breaking their confidential relationship with you.

Spouses and friends not associated with your organization can also provide valuable perspective. However, you'll need to give them permission to be honest, and to reinforce this permission several times during the discussion. You'll also have to give them time to work up to being fully candid. Remember, the key to promoting openness in others is your reaction after they start. If your response is laden with explanations and impatient reminders that they aren't fully informed of the situation (amazing how hard it is to *not* offer either) you will quickly shut off that source of perspective.

Whether your third parties are consultants or friends, the best way to start is to describe in detail the current problem or program, especially any doubts you have about it. After your presentation, the most useful questions to put to them will be these:

- Where are the gaps or distortions in my view of the problem?

- What does my intuition tell me might go wrong with my plan?

- What else do I need to find out to have a complete picture?

Such questions leave open a wide range of responses and demonstrate that you want more than a pat on the back. One initially disconcerting response to be prepared for is "Something's wrong, but I can't quite put my finger on it." Your natural inclination might be to dismiss your confidants' unease as vague and uninformed, or explain away their concerns by assuring them of all the work that has gone into checking out the facts, or accuse them of never giving you the support you need. I've been the target of each of these responses and, especially in my personal life, have used them all. They are understandable, especially if you are of a concrete turn of mind, but they will not help you penetrate the layers of benevolent noncommunication that keep you both satisfied and out of touch. Further, you will also deny yourself the support you could derive from these conversations. Instead, use more and more specific questions to help your third parties pinpoint *where* in your exposition they began to feel odd, and *what* thoughts they had at the time.

Whether or not anything substantial arises in the discussion, there is something marvelously supportive about explicating a problem and airing concerns and fears to someone who is interested in you, but who is not a direct party to what you're doing. I have often wondered whether this might not be the chief value that one derives from consultants, counselors, and other paid "friends."

Reestablish After Each Move

Each time your own status changes, it's wise to presume that the way others feel about you will also change. This is especially true if the change means that you have greater access to resources or to people of importance. Keep in mind that the forces reviewed earlier in this chapter are always at work, thus many of those who formerly were open with you may now be guarded or subtle. Assume this to be true even though they assure you that in their eyes you're still "good old you."

Sonja had been director of marketing and advertising for a Midwestern bank. When she was named vice president in charge of those same functions, she was astounded and hurt that her staff, with whom she had always enjoyed, she thought, a wonderfully open and informal relationship, began treating her more formally. Her secretary, whom she had known for years, began calling her "Mrs. Jones." Meetings that had been "free rein and fun" were now decorum itself, others waited for her to introduce a topic and raised their hands to be called upon. "Just because I'm now part of senior management," said Sonja, "doesn't make me into a different person. We were very successful before, and I'm damned if I want to lose that. I don't know what to do, because I don't know why it occurred. I don't think *I'm* any different."

I pointed out to her that since the sign painter had been busily changing the title on her office door an hour after she was informed about her appointment (or so I was told), and her in basket had been piled with congratulatory notes from her fellow executives, her staff might be uncertain about the way she wanted to be treated. I also reminded her of an absolute in human relationships: when a change occurs in one person, it will breed changed perceptions, some unwarranted, in those who are close to that person.

Accepting the inevitability of such changes will save you trying too hard, as Sonja initially did, to pretend that all was as it had been. Instead, raise the issue yourself, talk with others about how your new status will affect your job, which new distribution lists you'll now be on, and then make known your wishes for open dialogue and informal meetings. Also keep in mind, however, that your newly confident, commanding manner will continue to mark you as someone different than you were, and take special care to recycle all of the methods for reducing isolation that you've let slide.

To this point, we've dealt primarily with organizational sources of isolation and what you can do to reduce the impact of those forces on yourself. Let us turn now to two additional factors that can contribute to feeling estranged and without that sustaining sense of partnership that can keep one going in troubled times. One of these undermining forces is, not surprisingly, isolation from self.

Isolation from Yourself

One thing that never changes in our lives is the fact that we're always the stars of our own show. Unless we make conscious efforts to do otherwise, we view the world, ourselves included, from the perspective of that entity we think of as "I." The fact that our selves and our views of the world are so familiar to us makes it difficult to apprehend a fundamental fact: When one aspect of our lives changes, it will affect the way we think and feel about ourselves. For example, if your job title changes from manager to director, you will react to yourself as a different kind of being to the extent that status and title are important to you. Thus, you may speak slightly more assuredly, perhaps with less flamboyance than before, or even with a superior air. As others react to those changes, their reactions will promote in you a whole new set of perceptions of yourself, and so on.

Here are some of the changes in self-perception that a number of writers on the subject have identified as contributing to the sense of isolation often felt by those who have moved organizationally upward:

- Moving from someone who is a recipient of direction from others to one who is expected to provide direction to others.

- Moving from a technologist-doer of "real" things to a manager (or a manager of managers) who sits in meetings and talks to other managers or managers of managers.

- Moving from an ordinary human being to a star with an office on the executive floor who is a proven success and therefore is not to be contradicted.

- Moving from a person whose self-satisfaction comes from personal creativity and accomplishment to one who measures himself or herself only against external rewards such as money and things acquired, because the real work is done by others.

These changes are seldom openly identified, talked about, or even mulled over much, because most of us are simply unaware of them. You know only that you've been appointed director of advertising, and that a "vice president" after your name is now more than just a possibility. While you're sure you don't really care about such things as status, and you're perfectly aware of the danger of becoming too self-important, still, isn't it nice to have an office with three windows? It is unlikely that you will think much about the fact that the aspects of your life that previously left you feeling solid, oriented in direction, and knowledgeable about who you were may now be missing or all askew.

If unexplained uneasiness or boredom suggest to you that such is the case, the key to finding yourself is to seriously question whether the work you're doing has meaning and purpose for you. Once they are squarely faced, honestly examined and answered, you will have either regained a firm center, or you will have begun to consider how to change your life's direction. Keep in mind that the Small Wins approach suggested in chapter 3 provides a way to make significant changes even when your possibilities seem very limited.

I vividly remember a moment two years after moving into my own grand, three-windowed office, in which I suddenly realized that I was excruciatingly bored with sitting through meeting after interminable meeting. I began wondering why, at age forty-two, having moved so far up the ladder, I felt as if none of it seemed to matter anymore. With the assistance of a counselor who had been of help to me in the past, I began to see that the things I had most enjoyed in my work—planning, solving operating problems, and working closely with others to implement the solutions—were now being done exceptionally well by the large and competent staff I had accumulated. What I really wanted were the satisfactions I had felt two levels down in the organization *and* the income and perquisites that went with a big office on the seventh floor. Fortunately, I could see a possible move that, with a little risk and a lot of luck, might get me both. Within three months I was borrowing money and making plans to return to school for a doctoral degree that I hoped would be my ticket to life as a highly regarded and highly paid management consultant.

Isolation from Friends and Family

When executives have been asked to identify their major sources of support outside of their work organizations, the two most frequently cited resources were same-sex friends and family. Unhappily, it is also true that some Fast Trackers' relationships with friends and family have resulted in further alienation rather than support. Here are some reasons.

Friends. For many hard-driving people, a perpetual lack of free time and guilt because of it combine to reduce, and then eliminate contacts with old friends. Consequently, as travel and long hours continue to consume more and more outside of work time, most executives report that they give their families first call. While this certainly helps with family relationships, it eliminates an important source of personal support for some people, especially those who are unable to sustain a deep level of communication with their spouses and other family members.

The available data suggest that this problem is exacerbated for men, even those with many friends, because men tend to establish less intimate relationships than women, and, even with longtime friends, reveal less about their personal feelings. These findings have been borne out for me when, from time to time, I have been asked to provide consultation to longtime male friends. In each instance, I have learned far more about their personal lives and their feelings in a single hour of consultation than I had during years of getting together as friends, even though the consultations were focused on work-related problems. In contrast, my wife has had similar opportunities to provide professional counseling to female friends, with the opposite result. During the consultations, she discovered little that she did not already know from intimate, friend-to-friend conversations. So, for most male Fast Trackers, friends, while they can provide companionship, respect, and liking, are less likely to provide the sense of personal support that is often found in a relationship in which both parties are willing to bring their deeper feelings into the arena.

The remedies for this situation are not at all easy for most men. The most obvious is greater sharing of feelings with friends. Many men can do this during times of tragedy—perhaps because it is then most acceptable for "strong" men to do so. For them there is a recognition that the slow death of boredom or anxiety is also a justifiable reason for gaining the relief and renewed perspective that are the products of shared intimacy.

Intermittent sessions with professional counselors are an excellent possibility. Over the years, I have fulfilled this function for executives and professional men and women who thought they could benefit from an uncensored mulling over of current issues, doubts, and difficulties. In turn I have benefited from intermittent sessions with my own consultants and counselors. Unfortunately many people associate counseling with weakness or severe mental and emotional problems and are concerned that a visit to a consultant or counselor will be seen as "softness." This can be a costly misperception if it results in putting off work on personal issues that might contribute to the stress overload we'll address in chapter 8.

Family. For many executives, family relationships are an immense source of support. Since I am one of those myself, I've always felt both sadness for, even anger at, clients who seem to be willing to settle for less than a full measure of family life. Training and common sense have indeed told me that we each must make our own accommodations to life, and that I have been projecting my values into someone else. Nonetheless, I feel frustrated when a client who wishes for warm and uplifting relationships at home does little to ensure that these relationships will be in place.

Here are some of the sins of omission and commission that tend to diminish family ties.

The Executive as Guest in the House. Anyone bustling through a busy, important career can imperceptibly drift into seeing home base and family as yet another support system whose purpose is to move this star even higher into the heavens. The most apt descriptor I have heard for this by-product of busyness is "the executive as a guest in the house." In brief, this is the picture. Our heroes (includes both genders) travel 50 to 75 percent of each month. In order to get the most out of those travels they need the support of secretaries, travel agents, airline attendants, and a retinue of others whose major function is to keep these outstandingly productive people from doing anything but thinking great thoughts, writing them down persuasively, and making deals. At home, the family functions in the same way. Schedules are amended so that home life will be quiet and peaceful and will allow ample opportunity to deal with the contents of the briefcase, which is brought home every night and every weekend. Menus are designed to meet our heroes' tastes, and children are scheduled for "quality time," whether they feel like it or not. Other family members make sure that those drab accompaniments to life outside of work—taking clothes to the cleaners, for example—are handled with a minimum of interference. As Maryanne Vandervelde, author and executive wife, has pointed out, family members who undertake this complementary role in return for reflected glory, high status in the community, and all the other things that money can buy do so at the cost of their own development and the maintenance of a warm and intimate relationship.

All You Need Is Money. Money can become a distancing factor in fast track families—not too much of it, not the lack of it, but an unrealistic confidence in it as a solver of all problems.

Tad was a tough and determined man who had sworn he would be worth ten million dollars at age fifty and had to settle at age forty for four times that much. But he was not up to looking at his wife's face when he explained to me why he was annoyed with her. Her crime was that she had refused to use employees to solve the normal problems that come up in any family's daily life.

Mary, trying to start up her own interior design business while still mothering four young children, was frustrated and furious over the idea that money alone could solve the problems of adequate child care. Why could she not, Tad said, in the tone of one who has once again solved an elementary problem, hire two full-time nurses to take care of the children so that she wouldn't have to worry about it at all?

"Because the children are not just customers at your stupid bank," she hissed, "and I'm not just one of your vice presidents!"

"Could it be," I ventured (mostly to give Mary a chance to make her point a little less venomously), "that you want something more from Tad than money? If so, can you tell him what that might be?"

"I'm not really sure myself," Mary replied, "but I think what I want is for him to be interested enough to talk with me about who the best people are that I might be able to find and what kind of people each one of the kids relates to the best and the worst, and I want him to sound like he cares about them and about me." The last, I was pleased to see, was said with a little smile. Whether she was right about it, I wasn't at all sure, but she seemed to think as she took in the startled, almost sheepish look on his face, that she had finally gotten through to him.

Savant at Work, Idiot at Home. I've seen another sort of role dissonance, one not nearly so disruptive, perhaps, but nonetheless annoying. Some people, extraordinarily competent at work, are much less able at meeting the ordinary demands of everyday life. They may be able to toss off a first-rate business plan in an hour, but they can't remember to start the dishwasher, are cavalier about paying bills on time, and are not much good at helping the kids with their homework. Since expertness at business planning is usually not relevant to the lives of spouses and teenage kids, they may wonder (as mine have) how this incompetent manages to drag down so much money, often—mostly unintentionally—communicating that rather unflattering perception. It can be jarring to move from respected professional in one setting to village idiot in the other. While this role conflict has its humorous side, it can, in time, add to feelings of being unappreciated and without support.

That these forces can push otherwise loving people apart there can be no doubt, and to further muddle things, they become entangled with the personalities of those involved. This confusion of individual traits with the social pressures that successful Fast Trackers encounter often obfuscates the real sources of the problem. To Mary, it was obvious that her husband seemed to care more for his bank than he did for her or their children. To Tad his wife seemed strangely dependent and unable to deal with what seemed to him to be practical, easily solved problems. The real culprit was a subtle interactive chain in which each made mistaken inferences about the intentions and motivations behind the other's behavior. From there it was the usual short hop from lowered trust to less open communication, to more misinterpretation, and so on until the end result—suspicion and a mutual sense of isolation—was reached.

Awareness of these possible hazards can keep you from blindly stumbling into them and is certainly the first step to recovery, if you've already fallen in. Because of the complex interplay between personality and the dynamics of the fast track, outside assistance in identifying what's happening and in reestablishing a supportive relationship is almost always useful. If frustration and anger have already made open communication and reciprocal listening impossible, then outside help is not only advisable but necessary. (When all parties want the relationship to continue, it is also amazingly successful.)

However, if you are still talking, and listening, it is also very possible for you and your family to work through these role confusions on your own. A sense of humor and mutual concern for the welfare of all are the most important ingredients for success. To solve any sort of complex, many-faceted problem, the best approach is to take a variety of small and sustainable steps, rather than leaping for a total solution to one piece of the problem. There are more than a few self-help texts that can provide useful suggestions for resolving family problems. You'll find several in the reference list for this chapter.

Feelings of isolation and lack of support are endemic to the fast track. As you move up, you may find yourself feeling alone in the battle and with troubling doubts about others' sincerity. Your most important bulwark is the recognition that the further you move up through the ranks, the more important it will be to work at maintaining as much connectedness as possible.

The methods we've reviewed in this chapter should help you in coping with this less-dangerous, but, at times, disheartening, hazard of the fast track.

7

Alcohol, Drugs, Money Madness, and Other Just Deserts

Life in the fast track, enticing, risky, and overloading, can sometimes turn a harmless flirtation with alcohol and other stimulating or soothing drugs into a disastrous affair.

It is not that the fervor of a demanding career "causes" heavy drinking or the misuse of any of the other mood helpers currently making the rounds, any more than the ennui of a tiresome life, or the dissonance of being poor in an opulent society. The etiology of such problems invariably turns out to involve a complex interweaving of the genes that shaped us before we were born, what happened to us after that event, and the choices we've made along the way. Yet, while neither the fast track, nor the humdrum track, nor even the poverty track are solely to blame, it is equally true that each does have its own assortment of slippery places.

The trouble is that getting caught is usually a step-by-step process. No one sets out to lose control to alcohol or other drugs, or to squander money. Like other primrose-path situations, each further step is taken with the confidence that a choice can be made to go no farther, or to retreat if warning signals sound. What is unforeseen by most of us, especially by those of us blessed with more than a modicum of self-confidence, is that at a certain point along the path, our intention to hold the line will no longer be able to resist the pull of the attractions that set us on the path in the first place. By that time, we're more than ready for a drink, a snort, or a drag to help us swallow that most beguiling of self-deceptions, "It isn't really a problem because I know I can control it any time I decide to."

The realization of how even the most knowledgeable people can come close to losing control of their lives forced itself on my wife and me when we least expected it—at the brightest moment of our own joint spin in the fast track.

Almost ten years ago, at the end of a not unusually noisome day, we began to talk about several disagreeable truths that had independently been gnawing away at each of us: (1) we were looking forward to a cocktail—and sometimes two—every night; (2) "looking forward to" was starting to verge on "needing"; (3) we were pouring ever larger amounts under the rubric of "one drink"; and (4) after our nightly "relaxation," we were quicker to anger in occasional confrontations with our children. Consider that we were professionally trained people, self-aware, sophisticated, and absolutely above overindulging in anything, or so we thought. Luckily, we were not yet immune to shock, nor so completely immersed in the busyness of our lives that we avoided facing an unpleasant fact—we had, by imperceptible degrees, drifted into a place from which we might have indeed lost control.

Our initial response was frightened, but useful—stop drinking entirely. Then we began to mull over our current lives. Were we really incapable of harmlessly enjoying the undeniable pleasures of fermented grape and grain? Or had we, given the kind of people we were, simply been caught off guard by the events of our own ride on the fast track? Our consulting practice had suddenly taken off. Of two books of ours recently published, one had become a best-seller and had thrown us into the frenetic pace of author promotions and multiple media interviews. We were dazzled by the celebrity status accorded us by our friends and clients—"we saw you on the *Today* show" has its own intoxications. Even worse, we found ourselves with more discretionary money to spend than we'd ever expected to see. In the center of this excitement, and actively competing for our attention were six children in widely varying stages of life. Our real task, and not an easy one, was not simply to "cut down on booze," but to find the balance between growth and stability that was right for all of us. One indication that we had found it came six months later when we realized that a cocktail every night had become an occasional drink, that hard liquor had become mostly wine or beer, and "God, I need a drink!" had become "a little wine sounds like fun."

Sadly, some Fast Trackers of high promise, are not as fortunate as we were—the thrills and pressures they encounter do, in truth, override their ability to cope. Without fully intending to, they grasp just the sort of props that they finally cannot control. The costs to them can range from a career that does not reach its potential, to a decimated personal life. Frequently, the line is crossed just when they least expect it, when everything seems to be going well.

Harvey Lufts, Vice President for Corporate Communications in a burgeoning Northwest health care company, was such a one. Here is what Pete, one of his former coworkers and now a subordinate supervisor of Harve's, had to say:

"Harve was good—one of the best PR people I've seen in my eighteen years in the words business. He had a wicked wit—occasionally he would turn it on me; actually, he could be very nasty at times—and he could write well about anything. But, more to the point, he had a way of making you feel special because he had accepted you as being an OK guy. But Harve was never satisfied with just being good or with the fat raises that he got, or even with being the top person in the unit. It was strange in a way. Here was Harve, on the surface the world's greatest cynic, but underneath you could tell that he envied the people who had position and big bucks. Maybe we all do, but with Harve it was more than just something you think about every once in a while. He kept pushing and pushing on the old man— he'd known him for years and they played golf together—to make him an executive. Well, he, the CEO, really depended on Harve, and I think he wasn't too hot about moving him out of the front lines, but he finally went along, and Harve was promoted to Vice President for Corporate Communications.

"I had hoped that it would finally cure Harve's itch, whatever it was, and that he would settle down. We actually did need a leader who could make this unit into something more than just a bunch of speech writers, and issuers of news releases. That's why, although I hated doing it, I finally blew the whistle on a guy who used to be my friend. Because, the fact is, after he finally got what he wanted, Harve just seemed to fall apart. He'd always been pretty friendly with the bottle, how many ex-newsy's aren't. But when he was finally 'knighted,' so to speak, it became something else.

"Picture this—Harve's typical workday for the last year. He came in early, by seven-thirty almost every morning—I don't know how he did it. Considering he'd go straight to his office, not stopping to have coffee with the rest of us, I guess that's when he'd do his paperwork. Around ten o'clock every morning, he'd pass by my office on the way to the john without saying a word to me, then he'd make the rounds, stopping in to see how everybody was doing, smiling and friendly as can be, moving like a streak. At lunch he would sit with the old crowd—I don't think he ever really liked any of the other VPs—always the life of the party. At 3:00, he would go out to his car to get a book or something and be back fifteen minutes later. Work hard until seven or seven-thirty and then, if anyone else was still working, he'd suggest stopping off at Seattle Square—that's the bar around the corner—for 'a few relaxing drinks.' He never quite seemed drunk, maybe sometimes a little flushed, especially when we'd get together after his three o'clock 'break.' And there was that 'high' that lasted through lunch.

"When we were on the road, especially at conventions, Harve would close the bar every night. But, what the hell, a lot of other guys—including some of the senior senior brass—did too, and he was generally ready to go in the morning. Only twice in all the time I traveled with him did I have to pick up after him. The worst time was the morning he woke me up at eight to tell me that he was 'poisoned'—that was his word for being sick and hung over—and I'd have to go on for him at 9:00.

His notes were a mess, but I managed to suffer my way through it.

"You know, none of that is what pushed me into going upstairs and laying it on the line. There were two main reasons, I guess. For one, we needed leadership and a good front man, and Harve wasn't providing us with either one. Another thing was that I was beginning to see the effects of all that boozing on him. He began to look different. The nose, the eyes, a little shakiness. . . . It just seemed crazy to have someone like that as our chief spokesman. What was really weird was that nobody upstairs ever seemed to notice anything, or, if they did I didn't know about it.

"Was I just jealous of his promotion? Sure, I've thought of that, but I don't think so. What it probably comes down to is this—what seemed OK in a word jockey, seemed awful in a vice president."

Harve's story did not have a happy ending, and in that sense, it is not truly representative, for the available evidence suggests that educated, employed, and stable individuals like Harve have the best prognosis for regaining control of their lives, *if* they have accepted that they indeed have a problem and that its cost is now unbearable. That was precisely what Harve could not do.

Harve's boss Jim, an intermittent client of mine over the years, had brought me in to help him out with "a sensitive situation," which turned out to be Harve. After a bit of preliminary nosing around, I was as puzzled as Pete had been about Harve's promotion, and I queried Jim about why he had not seen the signs of Harve's growing dependence on alcohol, and probably cocaine? But Jim uncharacteristically sidestepped the question. Harvey was dependable, he insisted, always coming through, and, even more important, immensely skillful in dealing with both the press and the public. Yes, he had known that Harve was a heavy drinker, but he had felt that the company "owed" Harve the promotion, and "it seemed to mean a lot to him."* We worked out what seemed at the time to be a reasonable plan. Harve was offered a one-month leave of absence, at full salary, if he would enter a residential treatment center.

On the expectation that he would stay for the full twenty-eight-day program and faithfully attend the follow-up group counseling sessions, he was promised a return to his vice presidency, contingent on no further drinking on the job. I sat in when Jim discussed the plan with Harve, mostly to bolster Jim, but also to suggest to Harve that he avail himself of some interim counseling through the company's employee assistance service before he made up his mind. He, however, needed neither me, nor anyone else. He was sure that (1) he did not, at least at that point, have a problem that he could not solve by himself, and (2) he certainly was "not going to accept anything from an organization that accuses you before all the facts are in and is only interested in squeezing out of a person everything it can."

Shortly afterward, Jim called to tell me that Harve had taken an appointive job as chief information officer with a large state agency. After two years in his new job, Harve's health—probably undermined by two more years of quiet, steady drinking—gave out; he was dead

---

*Many practical men and women of affairs who regularly make quite difficult personnel decisions seem almost immobilized when they must deal with personal dysfunction—mental illness or substance abuse, for example. Perhaps it's because, at work, we mostly see each other "on stage," as Erving Goffman has termed the presentation of self held up for others. When we glimpse the disarray "backstage," we are often shaken.

at age fifty-two. One gentle irony: because his addiction—under partial control at work, but blooming at home—had years before bereft him of family and close friends, the funeral eulogy was delivered—most eloquently—by Pete, that same old friend who had finally made it impossible for Jim to look the other way.

My experience with Harve bothered me for a long time. Because of it, I debated for some time whether or not to include, in this book, a chapter on this topic. I knew there was already an overabundance of books, articles, and films about the use and misuse of heady, but harmful, substances. Moreover, I wondered, was there anything that I might add that hadn't previously been said by others, better and more pointedly, since it had been many years since I had been directly involved in the study or clinical counseling of substance abusers. My thoughts kept returning to a pessimistic, but regretfully not invalid, maxim that those most in need of help are often the least likely to profit from it. Even so, I found myself wondering if, as it had for old Scrooge, a glimpse at the slippery places in his future, put to him before he had nothing left but denial to fight with, might have changed the ending of Harve's story. My answer to that question was a relatively optimistic, "maybe." While it is true that many Harves cannot acknowledge that their lives are out of control until they have bottomed out, I have personally known a number who have heard the tocsin and heeded it before such disastrously heroic measures were needed. Given the right information, and a template with which to gauge the degree to which they were at risk, they were able to put their lives in order.

What follows, then, gleaned from my acquaintance with more than a few thus beguiled Fast Trackers, is a brief look at the places that seemed the slipperiest, some thoughts about why, and a few suggestions for staying in, or regaining, control.

SPECIAL RISK FACTORS OF THE FAST TRACK LIFE

A Fertile Ground for Growing the Jitters and the Blues
The fast track is a breeder of what psychologist E. Torrey Higgins calls self-discrepancy problems. The notion is simple. We feel awful when we discover discrepancies between how well *we* think we're doing whatever we're supposed to do, and what others who are important to us, or our own secret selves, expect from us. Further, Higgins suggests, the kind of awfulness we'll feel depends on the exact nature of the discrepancy. So we feel *anxious*—that painful sense that doom is about to descend—when our perception of our behavior doesn't mesh with what *others* expect of us, and *depressed*—the "what's the use, it'll never work out" blues—when the dissonance is between what we think we do and what our idealized picture of ourselves tells us we ought to do. While both anticipatory anxiety and depression have been linked to the heavy use of both alcohol and other drugs, feeling down seems to be especially conducive to seeking bottled comfort, while a craving for cocaine and marijuana are more related to anxiety. At this point, it's not completely clear which causes which. People who feel uneasy, apprehensive, or down, will welcome relief from any source. And, naturally, those who suspect, even if it is only fleetingly, that they might be treading a dangerous path, will feel anxious or depressed about it. However it starts, the circularity of the process is evident: the effects

of immoderate use increases our own and others' disappointments in us, occasioning more of the worry and melancholy that we were trying hard to alleviate. To the extent Higgins's theory is true—and there is substantial evidence to support it—if we didn't care what others (remember, "others" includes our ever-evaluating parents, alive or dead) expect, and we didn't expect much of ourselves, we might be poor and friendless, but we'd also be contentedly happy. Unfortunately, those of us who inhabit the fast track will never be able to test the truth of that recipe for contentment. We care—possibly too much—about how well we're doing. When our high personal expectations and concern for the respect of others encounter several fast track realities—aided, at times, by a few personal characteristics that make some of us more vulnerable than others—the conditions exist for generating the emotional pain that cries out for rapid relief. This, in turn, abases us in our own or others' eyes, creating worse discrepancies that. . . . And so on. The chief fast track contributors to this cycle we've already touched upon: fear of dropping the ball, exhaustion from continuous overload, and the excitement of the chase.

Concern for Dropping the Ball. By virtue of both your job and your personality, you attract responsibilities. If you're an executive, you have the authority to spend or conserve scarce resources. You can make jobs, hire people to fill them, and then fire them (under the impersonal rubric of "layoff," perhaps) when they are no longer necessary. You routinely and regularly evaluate others, and upon the opinions you form depend their promotions, demotions, salary levels, and the munificence or puniness of their bonuses. In short, the welfare and general satisfaction of many others hangs on your wisdom, fairness, and all-around perspicacity. Moreover, you are often required by higher ranking executives to quietly produce short term results that are only possible in the long term. Similarly, as an independently practicing professional or individual entrepreneur, while you may hold sway over fewer others, you still make decisions that affect the fortunes and—in a very particular way for physicians and lawyers—the lives of those with whom you do your business. You may not have consciously thought of yourself as a determiner of others' well-being in quite this way. But if you are like almost every Fast Tracker I've known, you *have* felt the goading of inner demands that you will: always do your best, always *be* the best, never make mistakes, beat the competition, make it to the top, and in a hundred other ways, be a somebody. Intersticed throughout this load of exhortations to succeed is the usual collection of social injunctions: provide for your family, be a perfect parent, repay the community for the bountiful life you lead. And while these sorts of expectations are not solely the lot of Fast Trackers, they are likely to be implanted more deeply, and with more emotional potential in you than in those who are not members of that select group.

For you who have already moved well up the ladder, there is the added fear of demotion, deposition, or dead end. The higher up you are, the farther you have to fall, or at least it seems that way to many of my clients, given the amount of worrying they do about it. The real degree of risk naturally depends upon many factors, including the field you're in. A hot jazz pianist with two hit albums can be in demand one year and old stuff the next, and I have seen more than a few middle-level managers summarily informed of their dismissal and escorted to the plant gates within the hour. That is seldom the case with corporate-level executives, who are usually well buttressed until they find a new place to light (however, that safety net often disappears when their jobs have disappeared in a merger). Even when the possibility of a sudden loss of income is slim, however, many senior managers are continually apprehensive because they know that for them, a continuing paycheck—even a munificent one—can't compensate for the "disgrace" of having been found wanting.

Overload. In chapter 2 we delved deeply into the fast track's frenetic pace, which can sometimes overwhelm your ability to keep up. When that happens too often, you can find yourself, like Alice Through the Looking Glass, running hard just to keep in place, moving from catch-up to crisis in a gradually eroding cycle: periodic exhaustion followed by helpless anger, a nagging sense of inadequacy, and finally frantic—and therefore inefficient—attempts to slow down the unslowable. Result— worry over the consequences at night and the moody blues during the day. Enough to drive some people to drink.

The Excitement of the Chase. Life in the fast track is a stimulant. New crises or opportunities continually turn up, your days are occupied with weighty tasks and high-status, important people. You make risky decisions, some of which even pay off. But, it's not solely the track that makes the excitement, it's also the way your own chemistry reacts to both the opportunities for mastery and the delicious fear that the tiger might turn and bite. When your ever-ready endocrine system favors you with its adrenocortical-endorphin special, you feel a complex "high" that invigorates, feels *wonderful,* and soothes away any lingering self-doubts left over from childhood. Over the years, as I've engaged my Fast Trackers in discussions of the best aspects of their careers, they've soon mentioned the exhilaration of moving from problem to problem, considering, suggesting, deciding, always engaged and pumped up. However, like any chemical lift, this internally produced cocktail can be habit-forming, and can be part of a familiar addictive cycle: a thrilling emotional flight followed by a crash as the stimulating chemicals are metabolized out of the bloodstream. These low periods can be magnified by the periods of exhaustion or disorientation that often follow prolonged overload; at length, their Fast Tracker bodies simply cannot sustain the level of stimulation they need for that rush of feeling they've grown to crave.

A few simply turn up the crank—they take on more, work longer hours, push for faster promotions. While that may work for a while, at some point they will either learn to get along with the occasional highs that the rest of us settle for, or accede to the temptation to increase their dosage with those always at hand bottled or powdered substitutes. After a time, these too lose their potency, and a second downward cycle begins in which more and more of the drug is needed to quiet anxiety or sustain a nondepressed state.

While an understanding of this forlorn pattern is useful for anyone who wants to stay out of trouble, it's also important to remember that it usually *doesn't* happen. Most people who use liquor or drugs from time to time, and in moderation, don't get caught up in an addictive process, and many who do can regain their balance when they realize early enough that their lives are getting out of hand. Unfortunately, there is not yet available (nor

much indication that it will be soon forthcoming—
controlled research on substance abuse is difficult because so many factors are uncontrollable, hard to define,
and even harder to measure) a surefire diagnostic tool
that can tell you in advance into which category you will
fall.

Money, the Nondrug Exhilarator

While money is a somewhat different "substance" from
the others we've discussed, its improvident use provides
many of the same emotional satisfactions as chemical
"uppers" and "downers." Obviously, "money madness,"
spending more of your resources then you can afford, is
not a folly exclusive to Fast Trackers. "Money problems"
have been often cited among the most frequently found
disrupters of domestic bliss. As anyone who has tasted
the sweetness of extravagance knows, an unbalanced
income-outgo equation inexorably will compound itself
into a "get behind, borrow more, get even more behind,
borrow more" cycle. As long as periods of high spending
are followed by catch-up times of enforced frugality, the
game can go on indefinitely. In fact, some pessimists have
suggested that it has become the norm of middle-class
American life (well, studies do show that pessimists generally have a more objective, if less sweet, view of
things). However, a number of financial realities of fast
track life can easily tilt the game board and make very
well-paid executives, entertainers, and sports figures often appear to be habitually poor money managers.

Isn't It Great to Feel Free with Money. Many Fast
Trackers find that they have so much money to spend
that it takes on an unreal quality. I have seen both irrational penuriousness in very well-off clients, and ram-

pant profligacy in newly appointed junior executives.*
Both observations have reinforced an impression that for
most of us—regardless of our experience in handling
money at work—personal wealth above a certain quantity takes on a "play money" quality. (My guess is that
the amount of money required to produce this effect depends on individual experience early in life.) The attitude is one of carefree disregard of the potential
consequences of writing checks without keeping track of
the relationship of income to outgo. The driving thought,
as it has been occasionally expressed to me, is "it's such
a pleasure *not* to have to worry about whether there's
enough money to pay the bills."

Spending money without judicious thought, like other
stimulants, can enhance and extend the excitement of
the chase. Similarly, such spending can fulfill early fantasies of omnipotence, or freedom from parental re-
straint, and be "proof" that maturity and adult status
have finally been attained. In plain words, throwing
money around can be fun and therefore seem a reasonable reward for overwork and responsibility.

Pressures to Live Suitably. You would be unusual if you
did not have beliefs, if a bit fanciful, about how those

---

*In this connection, I think of C. Northcote Parkinson's "law" of busi-
ness budgeting, which suggests that consideration given to budget
items is always inversely proportional to the amount. He points out
that most people cannot really experience the meaning of three million dollars and that, while believing that they are applying careful
judgment to their decisions, in truth, they have only a vague notion
of what that sum might purchase. On the other hand, almost everyone knows quite well what five hundred dollars will buy, thus decisions involving those amounts are accorded the detailed examination
that the larger sums ought to have had.

who have "made it" are expected to live. Your new subordinates and colleagues alike may indeed expect that some change in your lifestyle will mark your elevation to the new rank. The pressures to live up to a standard of affluence vary widely by community, professional identification, and kind of organization, but house size and location, and automobile make often become standards by which "success" is measured.

Besides, outside pressures or not, where's the fun of rising in the world—at least so say the ads in stylish magazines—if not in moving higher up the hill along with the other somebodies who, like you, have "made it." Roomier or more esthetically pleasing quarters, and an auto that is an engineering miracle are, in themselves, not unreasonable ways to spend additional income, if the funds are sufficient for the task. Keep in mind, however, two unexpected threats to solvency that can arise in a fast track financial life.

Now You See It, Now You Don't—Your Income, That Is. A substantial proportion of many Fast Trackers' incomes is both intermittent and irregular, coming in the form of bonuses, royalties, fees, and the like. These payments can at times, and often unexpectedly, fall short. Car, mortgage, and loan payments, on the other hand, come due with a regularity that is indifferent to adverse market conditions, unexpected delays in the settlement of contingency cases, and other exigencies of work life. Fueled by the excitement of a recent promotion, your native optimism and self-confidence may engender a too-rosy interpretation of how much will be forthcoming, or how soon it will arrive.

Even worse, because they defy prediction, are organizational restructurings that can eliminate you, your job, or your prospects for *any* supplemental income. Some examples I've seen recently have been: a decision to sell a division to the highest bidder, who wanted only the capital equipment and not the people who ran it; a new senior executive who was uninformed about, and therefore disinclined to support, the technical area in which my client was expert, and, of course, the demise of several "absolutely secure" vice presidential jobs, courtesy of the merger/acquisition process.

Money is not a physically addictive substance, and it is unlikely that we will see a proliferation of money madness clinics or a national campaign to "say no to personal spending." Yet it would also be unwise to underestimate the degree to which, unheeded, these pressures and temptations are capable of derailing your career or causing undue disturbance in your personal life. Tim Conway—good-looking, well educated, a very smart and charming man—certainly found them so.

Tim had been hired, at double his former salary, into the newly established job of East Coast bureau chief for an international publishing house. His position had been set up because the CEO had decided to impose tighter corporate control over the collection of semiautonomous magazines that were a major source of income for the company. As the corporate vice president who headed the magazine side of the business had put it—"those magazines have operated as inefficient little fiefdoms for years. Their costs are way out of line, and they're not contributing what they should to the overall profitability of the corporation." He also had candidly informed Tim that several of the more powerful magazine publishers in the chain had adamantly disputed the value of such a "coordinative" position ("coordination" was the rubric under which Corporate had chosen to disguise its true intent, which was to force them to cut costs) and, or so the rumor mill said, they were privately plotting to make it impossible for Tim to succeed. Nonetheless, Tim felt confident that he had the support of senior management and that the ideas he had for improving both quality and cost effectiveness would soon win the backing of all but the least capable publishers. On the strength of assurances from the corporate CEO himself that he would not be abandoned, Tim bought a "suitable" house that stretched to the limit even his munificent new salary. It was not that he had moved ahead blindly, as he later assured me. He had properly worked out the necessary arithmetic to prove that, with bonuses he would surely receive when his initial projects showed results, he could manage the hefty house payments. But, as he also later admitted, in the sheer excitement of more money than he had ever in his life expected, anything seemed possible.

I first met Tim eighteen months later. By then, he was thoroughly depressed, disheartened, and defeated. Those recalcitrant but politically skilled publishers who had resented his coming had not openly defied corporate policy, they had simply worn Tim's boss down with constant complaining about the size of Tim's budget (the funds for which, they took pains to point out, came from their own profits), the length of time it was taking for Tim's programs to show results, and his lack of sensitivity to the realities of managing a highly creative enterprise. Did they think he should be fired? Not at all. All they wanted was that his staff of twenty-five be reduced to "three or four good people who can help him keep an eye on what we're doing."

"They know full well that there's no way for me to do anything effective with a staff of four in an organization that's publishing in eight languages in twenty countries around the world. My boss is trying to soothe my feelings with the usual crap—Corporate still has confidence in me, and all it means is slowing down a bit, but I feel completely let down by him. And I also know that sooner or later some other corporate shark is going to gripe about how much I'm being paid. It'll be years before I can show the kind of results that would pay off in any real bonuses. The worst of it is, I've got to swallow the insults and stay in this dead-end job because I can't afford to quit. We bought a gorgeous house when we moved here that we can barely make the payments on, and I've been borrowing money for the past year just to keep afloat. I can't afford a week without salary, much less the months it would take to find a decent job. Hell, I don't even know if I could, because right now I'm the publishing world's biggest joke. Of course, we can always sell the house, but I'm not about to uproot Millie and the kids again after moving them halfway across the country. Anyway, seven-hundred-thousand-dollar houses are not that easy to unload."

As it did Tim Conway, "money madness" can afflict any of us when the conditions are right. It is not simply the result of a sudden increase of income or pressures to live up to rank and privilege. These are merely road hazards to be cautiously circumvented. Like the other potentially self-harming predilections we've examined in this chapter, we become "mad" only when, intoxicated by the sometimes heady vapors of the fast track, we accelerate when we should slow down.

Personal Risk Factors

While the hazards that we have examined thus far are potentially dangerous to all Fast Trackers, there are several personal factors that have been shown to increase the odds that the use of drugs of any sort, recreational or prescription, legal or illegal, might get out of hand. Those most clearly implicated are genetic inheritance, having been raised in a dysfunctional family, and a tendency toward dependency.

Inheritance. There is evidence—although it is far from definitive—that there is some degree of inherited susceptibility to alcohol addiction. For example, the biological children of alcoholics are somewhat more likely to become alcoholics themselves, even when wholly raised in families that did not abuse alcohol. Even so, more don't than do. While little is known about how this tendency is passed on, there is some indication that both sons and daughters of alcoholics respond *less* than other people to the stimulating effects of alcohol. Thus, they must drink more to feel its pleasant effects, and that may condition their bodies to needing heavier doses.

Dysfunctional Families. If you were brought up in a family in which one or both parents were heavy drinkers, you're more likely than those of us who were more fortunate to find yourself in the same tangle as your parents. There are substantial findings that growing up in a family in which one or both parents were heavy alcohol users can also put you more at risk. Many authorities, drawing upon considerable clinical experience, have generalized these findings to other sorts of severely dysfunctional families, those who were excessively repressive or physically abusing, for example. Children of such families often grow up to be distrustful of others and of themselves, overly concerned with staying "in control" of everything and everybody, overly responsible—acting

out as adults what they were forced to do as children—
and out of touch with their own needs and feelings. As
one of my clinician friends put it, "the wonder is not
that some drink too much, it's that the others don't."

A Tendency Toward Dependency. Every human being
is saddled with an inner battle between the urge to be
self-sufficient and independent, and the equally insistent
wish to be totally cared for. Although much of this struggle transpires far out of sight, surfacing from time to
time—ages two, seven, and sixteen come to mind—the
eventual decision to take care of ourselves is never easy
or simple, and even then it is not made once and for all.
I continue to see signs of "incipient dependence" in some
of my most prestigious clients, and, I am forced to admit
ruefully, even in myself. Well, we must all, at times, be
dependent on others—when we are ill, for instance. And
as interdependent social creatures, we continually engage in "I'll help you here, if you'll help me there" ne-
gotiations with others. However, for some very bright
people the wish to be taken care of wins out and, although they wear the behavioral trappings of adulthood,
and, through charm or talent, may have initially moved
well along the fast track, they secretly doubt that they
can succeed on their own. If they're "lucky" (actually,
it's the worst luck possible) they'll find someone who is
looking for another someone to take care of. The upshot
of the marriage of these reciprocal needs is often a sticky
relationship that continually satisfies and frustrates both.
Therefore, it's not surprising that this sort of convoluted
pairing is often cemented by drugs that temporarily ease
self-recriminations and mutual disappointment, and, incidentally, keep the dependent partner functioning
poorly enough to justify to both the need for continuing

the relationship. (Not all dependent people use drugs to excess. There are other kinds of cement—chronic over-spending, for example.)

Here is a checklist that can forewarn you that you might be allergic to your own dependency needs:

- Are you often counterdependent, that is, do you often feel resistant to, or angry at, legitimate requests from authority figures?

- When trouble hits, do you hope that everything will turn out all right instead of realistically assessing the thorny situation and doing what you can to fix it?

- Do you want—need—others to do little things for you, or in other ways constantly show that they "really do" care about you?

- Do you do one unasked-for favor for others which in your mind repays them for all of the "little things" they've done?

- Do you find yourself borrowing small amounts of money which you somehow "forget" to repay?

- Are you chronically late to meetings, parties, family get-togethers?

Kept in check, a little inclination toward dependency is harmless, simply a sign of your vulnerable humanity. If, however, having heaved a sigh and brushed aside your natural dislike for seeing yourself as less than ideal, you admit to more than a few of these dependency indicators, consider yourself especially open to the unwise use of alcohol or drugs.

COPING WITH ALCOHOL, DRUGS, AND MONEY MADNESS

No one really knows why some people can use mood-altering substances without any noticeably adverse effect, while others cannot. Similarly, we know little about why some of those who have been caught can make their own way out of the trap, while others, ostensibly alike in circumstance, can do so only with considerable outside help, and then only after making shambles of their lives. However, there is general agreement among authorities of every theoretical persuasion on the essential steps for preventing or gaining control over the immoderate use of alcohol and other drugs, whether the problems are large or small. They are: becoming aware of the personal risk factors in your life, recognizing that you have a problem and that whatever you've been doing to try to solve it hasn't worked, and accepting the help of others when necessary.

Know When You Are Most at Risk
Knowing which circumstances in your life situation and in your own uniqueness can put you most at risk can alert you to be especially careful not to start down a path from which you may have difficulty extricating yourself. For example, I have learned that when I am starting on a new chapter in whatever book I'm working on at the time, my anxiety level rises dramatically. It is on those few days—certain that my brains have turned to mush and that I will never again turn out a paragraph worth

reading—that experience has shown me I will be achingly tempted to precede dinner with a drink and follow that drink with another. Knowing that the urge will be there, at least until my "creative tension" has actually produced something creative, has warned me that on those days, I must pour just one glass of wine and then put the recorked bottle away where it is out of sight and ready reach. Of course, I could simply resist the impulse to pour that second glass, but there's little sense in making life harder than it need be, and it's at the instant that the inclination hits me that I will be most open to finding good reasons to do something I would later regret. The point is to use knowledge of yourself to help you pay objective attention (well, as objective as we human beings can ever be about ourselves) to what's happening. That is the special kind of awareness that will help you keep in control precisely at the moment you feel least like doing so.

The events that increase vulnerability differ dramatically from individual to individual, but they are frequently, at base, somehow connected to fears about personal adequacy. For example: is your life in the fast track especially trying for you at this time? Is it edging past your ability to cope with equanimity? Perhaps you've just moved into a more demanding job and you wonder if you will succeed. Or maybe you *didn't* get that more demanding job and are relieved and yet ashamed that you are relieved. Do worries about unmet responsibilities and barely adequate work keep you awake? Answering these and similar questions may help alert you to your own areas of thinnest skin.

Keep in mind, however, that excitement also sings its own siren song. Has your life suddenly turned exciting; you love it and want more and more? Or has the thrill of a recent promotion faded into a new daily grind, leaving you vaguely disappointed?

Needless to say, these common life experiences cannot, of themselves, turn you into a substance abuser. Yet I have mentioned them because they have frequently triggered rounds of tension and uncertainty in many of my fast-tracking clients. Think of them as illustrations to start you on the task of compiling your own list of personally threatening situations, which I urge you to do, being as specific and descriptive as you can. "I get overwhelmed with feelings of being a failure when I start a chapter" is far more useful as an alerting signal than "I'm anxious about writing well," even though the latter statement might be equally true. Then, when that event on your list is imminent, or when it suddenly appears in your path, you will stay vigilant for a creeping increase in your use of alcohol or other drugs, or impulsive shopping to alleviate self-doubt or despair.

Accept What You Cannot Change, Change What You Can. You did not choose your heredity or the way you were parented, but you are nevertheless stuck with the results of both. While you cannot do much with the former, it is possible to ameliorate some of the mistakes your parents may have made by learning more about how those mistakes shaped your view of the world and *unlearning* those parts that are irrational, confused, and hurtful. The process is known as psychotherapy, and most people who engage in it are at least to some extent glad they did. If you choose not to do so, it is still useful to make yourself aware of what in your background might incline you to alleviate internal tension by drowning it. Your purpose will be neither to accuse nor to excuse yourself, but simply to increase your watchfulness in those situations that might lead to a slide. For example, to what extent do you fit the dependency model? It may be hard for you to look squarely at that image of yourself because all Fast Trackers are supposed to be fully mature, independent, personally secure, and strong. I remind you that many people of great attainment, certainly I have known several, have been deficient in one or all of those wonderful characteristics (most people know that, because they clearly see the deficiencies in their bosses, but somehow believe that *they* should be above such human failings).

Barriers to Acknowledgment

Acknowledging that you have a problem—that is, what you're doing is costing you more than it's giving you—will seldom be deterred by a lack of information. Like most people who have begun to slip you will be bombarded with your own inner doubts, especially in moments alone, and complaints, hints, and pitying or resentful looks from those closest to you. The gist of these messages will be that the behavior that seems to you to be sharp and well controlled is, in fact, irresponsible. The difficulty is in taking these messages seriously, when your intellect is working overtime to deny their truth. Breaking through to a bare and undisguised look at your fallibility is an invariably trying experience (at times, it can also be exhilarating and tremendously relieving). To complicate matters, several fast track factors can keep you from tackling this always onerous job early on, when regaining control is easiest: the social acceptance of mood-enhancing substances; the ability of some to compartmentalize their behavior; and the particular availability to Fast Trackers of partially true justifications for seeking rapid relief from tension.

When Is a Problem a Problem? It's not too hard to understand why many people have difficulty in knowing whether or not they have a problem with mood enhancers. To understand how and why, we must acknowledge some facts about these age-old companions of the human race. They do their intended job—a "rush" when we want high spirits, a "lift" when we want to stop fretting—exceedingly well. In a relatively pleasant and easy-to-take form—and without the expense and bother of three years on the couch struggling with our psyches—they gift us with instant relief from care. Is it any wonder that they have been part of the human predicament in every age and in almost every place? Given their amply demonstrated potential for causing mischief—hangovers, impaired judgment, loss of vigilance, the possibility of physical or emotional dependence, long-term wear and tear on the body—they have been amazingly resistant to periodic efforts to outlaw them.

There are several important points to be made about this amply demonstrated affinity between us and them. The first is to restate that a life that has been fed on excitement, or one that is filled with tension, is likely to increase our interest in, and possibly our dependence on, those convenient and time-tested little helpers.

The second is perhaps obvious: once most of us have experienced the pleasurable or tension-relieving powers of alcohol, or any of its powdered cousins, we are unlikely to want to give them up until we have concluded that they are taking more from us than they are giving. Third, many people can partake of alcohol, marijuana—and, perhaps (research on middle- and upper-class occasional users has been sketchy), even cocaine in its unpurified form—in moderation, and therefore without observable long-range costs.

The result is that while we may—albeit, at times with pity—denigrate drunks, speed freaks, coke abusers, and pot heads, we show an amazing tolerance for the less extreme, but nonetheless immoderate,* use of drugs for fun and forgetfulness. In other words, you can drink a lot—as did Harvey Lufts—and still not be seen as a drunk.

Compartmentalized Addiction. Recognition that an addictive problem exists is complicated for Fast Trackers by a fact that has only recently become apparent: many very heavy users can continue to perform well on the job. Some simply restrict their imbibing to off-work hours. Others manage by virtue of a seemingly enormous tolerance for the effects of the drug—Harve was one of those. In either case, though, payment is exacted, in terms of a personal life that is in shambles, or in physical impairment.

Carla Lacey was a building executive who reviewed plans, managed the construction of interior layouts in mammoth office and apartment buildings, and negotiated corporate leases for very large properties. Almost every evening, however, she downed cocktails or wine, or both, until, usually by nine o'clock, she fell into a drunken sleep in front of the television. For years she followed a pattern of periodically "cutting down on the booze" to show that she indeed had control over her drinking, gradually slipping back into her old routine,

---

*However, what is considered immoderate has varied widely from generation to generation. The acceptance of substances other than alcohol also varies by community. But in metropolitan areas, the common habitat of Fast Trackers, the social limits are usually toward the tolerant end.

until the threat of divorce from a too-long tolerant husband, and the support of friends, one of whom had faced a similar problem, finally moved her into an outpatient recovery program. She has remained in recovery, aided considerably by a decision to give up her tension-producing executive position to return to less emotionally demanding on-site supervision.

Interestingly, neither her bosses nor subordinates were aware that she had a drinking problem, and they were shocked when she asked for a demotion to construction supervisor. Her executive skills had been judged first-rate, her demeanor "exacting and responsible, yet friendly and fair." Ironically, Carla's extraordinary competence and tight control during the day seemed to her to be incontrovertible evidence that her nightly efforts at "relaxation" could not be signs of impending alcoholism.

If Anyone Deserves a Lift, It's You. As a Fast Tracker, you have a supremely plausible justification for overindulging in forbidden sweets—your truly heavy load of work and worry. Harvey Lufts's "I've earned a little fun and I deserve it" could apply to most Fast Trackers. So could Carla's favorite, "I have a right to relax with the load I'm carrying."

Unfortunately, these immensely appealing rationalizations do not show themselves in that guise at the moment you are trying to decide whether or not to pour that second drink. Instead, they sit to one side of your center of awareness and nudge you into disregarding injunctions from your logical self to "stop now." The helpful thing about recognizing them as rationalizations is that they won't work nearly as well. Writing down your favorites or even telling another person—preferably one

who will be with you when you're likely to use them—
will help to minimize their power, and may also provide
you with an occasional, if rueful, laugh at yourself.

When and Where to Get Help

The sorts of problems we've been examining in this chapter are seldom easy to deal with, nor do they often simply disappear on their own. Thus, it may indeed happen,
sometime in your fast track journey, that you will have
to face the fact that you have become enmeshed in a
behavioral pattern that is threatening important aspects
of your life. Drug- and alcohol-related problems are
complex—an intermix of potent chemicals, your physical
responses to them, and whatever psychological imperfec-
tions you may have brought along with you. For these
reasons, they are not easily managed alone. However, if
you have caught it early enough, and understand something of what in your life and in yourself tilted you into
trouble, you might well be able to regain control simply
by setting limits for yourself and sticking to them.

If you try it on your own, keep alert to these two indications that you might do better with some outside
support. The first is a realization that your attempts at
self-control have evolved into repeated cycles of absti-
nence, usually accompanied by severe anxiety or depression, followed by a resumption of the maladaptive
behavior you were trying to change. The second will be
your awareness that you are once again rationalizing
your actions to yourself and others, and doubting your
own efficacy to change. At this point, the wisest course
is to seek some sort of outside help, sooner rather than
later, because your ability to remain productive and
committed at work and at home may otherwise begin to
deteriorate rapidly.

Many sorts of help are available from very different kinds of organizations—the choice is wide. When you are ready to begin, you can get confidential referrals from your physician, family counselor, community mental health clinic, or similar resource. Look for a person or facility that starts off with an assessment to determine, with you, which specific approaches would be most useful. Most will involve individual counseling (even lay organizations such as Alcoholics Anonymous utilize peer counseling) along with group work, and require participation in some sort of supportive self-help program to sustain the gains made in the treatment process.

Once in a recovery program, the odds are in your favor that you will regain the ability to choose the directions in which your life will go—at least to the extent that any of us has that ability. However, you are also likely to find that, as with any sort of developmental process, slips and backslidings are commonplace. What will differentiate these brief relapses from the recurring cycles that led to your need for outside help will be an unwavering acknowledgment that where you were is not where you want to be, and that you can do something about it.

8

When the Going Gets Rough for the Psychologically Tough

Phil Simmons, an experienced and highly successful executive in a Fortune 500 company, showed all the signs of a man who had been pushed past his limit.

"You know, Bob, it was you who did this to me," Phil said as we sat down to talk. He was smiling, but not altogether convincingly. "Maybe you don't remember it, but at one of your infamous team-building meetings about a year ago, some of my esteemed colleagues, while generously allowing that I'd shown great ability at pulling reasonable profits from divisions that were already doing well, questioned whether I had the stuff that we need right now, when we're having to fight hard for every bit of market share we get. I didn't pay much attention to it at the time because, hell, our profits were up and the market was hot. But Herb [the CEO] evidently did. After twenty-five years of successful line experience, he sidetracked me into this high-level staff job. I have a fancy title, and I'm drawing an executive vice president's pay, but I'm hating every minute of it.

"The crazy part is, there's actually a hell of a lot of important work I could be doing. Herb is chomping on me to get the management information system mess straightened out, to trim down International, and to see that we finally have a decent corporate succession plan. The trouble is, I just can't get myself moving. Thus far I've been able to crank things along mostly by assigning enough projects so that at least something gets into the works."

At this point Phil blinked away some tears. "Damn it, I'm sorry, Bob. Nothing like this has ever happened to me before. I've always been a self-starter, and I've loved coming to work most days. But for the last two weeks I've been dragging in here at ten in the morning, shutting the door, and sitting on my ass, staring at a mountain of paper that just keeps growing. Frankly, I think I'm about done in. My wife is already worried about what's happening to me—I couldn't get out of bed this morning—and I am too. The sad fact is that I'm frustrated, bored, and depressed. At age fifty-six, when I should be at my peak, I feel like a failure, and I'm ready to quit."

Phil was a capable executive who had been moved into a highly responsible job and suddenly found himself unable to perform. The cause, quite simply, was stress— not tension about the job itself, but from a stressful reaction to Herb's "sidetracking" him from his line vice presidency. That reaction included buried anger, and a feeling of trapped helplessness—the classic recipe, as we will see, for destructive stress.

Almost by definition, being on the fast track means having to cope with stress. Nor is that always bad. In fact, most kinds of stress are good for you. Stress energizes you to rid yourself of the stress producer. It plays a role analogous to that of the physical pain that warns you that something in your body is amiss. It can even contribute to your self-esteem by affirming that what you're doing in the world must have real importance because it's so much trouble to do. Several kinds of stressors, however, such as feelings of frustration, of powerlessness, or derogation from those you respect or care about, *are* closely correlated with a variety of adverse physical and mental symptoms. Below a certain limit—where the limit is depends on a variety of personal characteristics—even the harmful kinds of stress are tolerable for most people, particularly for the sort of person who ventures into the fast track. But beyond that quantitative limit, relatively small increments can reduce the quality of our decisions, undermine the body's defenses, and provoke us into a variety of self-defeating behaviors.

Actually, most successful Fast Trackers tend to be rather psychologically tough. That is, they are able to stay calmer than most when things haven't worked out as they should, they keep their wits about them during emergencies, and they are less likely to feel overloaded when tasks or responsibilities proliferate. Even when something tips them out of emotional balance, they tend to regain their footing sooner than those who are less psychologically hardy. Psychologist Raymond Flannery has called people like this "stress resistant" because they seem to be able to function well in environments that many others would consider too stressful.

Yet executive burnout—Phil Simmons's condition certainly appeared to be a candidate for that label—is not uncommon, and Fast Trackers in the professions and the arts also experience high levels of painful stress. The reasons for this seeming paradox are not hard to fathom.

Stress resistance is not an all-or-none affair. Some of those who have achieved success are inherently more vulnerable than others to the perturbations of the fast track—an environment laden with overwork and multiple aggravations—and they will reach their limits sooner. As for those who are toughest, ironically it is their very ability to remain productive in the face of confusing and complex conditions that can gradually erode their coping reserves. Often prideful of their capacity to work under fire, they tend to ignore or dismiss signs that the buildup of emotional tension may have exceeded the limitations of even their oversized ability to endure.

Whether you are supertough or just sort of tough, the steps involved in coping with stress are the same. First, you need to learn to recognize the signs that your emotional load has become too heavy. Second, you must do what you can to reduce that burden to tolerable levels before it begins to affect your performance and your personal life. Finally, you can increase your capacity to handle the continuing rush of stressful events by taking advantage of recent findings about the nature of psychological toughness.

In the preceding chapters, we've examined the facets of fast track life most likely to contribute to stress overload. If you consistently put into practice all the coping steps I've suggested, it's possible that you might never become excessively stressed. However, even in that optimistic scenario, misadventures can occur, situations can devolve from bad to awful, and even the most effective coper can be pushed to his or her point of no return. Accordingly, in this chapter we'll review the most important signs that you might have exceeded your own personal stress limit, as well as some recent findings about the nature of harmful stress and how to cope with it.

Finally, with an eye to the future, we'll consider specific ways for you to make yourself even more stress resistant.

SIGNS THAT YOU'RE REACHING THE LIMIT OF YOUR STRESS TOLERANCE

The following checklist can help you determine whether, at any given time, you are approaching your own stress limit. Check any of the symptoms that apply to you.

- A sudden change for the worse in your physical state that lasts more than two weeks. For example:

  — intestinal distress
  — rapid increase in pulse or heartbeat not brought on by exercise, sex, or the Super Bowl
  — sleep problems, such as difficulty in falling asleep, or awakening in the middle of the night and being unable to return to sleep
  — feeling tired early in the day
  — increase in "nervous habits" such as nail biting, twitching muscles in arms and shoulders, or facial tics

- Mental symptoms such as

  — persistent thoughts about the uselessness or meaninglessness of your life
  — difficulty in concentrating, tendency to impatiently rush a solution to a complex problem
  — repetitive thoughts about quitting, retirement, or telling off your boss

- Changes in your emotional state that last more than two weeks. For example:

  - constant or recurring feelings of anger and resentment at coworkers or family members (in calmer moments you will wonder "Why was I so upset?")
  - a marked increase in general irritability
  - feelings of fear or threat that leave you agitated and unable to sit still
  - feeling down, unworthy, ashamed, or guilty

- Changes in your day-to-day life routines, such as

  - increased use of alcohol or other drugs
  - changes in eating habits, eating less or more, or an increased hunger for sweet, salty, or rich foods
  - an abrupt change in your attitudes toward money, such as becoming unusually tightfisted or engaging in sudden shopping sprees
  - loss of interest in activities you ordinarily enjoy, including sex

Most of us have thoughts or reactions of this sort from time to time until a victory at work, a refreshing weekend, or a vacation renews our natural capacities for emotional rejuvenation. If, however, you find yourself suffering from more than one or two symptoms on this list, pay serious attention to what is happening in you and in your immediate situation and consider the coping steps discussed in this chapter. Remember, the best time to act is when you first realize that these symptoms have become a part of your life. That's when you'll have the best chance of pulling yourself out, because your stress overload has not yet begun to rob you of the capacity to take control.

THE NATURE OF HARMFUL STRESS

Until recently, much that was written about dealing with stress focused on methods for helping us after we have already been pushed over our individual stress limits. Relaxation techniques such as meditation and yoga, physical exercise that helps to rebalance a variety of bodily functions and to dissipate feelings of anger, dietary control, and a variety of prescription and nonprescription drugs ("Lighten up with your favorite brew") have all been recommended. While such methods can be useful in minimizing the effects of stress, they do little to help you learn how to keep out of trouble in the future. To better understand the reasons behind the coping suggestions that will follow, let's look at the current state of knowledge about work-related stress.

It's becoming apparent from a host of recent studies that a stressful situation itself is not the cause of adverse effects to productivity and health, the real culprit is the emotional state that is aroused in us while those exciting things are happening. Further, it is only negative emotions—anger, frustration, fear—that are harmful. Interestingly, the way you feel in a difficult situation depends to a great extent on how you expect to feel. If you walk into your boss's office expecting to feel afraid, the evidence is quite strong that you will. On the other hand, if your anticipation is that you'll feel challenged by his critical comments, then that's the way you'll feel. Your expectations, of course, will depend upon what you've run into in the past and how well you think you've handled it.

The emotional themes that trigger harmful stress re-actions are as varied as the individuals who experience them. But they all seem to involve the belief that we've lost something important to us or the anticipation that such a loss is imminent or inevitable. I'm not speaking here of a loss of material things, unless those things also have an emotional meaning. While a reduction in salary might mean less convenience in your life, it will not in itself arouse the negative feelings that can throw you or your body off course. But if salary represents self-esteem, status, and respect in others' eyes, or the recognition of your own competence, the loss of those important ingre-dients can trigger the kind of emotional response associ-ated with debilitating stress.

Actually, in most cases our recuperative powers will help us recover from losses, even those more important than a few notches in our annual salary bracket. The extra ingredient that seems necessary for our defenses to stop working long enough for us to feel inundated is lack of control, or rather the *perception* that we cannot con-trol or influence the outcome of the situation. As we saw in chapter 2, an inordinately high job demand will not in itself tear you down. But if you believe you have little say over how the work will be done or the rate at which the work will hit you, even a moderate increase in workload can lead to weariness, and, if it persists, to exhaustion, psychosomatic illness, or even depression.

Recent studies have provided an interesting physiolog-ical explanation of this intricate relationship between negative affectivity, perceived loss of control, and break-down of both physical and mental defenses. For exam-ple, under conditions of very high effort, even to the point of overwork, if the workers have high levels of con-trol, there is *no* elevation of blood cortisol, a powerful central nervous system hormone associated with dysfunction in the autoimmune system. When the level of control over the job is low, however, cortisol levels rise significantly. Similarly, in studies with both the elderly and with children who were taught to deal more effectively with daily problems, their improved coping skills, and the increased feeling of control that those coping skills gave, produced a measurable lowering of cortisol levels.

This, then, is the script of the intrapersonal soap opera of stress. It begins with a blow to our ego or self-esteem, or a kick in one of the motivational areas most important to us—recall the discussion of power, achievement, autonomy, and affiliative needs in chapter 6. If we believe that we're powerless to dodge the kicks, and we're unable to get out of the situation entirely, then the level of personal stress will rise and continue to rise until we find some way to regain control. With all of this in mind, let's return to the case of Phil Simmons and see some of these factors in action.

In actuality, Phil's new duties required a person of considerable interpersonal skill who could be forceful even when not backed up by line authority—precisely the qualities that Herb had in mind when he chose Phil for the job. Was Herb also influenced by others' doubts about Phil's ability to compete with the proper degree of ferocity? If he was, he never directly cited those doubts as a reason for moving Phil from his line vice presidency. The reason he did give, however, points up both the futility of trying to protect others from reality and an equally cogent fact of human relationships: it is our interpretation of reality rather than the reality itself that engenders personal stress.

Herb, it turned out, had decided that if Phil could pull

off even one of the complex assignments he had been given, he would be the prime candidate to fill the soon-to-be-vacant position of chief financial officer. "I know he doesn't have an accounting background," Herb said when he told me about his plans for Phil, "but he would have plenty of those people on his staff. What we really need right now is someone who can bring our whole administrative apparatus into the next decade." Herb had chosen not to inform Phil of his intention for what he thought was an excellent reason: he knew that Phil was ambitious and thoughtfully did not want to place added stress on him by talking about a promotion that was not yet assured. But because Phil was lacking this information, he perceived the situation in a way Herb did not intend. To Phil, the facts were plain: he had been weighed in the balance and found wanting.

Several factors kept Phil from confronting Herb about the move. For one, the change took him by surprise. For another, though he was proud and ambitious, he was also a good soldier, and he could not bring himself to complain to his boss. In addition, believing that his fellow executives, most of whom he had thought of as friends, lacked confidence in him—perhaps had even set him up for "demotion"—he had no one at work in whom he might confide. Ironically, it was his high need for achievement that made him so vulnerable to what he saw as an apparent loss of respect from his superior and peers.

While Phil's initial intention was simply to swallow his pride and get on with a job that seemed full of opportunities for action, he actually underestimated—as many executives do—the degree to which his sense of angry helplessness left him vulnerable. He quickly began to show signs of emotional overload: passivity, inability to shift perspectives, and sleeplessness. These, resonating with shame over failing to meet his obligations and an alarmed bewilderment over his rapid deterioration, brought him to the state of profound dejection in which I found him.

HOW TO COPE IN A STRESSFUL ENVIRONMENT

How do we cope with destructive stress? Later in this chapter we'll look at preventive measures that can build up your stress resistance. In this section we'll look at short-term techniques for relieving current stress, beginning with some popular methods that, unfortunately, don't work.

What Doesn't Work

If helpless anger and frustration are the culprits that turn stressful situations into emotional disasters, it's not surprising that the most effective ways to cope all involve regaining some modicum of control. By the same token, the tactics that offer little relief do little to restore a sense of control. The ineffective tactics that are used most frequently include suppressing feelings, fault finding, distraction, and devaluing.

Suppression. Much of life is a succession of irritating events—pencil points breaking, traffic tie-ups, independently minded children—that we usually manage to ignore. After pausing for a groan or swear word, we swallow our annoyance and move productively on, focusing our attention on tasks that should more rightfully occupy us. Psychologically tough people are particularly adept at suppressing their feelings, at least until the work is done.

Much of the time, this process seems to work satisfactorily because often the physical arousal that accompanied the suppressed feelings dissipates when the crisis is over. But when hurt remains unresolved or is continually reinforced, this simple "ignore-it-until-it-goes-away" approach breaks down. Unfortunately, when events are personally threatening to us, pushing our negative feelings out of mind becomes self-defeating. It's not easy to ignore the emotional equivalent of a punch in the stomach. Even if we could, the complex chemical changes that accompany strong feelings would continue to affect our nerves, muscles, and minds. Phil's initial attempts to "forget" what had happened did little, if anything, to assuage his anger and hurt. Interestingly, he did not initially report feeling angry at Herb, and he passed off as trivial the umbrage he felt toward his fellows for raising doubt in Herb's mind. Of course, his stress symptoms told a different story.

Fault Finding. Blaming has always been a tried-and-true method for resolving hurt feelings. Like suppression, in most circumstances it's probably harmless. Some authorities even suggest that fault finding is beneficial in the short run, one more of the buffering tactics we've all learned to use to muddle through life's tribulations. There are, however, several trade-offs that can substantially reduce its beneficial effects.

First of all, blaming is often an engaging substitute for self-awareness, lessening the opportunity to learn from whatever difficulty we have encountered. Second, as it did with Phil, fault finding may also substitute for fact finding. It was Phil's attribution of blame to his cowork-

ers, in part, that kept him from checking out his perceptions with Herb. Third, whatever momentary satisfaction blaming provides—and it does—is often at the cost
of hostility generated in those we've blamed—especially
since we may be accusing them unjustly or on the basis
of incomplete information.

Distraction. Most of us learned early and well to distract
ourselves when feeling upset. The message we've internalized is "When you feel bad, you'll feel better if you
eat something, have a drink, or an affair, or spend a lot
of money." Unfortunately, such "cures" often exacerbate
the illness. We end up fatter, drunker, divorced, and
poor, and still hurting from whatever it was that set us
off in the first place. Even worse, we may be distracted
not only from our feelings but from trying to do something that will remedy the situation.

Devaluing. A tempting way to deal with feelings of
shame or guilt is to make believe that you don't really
care much that you feel that way. Devaluing is different
from the kind of deliberate rethinking of the sort I've
suggested in previous chapters, where you might, indeed, assign less importance to something you had previously overvalued. While you may have learned as a
child that winning was more important than, say,
friendship, having acknowledged that belief, you might
further explore and reexamine the truth of that value or
you might settle for it as it is. Either way, you're more
in touch with yourself. Devaluing, in contrast, involves
pretense, and fosters that sense of self-estrangement we
discussed in chapter 6. Phil would have been engaging
in this tactic if he had said, "I don't really care what

those sons of bitches think of me" when he really did care.

Shortcuts to Stress Relief. There have been some recent findings that anxiety-reducing drugs do, in fact, provide many of the short-term physiological benefits as the psychological toughening activities recommended later in this chapter. Like those activities—mental challenge, humor, and regular exercise—they stimulate hormones in the central nervous system that counteract the debilitating effects of stress. Wouldn't it be nice, especially for those of us of sluggardly tendencies, if taking anti-stress pills could accomplish the same thing?

Unfortunately, while anxiety-reducing drugs may provide short-term relief, they can also interfere with the development of stress resistance that will help see you through in the long run. One plausible reason for this effect is the passive nature of taking medication as a response to a problem. Passivity tends to reduce the sense of self-efficacy—the belief that we have the ability to take charge of ourselves and our situation—and thus increases our vulnerability. From there it's a short step to that same cycle of perceived powerlessness, dejection, even less effort, even less sense of control, and greater dejection. The best antidote to helpless frustration and the stress it brings is the feeling that you are captain of your fate—and taking drugs is less likely to nurture that feeling than it is to corrode it further.

What Does Work
In contrast to the essential passivity of coping tactics that are of little help, those that help leave you feeling more in control. They include looking on the bright side, calling on support systems, cutting down on surprises, gain-

ing perspective through humor, actively relieving the effects of stress, and developing a Small Wins Strategy for regaining control.

Looking on the Bright Side. While a pessimistic outlook on life may mean a more accurate perception of all of the rocks over which you *might* stumble, an optimistic view—realistic or not—leaves you feeling that you are capable of jumping over or sidestepping them As a result, you feel more in control, and that, in turn, makes you feel less overwhelmed.

Recall that stress doesn't equate to what happens, but rather to how we perceive what happens. Suppose you were to react to being demoted by saying, "Well, I've been demoted, and I don't like it, but it's happened. On the positive side I still have a job and I'll be learning about a new facet of the business. Meanwhile, I'll have more time to spend with my family and for myself." Reacting in this way won't get you your old job back or completely alleviate the resentment you feel. But it can predispose you to avoid the passivity trap and set to work on a plan for regaining control.

For Phil, the bright side was not work related at all. He came to recognize how little he had appreciated the strength of his spouse and how much she cared for him. Although it was a bittersweet recognition, it was while telling me of his feeling for her that he first showed signs of reanimation.

Calling on Support Systems. It's at times of emotional overload that support from others—a confidant, an informed outsider whose perspective you trust—can be most helpful. If Phil had not felt so estranged from his colleagues, he might have confronted Herb at the time of his disappointment, an act that would have saved both him and the company from a wasteful misunderstanding. The support-building steps outlined in chapter 6 will put into place a backup system that will help in coping with stress overload.

Cutting Down Surprises. Picture yourself in the dental chair. The dentist is poised, drill in hand, ready to prepare one of your teeth for a filling. If she says, "This won't hurt at all," and you then feel a sensation that you interpret as pain—it may actually be a bit of heat or vibration from the drill—your stress reaction will be greater than if she had said "This might hurt a little" (and you trusted her word). Further, if she said, "You'll feel a little vibration and heat for the first minute or so and then you may feel some sharp pain, but I don't think it will be too much for you," you would be able to withstand the pain (within limits, of course) without the underlying emotional distress you would have felt if the pain had come as a surprise.

The same effect holds for situational pain. If regaining a sense of control is the best way to climb out of an emotional hole, knowing ahead of time that you're going to fall into the hole minimizes the distress you feel when you hit bottom.

To cut down on surprise understand your own stress points, plan for disasters, and mentally rehearse tough encounters.

Since the emotional effects of a stressful event are within you rather than within the event itself, one way to keep from being hit so hard is to know which events tend to trigger angry or self-blaming feelings in you. Don't be sidetracked by a concern for whether they ought to, which is distracting and irrelevant. Instead, take notes as soon as possible after an event that has left you feeling hurt, angry, or frustrated. Be as specific as you can in your note taking, describing rather than evaluating your sensations. Phil's notes, for example, might have read "When I saw that comment that my colleagues did not think that I was an aggressive enough competitor, my stomach clenched and my upper back tightened up. I felt betrayed that my friends had said that about me."

Later, review your notes and reflect on why you felt so distressed or angry. Often, you will discover that some deeply held notion about how people should relate to you was violated in the encounter. For Phil it might have been "If anyone I care about sees me as deficient in any quality at all, I feel like garbage." Be wary of rationalizing your reaction by dismissing it—"Well, anyone would feel that way." Even if your rationalization were true, it misses the point, which is to understand how you react to certain red flags so that you can anticipate those very reactions. The more you know when "it might hurt a little," the less your body will react as if it hurt a lot.

Understanding your own stress points is a lifelong occupation. The benefits are not only self-knowledge—which, after the shock wears off, can actually be pleasurable—but the ability, over time, to lessen the degree to which you react excessively to perceived setbacks.

A second tactic for reducing surprise is contingency or problem prevention planning. By either name it can help you anticipate possible disasters and thus reduce their emotionally negative effects. Even better, looking ahead at things that *might* go wrong may help you prevent the disaster from happening in the first place. Surprise prevention, then, is an important secondary benefit of the work toward keeping your information networks open that we discussed in chapter 6.

A third tactic to prepare for possible setbacks is mental rehearsal. I've often led clients, disproportionately anxious about a forthcoming encounter, through a mental rehearsal of the eventualities they think just might occur, but I am mostly providing the motivation to do it. This is an easy technique to use on your own; you may have done something like it all your life without thinking of it as a special technique.

It's best to choose a quiet place where you can run through the particulars of the coming encounter. In your imagination, put yourself in the arena as clearly as you can. At each potentially stressful point visualize the worst, let anger, fear, or frustration well up in you and then gradually dissipate. Then move on to visualize how you will handle even the worst eventuality. Phil, for example, was apprehensive about his first face-to-face meeting with Herb after his discovery that Herb had intended to hand him a plum rather than a nettle. As he looked ahead he could only repeat, "I feel so damn stupid. I feel so damn stupid. No one will ever take me seriously again." After a bit, he thought and then decided that he would not complain or apologize. Rather, he would simply report as matter-of-factly as possible what his interpretation of Herb's action had been and how he had felt. When I asked, "And what will Herb's reaction likely be when you do that?" he said, with a half-concealed smile, "He'll feel like shit."

Gaining Perspective Through Humor. At least as far back as the beginning of written history, humor has been a curative of ills of both the mind and body. Since it is not events but our perception of them that induces both physical and psychological distress, a balanced and realistic view can help prevent the sort of overresponse that hit Phil. Nothing does that better than humor and most human strivings—especially those done with an excess of exertion—have a humorous, even ridiculous, side. Catching a glimpse of the comic side of your own or others' antics can take the steam out of the sort of emotional escalation we've been exploring in this chapter.

When Phil and I first talked, it took but a moment for his pleasantly businesslike face to fall even as he accused me, half-jokingly, of being the cause of all his troubles. Although I knew his remark was probably not totally in jest, at least it showed that he hadn't entirely lost his sense of humor. By the time he had finished the woeful tale with which we began this chapter, it seemed clear that he was exceedingly in need of a dose of reality. While banishment to a supportive senior management job at a vice president's salary had its disappointing side, it could in no way be objectively interpreted as a catastrophic event. I was encouraged by Phil's joking to try a little paradoxical humor of my own. "Look on the bright side," I said with the hint of a smile. "Now you can finally stop worrying about when you're going to make CEO." While my remark might not win any awards for wit, it did elicit a grin from Phil and a willingness to take the next step toward escaping the morass into which he felt he was sinking.

Studies have shown that self-directed humor of many kinds—exaggeration, paradoxical reversal, even such dark humor as "I think I'll have lunch and then shoot myself"—can be efficient mood elevators. The problem is that most of us find it difficult to see the comical side of our predicaments when we are feeling despondent, anxious, or agitated. It is during those times that a friend (or even a friendly consultant) can provide a service by making light not of us but of the ludicrous situations we are all adept at creating for ourselves.

Develop a Small Wins Strategy for Regaining Control. Since a belief that we can't influence what is happening to us is the root of harmful stress, the most efficacious means for reducing it is to do something that leaves us feeling more in control. Needless to say, that's easier said than done. Since by definition we started with the belief that there was no way out of the trap, advice to take constructive action can seem impossible to carry out.

The way out of that bind is to regain a measure of control by using a Small Wins Strategy similar to those described in chapter 3. Briefly, you'll devise a plan made up of small action steps, the first of which is within your present resources. Moreover, its accomplishment must leave you feeling that you've at least gained something on the goblins that are pursuing you.

Phil's initial Small Wins Strategy consisted of two steps. The first was a series of short meetings with his staff to bring himself up to date on what had been accomplished. The second step, much more difficult for him, was to make a phone call to Herb—now on a long field trip in Europe—to inquire whether reassignment would be possible (as it turned out, it was in performing this step that he learned about Herb's original intention in assigning him to the job) and to set a date for a follow-up meeting. I believed it was important that Phil accomplish his first small win—getting himself back in touch with the state of affairs in his area of responsibility—before he called Herb. First of all, it would get him moving, contributing to his sense of being an active rather than a passive participant. Second, simply entering his appointments into his calendar added something to that reawakening sense of purpose. Remember that the distance between you, stressed but still managing, and you overstressed and incapacitated may be very small. The modest gains that accrue as you pursue your Small Wins Strategy can tip you back within the limits in which you function well.

Relieving the Effects of Stress. Achieving some symptomatic relief from stress can help you pursue all the other coping strategies more effectively. There is now a voluminous literature in both the popular and the health care press about how to feel better if you are overstressed. (Some of the recommended methods also have a preventive quality, and we'll mention them later when we consider prevention.) There is good evidence to substantiate that all of the following are effective in reducing both psychological and physiological responses to emotional overload: noncompetitive physical exercise, relaxation techniques, hatha-yoga, meditation, and listening to music (as any teenager can tell you).

PREVENTING STRESS EFFECTS: DEVELOPING PSYCHOLOGICAL TOUGHNESS

With stress, as with most of the pitfalls discussed in this book, prevention is the best cure.

While it's likely that some of us are born with a physiology that makes us more stress resistant than our fellows, it's also likely that we can add significant increments to our given level of psychological toughness.

In reading through the methods that follow, you may recognize that several have been part of the repertoire of capable sports coaches, military training officers, and others who have been tasked with teaching others to function well under pressure. Recent findings from researchers of a variety of persuasions have provided a better understanding of why and how these methods help, as well as suggesting a number of refinements that increase the payoff for the effort they require. Since it is the essence of some of these methods that you push yourself almost to the limit of tolerable discomfort, your best bet is to set your mind to think of them as "fun" rather than as "work."

Mental Challenge

Every study of stress-resistant people shows that they display an inclination for undertaking difficult jobs, which may explain why Fast Trackers as a group tend to be psychologically tough. The underlying mechanism seems to be a state of mind that psychologist Walter Bandura has called "self-efficacy"—the belief that you will be able to survive, accomplish, and prevail, because you have managed to do so in the past.

Challenges increase self-efficacy when they stretch capabilities and courage but are not beyond them. For years we have known that the consistently best performers are those who set hard but feasible goals for themselves. Poor performers, on the other hand, typically set goals that are too ambitious, thereby ensuring that they'll fail and then feel inadequate. Interestingly, when, by chance, they actually reach their improbable goals, they ascribe their success to luck rather than to their own efforts. Consequently, they do not increase their self-efficacy.

Humor Again

If seeing the humor in a pratfall helps you bear the pain of a bruised rear end, developing a humorous perspective on life in general also confers a degree of preventive protection. (Interestingly, seeing the funny side of common stress-producing happenings has been shown to elicit an increase in the hormone catecholamine, which is, in turn, accompanied by a minimization of the physiological effects of stress.)

The kind of humor that is effective as a stress preventer is self-directed, but not belittling. As one of my colleagues has suggested, it's an attitude that reminds you to look at the denominators in life when the natural tendency is to focus on the numerator. That is, a horrible day at work won't feel quite as bad if you recall that one day is only 1/365th of a year, or 1/3650th of a decade, or 1/25,550th of a seventy-year life. But, then, that is exactly what is difficult to do when we're still smarting from a fall. What most of us need is an easy-to-use device that helps keep things in perspective.

One such device is the pain scale.* Imagine a scale that ranges from 1 to 100. A score of 100 represents an excruciatingly painful event, such as the total distress you would feel in losing both arms and legs in an accident. A score of 1 represents the least painful injury that is still noticeable—a mosquito bite that itches, for example. At a score of 75 we might place losing one arm and one leg, and at 50 one or the other. In that frame of reference, a score of 25 could equal a cut, let's say, that lays your arm open to the bone, 20 a clean stab wound in the shoulder, and 15 a thoroughly abraded

*The pain scale was adapted from Tom Miller's book *The Unfair Advantage.*

knee from a hard spill. Now we're down to a score of 10 for a painful boil where you sit down, and a score of 5 for a half-inch deep cut on your forefinger from a steak knife. Still left to be inserted somewhere on the scale from 5 to 1 are two very itchy mosquito bites, a bee sting (assuming you're not allergic to bee venom), and a skinned knuckle. (Of course, the details of your own pain scale will depend on the painful incidents you've experienced and your secret fears.)

Having gone through all the work of preparing this personal rating of horrors, you might as well take the next step of committing it to memory (if you've written it out, you will find it surprisingly hard to forget). The final step is the fun part. When an unpleasant event occurs and you feel your usual rush of anger, frustration, and dismay, pause for a moment to decide which of the amusements on your pain scale you would be willing to substitute for that awful event.

Imagine, for example, that you are driving across town to an important budget review meeting. Although you left home in plenty of time, traffic slows and then comes to a standstill. You are going to be late. Worried about the fate of your budget, you fume over the delay and berate yourself for not anticipating the possibility of a traffic snarl. It's a classic stress-inducing situation. Not only do you feel angry and frustrated but you are powerless to do anything about it. This time, however, instead of stewing you ask yourself "Where is this on the pain scale?" Would I, you wonder, be willing to sacrifice both arms if only the traffic would magically disperse? No? How about one arm, or even a leg? Still no? Then would I opt for a simple, clean stab wound in the shoulder just to be on my way? How about a painfully abraded knee?, or a bee sting?

Wherever you put this event on your pain scale, thinking of it in this ludicrous way will cut down on the time you spend in what rational-emotive therapist Albert Ellis calls "awfulizing," the predilection—very hard to resist at times—for reacting to an annoyance as if it were a catastrophe that is "terrible, awful, and beyond standing." The notion of a "pain scale" may be comic, but the physical and mental costs of "awfulizing" are not.

Although Phil Simmons may not have used exactly those "awfulizing" words, their meaning came through clearly as he recited the litany of terrible things that had befallen him. Perhaps he would have been unable to resist a smile if he had asked himself "How many limbs would I give up to get my old job back?" (On my own pain scale, most everyday "catastrophes" turn out to rate less than a 3.)

Aerobic Exercise

A wide range of evidence has demonstrated that even moderate exercise works both to relieve and to prevent the effects of harmful stress. Exercise can make you feel better after a stressful experience even when the exercise is taken hours after the disturbing event. In addition, regular exercise builds both physical and psychological resistance to future troublesome events.

There are a number of plausible reasons for this useful effect. For one thing, simply keeping at a routine that involves effort and some short-term discomfort can increase your sense of being actively in control of your life. Even if, as some cynics claim, it is an *illusion* of control, it seems to work anyway, for regular aerobic exercise helps to keep central nervous system hormones such as cortisol and catecholamine at consistently optimum levels. Thus your body is better prepared to deal with stresses when they hit. Then too, activity of any sort is the best single antidote for feelings of depression. Remember, however, an exercise program can itself become a source of added stress rather than something done for pleasure or as a means of improving your health if it becomes simply another arena for your insistent drive for success. This plaint from a fast-moving advertising director makes the case quite well: "I've been out on the court almost every night for a month, working with the tennis coach, and I still can't beat any of the top three players at the club. I haven't felt so frustrated and angry since I was cut from the football team in high school because I was too small."

Regular Exposure to Cold

Don't laugh: studies of both adults and children show that regular exposures to temperature extremes, particularly cold, seem to provoke many of the same physiological responses as hard physical exercise. You develop the temperature tolerance that is associated with psychological toughness by enduring temperatures that are uncomfortable but not debilitating. Since you are accustoming yourself to take discomfort in stride, the temperatures must not be so extreme that you feel overwhelmed by them—shivering uncontrollably, unable to think of anything but the cold, feeling weak and unable to cope. In practice, this notion suggests that you leave your sweater off in cooler temperatures, and tell yourself, when the air conditioning can no longer keep up with midsummer swelters, how glad you are that you're building your character. And after all, it's only a 1 on the pain scale.

Creating Free Time

In 1978 three paragraphs in an article by anthropologist Allen Johnson suggested a method for peeling off layers of harried anxiety. Since then, family, friends, and many clients have been delighted at its utility in keeping a highly programmed life from devolving into too little frisking and too much fretting.

Johnson, with his anthropologist wife, had been comparing how the Machiguenga Indians of Peru and urban French men and women spent their time in a variety of day-to-day activities. Although, naturally, the specific activities were different, both the French subjects and their Machiguenga counterparts devoted similar amounts of time to acquiring and preparing food, manufacturing, cleaning up, and child care. One area in which they were strikingly different, however, was in the amount of free time they were able to carve out of each day. "Free" in this context included sleeping, resting (which includes "doing nothing"), play, conversation, and generalized "visiting." It was especially interesting that the Johnsons differentiated free time from "consumption time," which included eating, engaging in religious and political activities, viewing sports or entertainment, travel, watching television, and reading newspapers. While the two groups spent almost equivalent amounts of their free time sleeping, the Machiguenga spent considerably more time than the French resting, playing, and visiting. Johnson further reported that during the time he and his wife spent with the Machiguenga (approximately eighteen months spread over three visits), they experienced a sense of relaxation and a leisurely pace that quickly evaporated each time they returned to their normal high-pressure life.

As I read his account, I was struck by the thought that

free time—that is, time spent neither in "consuming" newspapers or television programs nor in structured activities with a fixed beginning, end, and outcome—might be an easily attained key to a less stressed life. I was particularly fascinated by the distinction between consumption time and free time for it made sense of several things that had puzzled me for years. I had often noted in myself and family members noticeable signs of fatigue and even a little melancholy following several hours of television viewing. In contrast, the all-too-infrequent interludes of just sitting around or aimlessly visiting with friends or floating down a slow-moving stream engendered renewed energy. From my own experience the evidence suggested that free time indeed restores, while consumption time adds to one's load of stress.

The possible value of free time as a stress buffer also shed light on an interesting phenomenon I had noticed during periodic visits with my wife's family, farmers for generations back. They displayed an amazing equanimity in the face of the natural catastrophes that farmers are constantly subject to—sudden spring freezes, hailstorms before harvest, too little water when it was needed, too much water when it wasn't. It certainly wasn't that they were unaffected—their very livelihoods were at stake—but there was much less storming around than I had seen in my big-city clients when hit by less personally damaging adverse events (and less than I had indulged in when an important client chose a competing consulting firm). I realized that what I had previously considered an odd aberration of rural life was the very thing that the Johnsons had alluded to, the inordinate amount of time that rural folk spent "just visiting." Chatting about such inconsequential questions as "What was the make of the truck that Tom used the day we hauled all of those fence pickets out to his place?" I now saw as far from useless. It was stress-preventing Johnsonian free time.

My wife and I soon discovered that planned "free time"—yes, the term does seem paradoxical—produced clearly observable decrements in our feelings of being rushed, overprogrammed, and generally tense. I then began suggesting it to a succession of appropriate clients. It was not easy to persuade already overworked individuals that they would accomplish more at less personal cost by building free time into their schedules. Once they brought themselves to try it out, however, for almost all, the payoff was rapid and convincing. Unfortunately, almost as rapid was a return to schedule overcrowding at the expense of that seemingly self-indulgent free time. I have yet to find anyone completely able to resist this inevitable erosion of time simply to be. Many clients, however, have learned to use signs that they have become tense, anxious, or abrasive as a signal that they once more need to carve out the time for this valuable activity, or should we say, lack of activity.

What makes time free is very personal. For me, reading light detective fiction while listening to music is relaxing, whereas reading suspenseful spy thrillers is not. Chatting with my kids about life is free time; telling them how they should live it is not. Wandering through a museum with no intention to cover a given amount of territory is rejuvenating; attending lectures—even interesting ones—is not. My conclusion is that free time should have no accomplishment or competition to it, either directly or vicariously. In other words, attending a ball game might be free time if you spend it enjoying the sunshine and the players' display of skill, but it would be consumption time, or even work time, if you really care about which team wins. The point is not that emotionally participating in competitive contests is a bad idea, but only that it is probably not effective in reducing harmful stress.

Fast Trackers have several areas of special vulnerability to stress. They are usually overmotivated, driven to seek power, to achieve, to be seen as important. They expect great things of themselves, partly because they are aware of their own talents and partly because they're heeding that parental injunction we visited in chapter 2: "No matter what you've done, it's not yet good enough." As a result, even relatively minor slowdowns can seem immensely frustrating. At times Fast Trackers feel they "deserve" success simply because they want it and work hard for it. When success seems to elude them—though what counts as "success" often is ill-defined in their minds—they feel angry, blocked, and unable to fathom what has happened to them.

Thus, learning to cope with stress is as important a skill for a Fast Tracker as being able to find financial backing for potentially profitable projects or creating an operational plan and budget. As Phil Simmons discovered, emotional overload can throw out of kilter your ability to pay accurate attention to what's happening—let alone deal with it sensibly. Phil never was appointed chief financial officer, but not because he had failed in the important assignments that Herb gave him.

After regaining his emotional balance, he proved that Herb's initial judgment of his competence was indeed correct. But it was also true that his brief period of floundering had left Herb just uncertain enough to decide that he needed to recruit a new chief financial officer from outside the firm. While Phil was disappointed and chagrined at his part in his own undoing, still, he understood Herb's dilemma.

On the positive side, Phil had gained a renewed commitment to his wife and family, an increasing appetite for the pleasures of free time, and a conviction that his life had come into better balance. And that leads us directly into our last chapter.

9

The Balancing Act

I have often been asked by my hurried and harried clients to tell them how to achieve a more balanced life. My first response, of course, is to remind them that when the methods that I've suggested in this book are put to use, a reasonably balanced life is often a welcome by-product. I then share with them some observations about the quest for balance that I've accumulated in my twenty years of helping dedicated people try for it. Having heard me out, they are at first disappointed and then relieved. Better yet, they seem even more ready to go back to work at the task of coping more effectively with their fast track lives.

Here is what I've learned about keeping your balance in a constantly shifting world.

Although everyone talks about "achieving a balanced life" I have yet to find anyone who has been able to do it for more than a day at a time. Even though experience has informed us otherwise, and especially when we see others who seem poised and unflappable, we continue to believe that somewhere a balanced and beautiful life is to be found. When it turns out that even those envied people are flawed and discontented, we sigh, feel relieved for a moment that we are not the only victims of an imperfect world, and transfer our projections of perfection onto others. The error is not in wishing for a time and a place in which everyone's needs, including your own, will be finally satisfied. It is in thinking of a balanced life as a state that can be once and forever attained.

———

"A balanced life" isn't a very accurate term for the task of paying equal attention to all of our important needs, wishes, and obligations, because it implies a state of being. Balance is not a static end point, it is a continuous process that regenerates itself by constantly going out of whack. This year you sought to redress an imbalance between career and family. But next year, you may realize that you haven't taken time for your favorite hobby in six months. You had tipped so hard toward your family that you lost the balance between what you owe your family and what you owe your own private self.

———

Whether it's part of the fun of being a Fast Tracker, or merely an unfortunate aspect of contemporary life, balancing the competing areas of your life is very much like walking a tightrope. Take the problem of dividing yourself between career and family. If you lean too far one way—say by lavishing most of your time, energy, and commitment on your career—you'll feel out of kilter and, with much emotional flailing, may throw yourself energetically too far the other way. The main point is, don't panic when you realize that you've somewhat forsaken an important aspect of your life. Wave your arms around a bit and lean a little in that direction.

As a Fast Tracker you won't have just one tightrope on which you must stay balanced but a myriad, among which you must hop and skip as the circumstances of your life change. Along with "career versus home life," you can expect to find "high pay right now versus learning for the future," "time with spouse versus time with children," "busy time versus free time," and so on. Even if you were to find a place around which all of your competing needs were in total equilibrium, any major event—a promotion, a move to another city, a new baby—will start the tightropes swinging again.

———

It's hard for most of us to give up a belief in "happily ever after." If you listen beneath the cynical banter at an after-work cocktail hour, you can hear a secret hope that when the *big* promotion, or the mammoth contract, has been landed, life will ever after be a place of perennial, peaceful fun. In fact, those who proclaim their disbelief in the goodness of the world the loudest are the truest believers. Their cynicisms are, like any incantations, efforts at warding off demons and summoning fairy godmothers to the rescue.

———

At different stages of our lives, we weigh the same things differently. What seemed trivial at thirty—long-term health needs, say—may seem vitally important at fifty. Therefore, the only time you'll know whether your life has been well balanced—that is, you've devoted proper attention to all that has been important to you—is when you are about to leave it, and then you probably won't care. The quest, then, is not for an impossible state of solid equilibrium, but for tricks of the trade that can keep you from swinging too far in one direction or another. Here are some suggestions for doing just that. You'll find that most of them recap the basic thrust of what has gone before in this book.

- Vital areas of your life that are starved often whimper quietly instead of shouting for help. So when your stress-absorbing capacity feels overloaded but you can find no immediate cause, look for an imbalance in the life areas most important to you.

- To keep from feeling overwhelmed when several of your "tightropes" are swinging at once, list ten answers to the question "What would most relieve my feelings of being stretched too far?" Prioritize your list and take some action on no more than the first three items.

- Incremental changes are less likely to throw you off balance. Use a Small Wins Strategy whenever possible. (Refer to chapter 3 for the specific steps to take.)

- Becoming caught up by unhealthy organizational practices can erode the solid center of your values and thus reduce your ability to determine what is really important to you.

- Keep a constant eye on the state of your conscience. Dissonance in that area unravels the strands of all of your tightropes at once.

- When you realize that you are losing the struggle to dance well on all of your tightropes, try to find a way to jump safely off before you tumble off into depression, despair, or divorce. Examples of safety nets I've seen are: an asked-for demotion to a slower-moving job; a transfer from a line management position to an active, but less frenetic, staff job; leaving the scramble of self-employment for a steadier, if less exciting, position in government, a voluntary agency, or a non-fast track company; a long (six weeks) hiatus from work achieved by means of combined sick leave (physician-ordered "stress leave") and accumulated vacation. Remind yourself that when one opportunity is forgone, another will almost invariably pop up. Since you'll never know whether the one you took was better than the one you missed, you might as well assume that it was.

Finally, always keep in mind that everything is more flexible than you think. That wonderful fact is what makes it possible to undertake a high-demand life with confidence that it can be both exciting and broadly satisfying.

Good luck, and take care of yourself.

Reference List

These chapter reference lists are just that—lists of books and articles for further exploration by those so inclined. In each list you'll find a mixture of popular discussions of fast track issues, scholarly texts on pertinent topics, and journal articles which summarize or exemplify the recent research alluded to in the chapter.

Chapter 1

Frost, P., V. Mitchell, and W. Nord. *Organizational Reality Reports from the Firing Line* (third edition). Glenview, Ill.: Scott, Foresman, 1986.

Kanter, R. *Men and Women of the Corporation* (Chapter 2). New York: Basic Books, 1977.

LaBier, D. *Modern Madness: The Emotional Fall Out of Success.* Reading, Mass.: Addison-Wesley, 1986.

Chapter 2

DeVries-Griever, A., and T. Meijman. "The Impact of Abnormal Hours of Work on Various Modes of Information Processing: A Process Model on Human Costs of Performance," *Ergonomics*, vol. 30, no. 9, 1987, pp. 1287–99.

Healy, D., and J. Williams. "Dysrhythmia, Dysphoria, and Depression," *Psychological Bulletin*, vol. 103, no. 2, 1988, pp. 163–78.

Kanter, R. M. *Men and Women of the Corporation*. New York: Basic Books, 1977.

Kepner, C., and B. Tregoe. *The Rational Manager*. Princeton, N.J.: Kepner-Tregoe Associates, 1976.

Miller, A. *The Drama of the Gifted Child*. New York: Basic Books, 1981.

Morrisey, G. *Management by Objectives and Results for Business and Industry* (second edition). Reading, Mass.: Addison-Wesley, 1977.

Morrisey, G. L., P. J. Below, and B. L. Acomb. *The Executive Guide to Operational Planning*. San Francisco: Jossey-Bass, 1988.

Moskowitz, R. *How to Organize Your Work and Your Life*. Garden City, N.Y.: Doubleday, 1981.

Oken, D., and D. Hay. "The Psychological Stresses of Intensive Unit Nursing," A. Monat and R. Lazarus, eds., *Stress and Coping*. New York: Columbia University Press, 1985.

Shaevitz, M., *The Superwoman Syndrome*. New York: Warner Books, 1984.

Chapter 3

Bandura, A. *Social Foundations of Thought and Action: A Social Cognitive Theory*. Englewood Cliffs, N.J.: Prentice-Hall, 1986.

Blotnick, S. *The Corporate Steeple Chase*. New York: Penguin Books, 1985.

Bramson, R. *Coping with Difficult People.* Garden City, N.Y.: Doubleday, 1981.

Ellis, A. *A New Guide to Rational Living.* Hollywood, Calif.: Wilshire Books, 1975.

Fisher, R., and W. Ury. *Getting to Yes.* Boston: Houghton Mifflin, 1981.

Giacalone, R. A. "On Slipping When You Thought You Had Put Your Best Foot Forward: Self Promotion, Self Destruction and Entitlements," *Group and Organizational Studies,* vol. 10, no. 1, 1985, pp. 61–80.

Gutman, D. "Sporting Life: Winners into Losers," *Psychology Today,* May 1988.

Karoly, D., and F. H. Kanfer, eds. *Self Management and Behavior Change.* Elmsford, N.Y.: Pergamon Press, 1982.

Kohn, A. *No Contest: The Case Against Competition.* New York: Houghton Mifflin, 1986.

Levinson, H. "Criteria for Choosing Chief Executives," *Harvard Business Review,* July-August 1980.

Russell, C. "Person Characteristic Versus Role Congruency: Explanations for Assessment Center Ratings," *Academy of Management Journal,* vol. 30, no. 4, 1987, pp. 817–26.

Taylor, S. E., and J. D. Brown. "Illusion and Well-Being: A Social Psychological Perspective on Mental Health," *Psychological Bulletin,* vol. 103, no. 2, 1988, pp. 193–210.

Weick, K. E. "Small Wins," *American Psychologist,* vol. 39, no. 1, 1984, pp. 40–49.

Chapter 4

Dostoevsky, F. *Crime and Punishment* (translated by Constance Garnett). New York: Random House, 1956.

Dweck, C., and E. Leggett. "A Social-Cognitive Approach to Motivation and Personality," *Psychological Review,* vol. 95, no. 2, 1988, pp. 256–73.

Fromm, E. *Man for Himself: An Inquiry into the Psychology of Ethics.* New York: Holt, Rinehart and Winston, 1947.

Goleman, D. *Vital Lies, Simple Truths: The Psychology of Self Deception*. New York: Simon and Schuster, 1985.

Harrison, A., and R. Bramson. *The Art of Thinking*. New York: Berkley Books, 1984.

Landi, A. "When Having Everything Isn't Enough," *Psychology Today*, April 1989.

Montaigne, M. "Of Profit and Honesty," *Essays*, vol. 3. New York: Dutton, 1910.

Srivastva, S. and Associates. *Executive Integrity*. San Francisco: Jossey-Bass, 1988.

Chapter 5

Kelly, C. "The Inter-relationship of Ethics and Power in Today's Organizations," *Organizational Dynamics*, vol. 16, no. 1, 1987, pp. 4–18.

McClelland, D. *Power: The Inner Experience*. New York: Irvington, 1975.

McClelland, D., and D. Burnham. "Power Is the Great Motivator," *Harvard Business Review*, March-April 1976, pp. 84–94.

Snow, C. P. *Corridors of Power*. New York: Scribner, 1964.

Chapter 6

Burke, R., and T. Weir. "Marital Helping Relationships: The Moderators Between Stress and Well Being," *The Journal of Psychology*, vol. 95, no. 1, 1977, pp. 121–30.

Langer, E. *Mindfulness*. New York: Addison-Wesley, 1989.

Mackoff, B. *Leaving the Office Behind*. New York: Putnam, 1984.

Mehrabian, A. *Public Places and Private Spaces*. New York: Basic Books, 1976.

Nelson, D. "Organizational Socialization: A Stress Perspective," *Journal of Occupational Behaviour*, vol. 8, no. 4, 1987, pp. 311–24.

Nichols, M. *Turning Forty in the '80s.* New York: Norton, 1986.

Vandervelde, M. *The Changing Life of the Corporate Wife.* New York: Mecox Publishing Company, 1979.

Chapter 7

Baumeister, R., and S. Scher. "Self-Defeating Behavior Patterns Among Normal Individuals: Review and Analysis of Common Self-Destructive Tendencies," *Psychological Bulletin,* vol. 104, no. 1, 1988, pp. 3–22.

Black, C. *It Will Never Happen to Me.* New York: Ballantine, 1987.

Brown, S. *Treating Adult Children of Alcoholics: A Developmental Perspective.* New York: Wiley, 1988.

Fischman, J. "Getting Tough," *Psychology Today,* December 1987.

Higgins, E. "Self-Discrepancy: A Theory Relating Self and Affect," *Psychological Review,* vol. 94, no. 3, 1987, pp. 319–40.

Johnson, V. *I'll Quit Tomorrow.* San Francisco: Harper and Row, 1980.

Kolata, G. "Alcoholic Genes or Misbehavior?" *Psychology Today,* May 1988.

Shaef, A. *Co-Dependence Misunderstood, Mistreated.* New York: Harper and Row, 1986.

Wholey, D. *The Courage to Change.* New York: Warner Books, 1986.

Chapter 8

Bandura, W. *Social Foundations of Thought and Action: A Social Cognitive Theory.* Englewood Cliffs, N.J.: Prentice-Hall, 1986.

Benson, H. *The Relaxation Response.* New York: Morrow, 1975.

Bramson, R., and S. Bramson. *The Stressless Home*. New York: Ballantine Books, 1986.

Dienstbier, R. "Arousal and Physiological Toughness: Implications for Mental and Physical Health," *Psychological Review*, vol. 96, no. 1, 1989, pp. 84–100.

Flannery, R. "The Stress Resistant Person," *Harvard Medical School Health Letter*, February 1989, pp. 46–47.

Freudenberger, H. *Burnout*. New York: Bantam, 1981.

———. "Today's Troubled Men," *Psychology Today*, December 1987.

Haley, W., and B. Strickland. "Interpersonal Betrayal and Cooperation: Effects on Self-Evaluation in Depression," *Journal of Personality and Social Psychology*, vol. 50, no. 3, 1986, pp. 288–91.

Hobfoll, S. "Conservation of Resources: A New Attempt at Conceptualizing Stress," *American Psychologist*, vol. 44, no. 3, 1989, pp. 513–24.

Johnson, A. "In Search of the Affluent Society," *Human Nature*, vol. 1, no. 9, September 1978, pp. 50–60.

Langer, E. *The Psychology of Control*. Beverly Hills, Calif.: Sage, 1983.

Levinson, H. "When Executives Burn Out," *Harvard Business Review*, May-June 1981, pp. 73–81.

London, M., and E. Mone. *Career Management and Survival in the Workplace*. San Francisco: Jossey-Bass, 1987.

McClelland, D. "Motivational Factors in Health and Disease," *American Psychologist*, vol. 44, no. 4, 1989, pp. 675–83.

McLeod, B. "Rx for Health: A Dose of Self Confidence," *Psychology Today*, October 1986.

Matteson, M., and J. Ivancevich. *Controlling Work Stress*. San Francisco: Jossey-Bass, 1987.

Miller, T. *The Unfair Advantage*. Skaneateles, N.Y.: Lakeside Printing, 1986.

Monat, A., and R. Lazarus, eds., *Stress and Coping*. New York: Columbia University Press, 1985.

Sethi, A. "Meditation for Coping with Organizational Stress." In Sethi, A., and R. Schuler (eds.), *Handbook of Organi-*

zational Stress Coping Strategies. Cambridge, Mass.: Ballinger, 1984.

Tavris, C. *Every Woman's Emotional Well Being: Heart and Mind, Body and Soul*. Garden City, N.Y.: Doubleday, 1986.

Watson, D., and J. Pennebacker. "Health Complaints, Stress and Negative Affectivity," *Psychological Review*, vol. 96, no. 2, 1989, pp. 234–54.

Wysocki, J., M. Chemers, and F. Rhodewalt. "Situational Demand and Self Reports of Stress and Illness: The Moderating Influence of Self-Monitoring," *Basic and Applied Social Psychology*, vol. 8, no. 3, 1987, pp. 249–58.

Chapter 9

Bateson, M. *Composing a Life*. New York: Atlantic Monthly Press, 1989.

Snow, C. *Last Things*. New York: Scribner, 1970.

Watzlawick, P. *The Invented Reality: Contributions to Constructivism*. New York: Norton, 1984.

Isolation, executive, 194–234
coping with lack of support
    and, 211–234
from family and friends, 15,
    206, 228–234
from oneself, 225–228
and lack of support, causes
    of, 201–211
third-party listeners and, 221–
    224

About the Author

ROBERT BRAMSON is an internationally known consultant and author. He is a leading authority on the prevention and management of difficult and nonproductive behavior, and on methods for obtaining optimal performance from executives.

Dr. Bramson's background combines varied work experience, from blue collar to executive levels, with training in psychology and organizational behavior (A.B. from UCLA, M.A. from San Francisco State University, Ph.D. from the University of California, Berkeley). His clients include major government entities, Bank of America, IBM, Varian Associates, Hewlett-Packard, Standard Oil of California, Pacific Bell, Electrical Power Research Institute, and Lever Brothers.

Past collateral faculty appointments include University of Southern California and San Francisco State University. For six years he was clinical lecturer in Psychiatry and Behavioral Science at Stanford University Medical Center, and at present he is a lecturer in management practice for the UCLA Engineering Management Institute.

Dr. Bramson is a co-developer of the Inquiry Mode Questionnaire (InQ) and for eight years has studied factors that contribute to, or inhibit, competence in thinking and organizational decision making.

He is the author of *Styles of Thinking* (with Allen F. Harrison), Doubleday, 1982; *The Stressless Home* (with Susan J. Bramson), Doubleday, 1985; and articles on organizational diagnosis, staff development, and managerial performance standards.

Dr. Bramson has appeared often on national and local TV and radio shows, and is a frequent speaker at conferences and association meetings. His work has been featured in newspapers and magazines nationwide, notably *Time*, *The New York Times*, the *Los Angeles Times*, *The Washington Post*, *The Chicago Sun-Times*, the *San Francisco Chronicle*, *Executive Productivity*, *Board Room Reports*, *McCall's*, *Ladies' Home Journal*, and *Reader's Digest*.

He is a member of the American Psychological Association, the Author's Guild, and Certified Consultants International, an accrediting association of applied behavioral scientists.

He lives in Oakland, California, with his wife, Susan, and their family.

6258